The Maintenance Man's Dilemma

THE MAINTENANCE MAN'S DILEMMA

The Extraordinary Life of an Ordinary Man

WILLIAM STOCK

The Maintenance Man's Dilemma

ISBN: 979-8-9909704-1-0 (Paperback)
ISBN: 979-8-9909704-0-3 (Ebook)

DEDICATION

For Sharon, who supported the maintenance man
always, loved him, and helped save his life.

Message from you

Sometimes,
Piss-shit full of vinegar,
talking too much,
mind in a single file,
I find a message from you,
like "Hi! You booby you,"
and I forget myself,
and forget myself, and smile.

Message to you

As tears trickling from long-dry eyes,
as soft words following a long pause,
as warm hands reaching slowly out,
as madness growing calm, as
strength,
work,
home,
joy,
I have known you.

FOREWORDS

B ILL STOCK IS A MAN of unpredictable nature. He is a rebel. In any discussion, were you to express an opinion, he might challenge you – even though he agreed -- just for sport. We go back a long way, having met in graduate school fifty-eight years ago. He is a good man, a good friend, and, as it happens, a good writer. Who knew? I did, decades ago when Bill and I co-wrote and edited *Abanarapor*, a mimeographed, counter-culture, publication handed out free to passing students as we walked across the Iowa State campus.

Bill and I were at the trial of the Chicago Seven—Abbie Hoffman, Jerry Rubin, etc.--- well, almost. We stood in line to enter the courtroom and were among the first told the galleries were full to maximum capacity. Oh, well. On the same trip, we went to the Art Institute of Chicago, where I became infatuated with French impressionists, a love affair that continues to this day.

A well-written memoir offers genuine insight into the author's life, chronicling not just his actions but also his motivations and lessons he learned along the way. In Bill's writing, his passion for life shines through, inspiring us with his generosity and his pursuit of being a good husband, father, brother, son, friend, and co-worker. His compassion for all beings is evident, and his fondness for dogs is particularly heartwarming, with his love for people coming in a close second.

Let me tell you how brilliant a guy my friend Bill Stock is. As a professor, he consistently earned high praise from his students. He has been an unqualified success as a business executive and team leader. And as an engaging memoirist? I urge you to read this book and judge for yourself.

CLIVE SOMMER
Independent Bookstore Owner,
Avid Reader, PhD in Mathematics

Fairly early in this adventurous, quirky, and poignant memoir, my friend Bill Stock recalls dropping a tab of Orange Sunshine (we both came of age in the Sixties). It came to him then, a young husband, that "he possessed an intense attraction to women, each woman, all women, not just Her." In the carefully crafted short sections of this book he—and we—ponder: How can he be with one woman yet long for many? How can he successfully maintain a home (a nest) while prizing travel (flight)? How can he act responsibly as both a blue- and white-collar wage earner, despite being at heart a spendthrift and lifelong gambler?

When his friends ask him about the appeal of gambling, he describes it as "floating on the wings of chance." Explaining his attraction to a late-life job as a maintenance man in a supermarket, he reports that "he liked unskilled, menial work that permitted his mind to think about whatever he wanted, whenever he wanted—*without rules* [my emphasis]." This is the same man who named his beloved dog "Free." Of course he did.

I have a personal interest in this life story, which fills me in on the fifty-plus years between first knowing Bill and meeting up with him again, late in life. As newlyweds and new parents, my first husband and I lived in student housing next door to Bill and his beautiful, shy wife, Sharon. I remember those days vaguely, through the haze of fresh motherhood. We played board games, listened to Bob Dylan, agreed on or sparred in bursts about politics, about everything. Sharon—who had a fine shock of brown hair, grave gray eyes, and a gentle but assessing smile—always seemed to have a cigarette in one hand and a Coke in the other. I recall Bill as a handsome, curious, argumentative, charming, and purposefully provoking presence. We were all bright young people. Bill was very bright. I think it is only on this second round of friendship in old age that I see, also, his creativity and compassion.

How does a free spirit and good man negotiate the puzzlement of it all as a son, husband, father, worker, friend, and traveler (there are vivid sections here on sensual Spain)? Read *The Maintenance Man's Dilemma* and meet Bill —and (as with any worthwhile memoir) you will also meet up with parts of yourself.

JEREDITH MERRIN
Retired English Professor, Poet

… I am different.
I am nourished by the great mother.

-- Number 20[1]

Lives are like a school of startled fish. No one
knows which way they will go,

-- Author

THE MAINTENANCE MAN'S DILEMMA

STARTED IN PUBERTY THAT ARRIVED a bit late, long before he worked at a local supermarket. This is not about that or then, rather about here and now, as time is short. His dilemma is women. How to be with them? What place they in his life?

For more than 40 years he thought little about relations with women because he took an oath to love Her until death parted them – and did. To be honest, he was not a perfect oath keeper. Nothing more about that now. Regarding his dilemma, before recounting it, knowing what a maintenance man does, helps.

Once each hour he sweeps the floor. As he passes up and down aisles, he stops and picks up trash that is a hazard to unsuspecting, inattentive, unaware, and possibly litigious customers. He replaces products that have fallen from shelves. A sweep takes 30 minutes. After a sweep he cleans bathrooms. Following a sweep in second hour, he polices trash bins, and empties those full or nearly so. Policing bins is an art. Because customers are indifferent to what they put in, and despite the fact he lines each bin with a plastic bag (to sequester liquids and obnoxious items), sharp objects and half empty drinks make spills and leaks probable. He puts the bag he removes in an extra bag or two to reduce chances of a leak on the journey from the bin through the store to the compactor. Leaks mean extra work and are another source of possible litigation should a customer slip and fall.

He repeats the same tasks in the second two-hour segment of a shift, and so on until it is time to go. A spill anywhere raises an alarm on the PA system as store employees call for clean-up. Spills are a side chore. As he pushes the clean-up cart, he mutters quasi-obscenities about careless customers and shelf stockers – the most egregious offenders.

Tasks of lower priority fill empty time as needed. This to say he is always moving. All that he does keeps his body busy, but not his mind. Boring?

Not for him. He loves the work. Suffice to say, his previous work focused on possible truths – of hypothetical constructs, theories, and hypotheses – so his mind – in a sedentary body – was busy and focused on that that might, or might not, be real. None of that for a maintenance man. Only sweep, clean, and police. No ephemeral or epiphenomenal constructs, only floors, toilets, and bins –all cleaned as fast as possible. Because the job is doing, not thinking, he amuses himself with thought. One thought is that he is like the ferry man Siddhartha met on first crossing a river, in a story by Hermann Hesse that the maintenance man read in college. Now his four days of work bring happiness.

He goes to the maintenance bay, picks up his broom, and starts a sweep. Only a few customers are in the store at eight in the morning so he concentrates on the floor just ahead of him, glancing right and left, steering the broom this way or that, picking up stray bits. On seeing a customer ahead, absorbed in shopping, he says "excuse me" or "coming through on your left (or right)" speaking in time – he judges – for the customer to hear him, decide how to react, do so, and, leave himself time to react. As a former mathematician, he knows it is impossible to calculate this in the real time it takes to reach the customer, so, he does not calculate, rather he does what he does a lot – he guesses, and says "thank you" as he passes.

You may imagine repeating "Excuse me, "or "Coming through on the (left or right)," and "Thank you" is boring, Yes, after a while, it is. Bending to serendipity, instigated by behaviors of customer(s), walkie-talkie announcements, the PA system, and other bits of life in the store, he creates a stream of alternatives that he utters as they form. Armed with riveting requests, commands, and humorous asides for persons in his path, he keeps moving.

As these utterances happen after he spots a customer, he encounters some customers who see him before he speaks, and move out of his way. To them he sends a hearty" Thank you." Compared to shoppers absorbed in lists and phones filled with deals and coupons, those who make way comprise a minority.

One phenomenon, which he calls an accidental crossing of paths, occurs regularly between he and a customer. You know the phenomenon: you are on your way one way, someone else is on their way another way, and your paths intersect. You both stop, mumble something, and return to your path. Before life in the store, he noticed women and men behave differently during such crossings. He noticed and deemed it a linguistic curiosity that most women said "I'm sorry," and most men did not.

Understandably, these crossings are more frequent in the store than elsewhere — given the end of each aisle is a blind turn, and people are looking for what they want, not where they are. Still, as a fully modern man, he thinks it is not right for women to say "I'm sorry." What might she say other than "I'm sorry." This is a manifestation of his dilemma: he wants to do something for them – but what?

He asks himself: should he directly tell women he thinks they are saying something wrong? He answers, "Probably not." It seems patriarchal, now proscribed, which reminds him of an earlier time

He was once a professor of statistics and used, with success, a Socratic method to teach the subject to mathematics- challenged persons. In his judgment, the method violated no boundaries. He tries it. As he sweeps, his mind is occupied with how to begin. It comes to him just as he turns a corner at the end of an aisle and nearly runs into a cart pushed by a woman who says, "I'm sorry." She maneuvers around the broom to shop on. Undeterred, as he steers his broom out of her way in the same direction as her, he says.

"Are you interested in human behavior?" which in other crossings is replaced by,

"Do you like behavioral science?" or simply by,

"May I ask you a question?" Any of these questions cause her to slow or stop her cart, cast a skeptical eye at him, and respond cautiously by saying something, for example, like "Yes."

Without malice of thought, intent, or action, more with joy, to himself he says "Got her" and begins a course of instruction. His goal is to have her explain why she said "I'm sorry." He tries several approaches, like

Getting straight to point saying, "Why did you say "I'm sorry."? Being so direct seems off-putting and elicits terse responses like "I don't know" or "It's a habit." Dissatisfied, he switches to an approach that is less direct, yet moves his agenda ahead – by asking a question like,

"You know how we got in each other's way a moment ago?" Followed by a somewhat hesitant, "Yes." (And by her look, he imagines her thinking," Where is this guy going with this?") He continues,

"Would you say either of us was at fault for nearly crashing into each other?"

"Not really." (One of a myriad of ways to say no.)

"Then why did you say I'm sorry?" This question aimed at the heart of the matter opens a door to a flood of responses. From,

"It's just something I always say" and "I don't mean anything by it" to

"I don't want a scene," "I do not want him to get angry" and "To avoid conflict," so he asks a final question,

"So, you really don't feel guilty or that you did anything wrong?"

While the response to this question is generally affirmative (e.g., "That's right."), some women do say they could have done something to avoid the situation entirely. Hmm... As more detailed inquiry is impossible, he thanks them, says he has kept them too long and encourages them on their way. He has a lot to think about, not the least of which is that their eyes were open a little wider the last time he looked in them before she continued shopping.

Given hundreds of such conversations – an adequate sample for him – he forms a conjecture. It is: women do not feel guilt for their part in an inadvertent crossing of paths yet they feign guilt, in the form of the expression, "I'm sorry" to avoid an adverse reaction from the other person, particularly if a man. Forming the conjecture leads back to the original nature of his dilemma. Believing himself correct, what should he do, if anything? In encounters after that, he shifts back to a direct approach, saying things like,

"No problem" or "It was inadvertent" or "It was a no-fault situation" or "It wasn't your fault" (but soon rejects responses that mention "fault," because it is as if he has assumed guilt). These statements provoke minimal responses, perhaps the hint of a smile, a nod, or an "uh huh," but no indication of introspection. This he finds unsatisfactory: no thought means no questioning means no change means she keeps saying "I'm sorry." Phooey! It is

Another instance of thinking "This needs to change," but not being able to change it in a manner he accepts. From here, for him,

It is a short distance to apathy, to relegate the matter to his heap of unresolved issues, to forget about it, and to move on to other aspects of life. As a human raised in our age of irony, he views the whole matter with irony, from which it is easy to slip to apathy, and from apathy to oblivion. Sometimes, irony suggests a response that is humorous. He uses irony to amuse himself and others. Instantly, he knows what he must do.

If a woman feigns guilt and speaks accordingly, then he will respond in kind. Now, when he and a woman accidently cross paths, and she says "I'm sorry" he feigns being a beneficent, magnanimous, patriarch of a large family of naïve, helpless women and says,

"That is alright. I forgive you" as he makes the sign of a cross, and moves on.

For him the matter is not resolved, but, in this instance, judging from wide-eyed, surprised, and quizzical looks his words elicit, he thinks a lot more thinking is about to occur. "That's right." he thinks. Let them figure it out. And what is more,

When they figure it out, they ought to say what is on their mind in an open, honest way – at least when they speak to men or, more precisely, when they speak to him, because he has neither time nor inclination to understand what obscure signs, ambiguous language, or feigned guilt, mean. There are the bins, the toilets, and the sweep to consider.

5

ANOTHER EXAMPLE OF HIS DILEMMA

EMERGES WHEN A WOMAN WANTS him to do something he does not. Store policy commands: Please the customer! Policy is on her side. To have the job, he endures the policy. When he receives a request, he should comply. But being himself, he may, or may not, do what she wants, as he simultaneously feels a need to be honest. The most trying request occurs near the bathroom.

In his store there are four bathrooms – two for men, two for women. One of each is on the second floor for employees only. Small and easy to clean, these provide no opportunity for this dilemma to emerge. On the main floor, there is one bathroom with four stalls for women and a second with two stalls and two urinals for men. The vexing request occurs at the door of the women's bathroom.

Just as he has or is about to start cleaning the women's bathroom, she comes and asks if she may use the bathroom. If he has started, she expects, asks, or demands that he stops work, leave the toilet, let her in, and wait until she is finished. After she has finished, he may clean again. If it were up to him, he would let them in and keep cleaning, saying: "If it's okay with you, it's okay with me." but social in- and prohibitions bar this option.

He could just stop, leave, and let her use the bathroom, but he is reluctant. Another woman might come along and ask or demand the same thing before the first finishes, and so on, delaying him for all eternity, meaning he would not finish cleaning before he had to sweep again. To not sweep is to not do his job. He cannot have that.

You might wonder how this goes. It goes like this.

He rolls the maintenance cart just short of the bathroom door to block neither the door nor the hallway. He takes the flag (CLOSED FOR CLEANING) off the cart and prepares to secure it between the jams of the door to deter entry into the bathroom. Before that he knocks hard on the door, opens it a few inches and shouts, "Maintenance." He waits for a response like "I'm in here" or "Occupied" or "Someone's here", upon which he backs out of the door, leans against the wall opposite, and waits. This is not the problem. This is an issue of right of way. She has it. He respects it.

When the toilet is empty, he puts the flag halfway up the jam and enters. He polices three trash bins, then moves to each stall to check toilet paper, flushable seat covers, and receptacles for tampon materials. He collects refuse and places it in one trash bag which he ties up for a trip to the compactor. Next, he goes and picks up a multi-purpose cleaner and paper towels from the cart, as well as toilet paper, a packet of disposable toilet-seat covers, and paper bags for the tampon receptacles. He re-enters the bathroom and replenishes the gaps. Thereafter, he sprays the counter, enters each stall, and sprays the toilet seat, lifts it, thoroughly sprays the underside of the seat and other parts of the toilet. Next, he wipes all sprayed areas with clean, dry paper towels, making sure to put the toilet seat down in each stall. He checks soap and paper towel dispensers to see if they need refills, he returns to the cart, gets the paper towels and soap he needs, and retrieves the aerosol air freshener. Finally, he re-enters the bathroom, installs the soap and/or paper towels, and sprays air freshener throughout the bathroom.

When it goes like this, it is perfect.

Without interruptions, cleaning all four bathrooms takes about 30 minutes. It is easier to clean the men's than the women's because there are two rather than four stalls, no tampon receptacles, urinals are easier to clean than stalls, and no air freshener to spray in the men's toilet. Thirty minutes puts him at the top of the next hour when he sweeps again.

An interruption by a single woman often goes like this. He is at the door, ready to put up the sign, when she walks up and sweetly, demurely, or deferentially says, "May I go in before you start?" and as he starts to reply, she goes on to say, "I won't take long" or "It'll just be a second" or "I'll be fast" and as he has not even begun to clean, he finds it impossible to say no, so he lets her go in. There is no reason to not step aside for her (other than it slows him down, which takes longer to explain than to yield). So, he steps aside. She has no right of way, but her need to pee, poop, or perform personal hygiene trumps his need for promptness. Over several shifts, these requests disrupt his thoughts and he begins to enter the bathroom as fast as possible to reduce this form of interruption to the lowest possible, and a more acceptable, level. So,

Inside the bathroom with the flag up he is confident he can proceed. That is, until there is a loud knock at the door, or the door just opens and she sticks her head inside, and subsequently uses one of two approaches. She may replace "May I go in before you start?" with just "May I come in?" Either just before he can say "No" or "I'm cleaning" or "It's closed," or just after, she adds, "I won't take long" or "It'll just be a second" or "I'll be fast." Alternately, she may take a more assertive approach that starts, "I have to get in here now" and continues to be assertive if he resists. She might add, as a sympathetic afterthought, "I won't take long" or "It'll just be a second" or "I'll be fast."

Early on he acquiesces, ends up leaning on the wall opposite the door, which is where he is as he decides she lied to him, because she is never fast, never takes a second, and, in his world of work, takes way too long. His first attempt to avoid this interruption is to simply block the door with the cart before he enters, but she still knocks or just loudly talks through the door. She shouts "How long?" and he responds "It's closed for cleaning" and she responds in a loud and exasperated voice, "NO, I said how long" and he says "Five or ten minutes." This silences her most of the time, but not always. On some occasions she goes to the manager, explains her problem and the two of them return to talk to him. In fact, the manager comes into the toilet and says, "You will have to let her in." Because the manager is his boss, when she tells him to do something, he does, so he lets the customer into the bathroom, steps outside, and leans against the wall opposite –hoping against hope no other woman appears while the manager is near and he is leaning against the wall.

He simply wants to clean the bathroom. He does not like a manager, accompanied by a vindicated customer, telling him to stop work, wait outside, and let the customer pee, poop, or perform personal hygiene. As a man of this modern age, he feels a little guilt that he feels so put upon by these women, and he imagines some would say, "He is a man, what do you expect?" To which, inwardly, he replies," I expect to do my work." So, in fact, he decides to make such requests moot in some non-threatening, non-male, manner. But how? The solution takes some days to arrive.

He decides he must present the woman, with or without a manager, a circumstance that she herself finds more unacceptable than the discomfort of not immediately peeing, pooping, or practicing personal hygiene. He tries to take her perspective. If you ask him, he will tell you he thinks he can do this, but is reluctant– there is always the further dilemma: Is his mind deceiving him in his attempt to role play a woman's point of view. Because self-deception is hard to detect, and a different dilemma, he takes a crack at it.

Illumination! It is a simple matter of changing his own behavior.

He changes the cleaning routine for the women's bathroom. He still races to get in the bathroom before she can ask to go in. He still blocks the door with the cart to deter her from pushing her way into the bathroom. He implements the change. First, he picks up the multi-purpose cleaner, enters the toilet and sprays every single toilet seat, relaxes, and starts the other cleaning tasks. It goes like this.

Whether she is alone, in a group, with or without a manager, when she asks if he will let her in, he says, "I just sprayed all the toilet seats with cleaner and haven't wiped them off yet." This causes a pause, so he adds, "It will take me a couple of minutes to go back and wipe the them dry" and then, "So if you wait outside, I will do that and when they are dry, come out to tell you." No matter what path she chooses, she does not keep pushing to get in. It turns out she is just like him – she does not want to sit down and get her naked ass all wet. As he mulls this over, his feelings are mixed because

In situations where she has a right of way, he respects it. When she makes her request before he starts, he manages sufficient grace to step aside. He rearranges the order of cleaning tasks in a way that allows him to keep working without stopping to lean against the wall opposite. He does not lie. These are all good. Still, she is in discomfort. This is not good. Perplexed, absent a soul-satisfying solution, he can think of nothing better. It is a case of "Now what?" and so he puts it in his pile of unresolved issues.

SOMETIMES

His dilemma Is quiescent, and he finds himself calm, quiet, ready to work. It was just so the day a new store policy arrived – the day he got to work and found keypad locks on all bathroom doors. Every employee received the entry code with instructions to open the bathroom when asked by customers. The change was meant to limit bathroom access by homeless persons, to reduce the amount of shit and piss on the floors, and to stop drug use in bathrooms (in the form of needles and a smell of burnt crack). An assistant manager put it this way, "Don't let homeless people use the bathrooms." Without thinking, he blurted, "I can't do that," to which she replied, "You must, it is store policy" and a store security man, listening nearby, added, "Right! Restrooms are private property. They are for customers only." The maintenance man had to do something, but what? First, he said,

"Let me say it another way. I will not do that." After he said it, he realized a reason he loves his job is he cleans – floors, toilets, trash bins – but does not police people. Refusing to keep homeless out of the toilets challenges the authority of managers who enforce the policy. By refusing, he might be fired or need to quit. The assistant manager repeats, "It is store policy, I do as I am told. If you have a problem, talk to Angela," His mind buzzed as he started his work day. He knew he would talk to Angela. And say what? And how?

Homeless people make him uncomfortable. If not mentally ill, he recoils from their life style. Being honest, he acknowledges he does not want them around, but he knows if they cannot use the toilets, they will behave as they do in San Francisco and piss and shit wherever, whenever. Please God, not that! He decides what he has to say when he goes to talk to Angela, who

Is a person always moving on some task or mission – in honorable pursuit of store excellence. He imagines she will insist on strict adherence to store policy. Nevertheless, between his first sweep of the store and cleaning the bathrooms he tracks her down. He says, "Can I talk to you for a moment?" She answers, "Sure, what's up?"

He says, "It is the locks on the toilets. I was told to keep the homeless out."

She says, "Yes?"

He says, "I cannot do that. People must be able to go to the toilet. Besides, I was hired to clean, not police people, homeless or not."

She pauses and then asks, "Do you mind that the doors are locked?"

He thinks a moment and answers, "No. It's a bother being asked to open the door, and doing so takes time, but, in itself, I don't mind."

"Well," she says, "Here is what I say to people who seem homeless: 'You know the bathrooms are private property, reserved for customers and employees.' Then I unlock the door for them." She also says, "Could you do that?"

After a pause to absorb his surprise at the humanness of her response, he knows he can and nods – no policing, just a simple statement of fact (store policy on toilets), then grant access, thereafter return to the joy of his work. So it goes, happily, until,

He notices and starts to think about customers who ask to be admitted to a toilet. His is an analytic mind. Whether he wants to or not, his mind dissects the speech of others. Why? He does not know. He just does, and doing so shapes his behavior for better and worse. Just like sweeping the floor brings him repeated accidental crossing of paths with customers and employees, the door lock policy brings him repeated contact with a subset of customers and non-customers with the same urgent need to use a toilet. At first, he expects

Customers to say, "Will you (please) open the bathroom door for me?" In fact, they never ask this. Instead, despite the urgency, they say, "The bathroom door is locked?" or "Do you have the code for the bathroom lock?" or other inquiries affirming the existence of locks on doors. His answer to all these is, "Yes," and his affirmation is not what they expect. Nevertheless, they continue an oblique path to a toilet or urinal by asking, "Do you have the code for the door?" Answer "Yes" or, if he is feeling self- important or expansive, "Yes, I do." More surprise – at times consternation – but still oblique, "Will you give me the code?" followed by his ironic, "No. (pause) I cannot. It is store policy not to share the code." (How liberating to say this!) Necessity prompts directness, so they reach the final question,

"Will you please let me in the bathroom?" to which he happily replies

"I'm happy to do so, and I must tell you that the bathrooms are private, only for store customers and employees." Saying this, he knows, on one hand, that he has been a smart-ass, but, on the other hand, he feels people, in their role as customer, ought to skip irrelevant aspects of a situation and get to the point – after all, he is a busy maintenance man. As a man busy with cleaning tasks, once he understands that such interactions with the codeless are ritual and require no thought, he drifts into a reverie of his work. His thoughts return to floors, toilets, and bins – no longer abuzz with policing the homeless, as he says – "As it should be." What of the maintenance man's dilemma? What dilemma? When he is in a reverie, when no woman smiles benignly at him, nor softly requests something of him, nor, knowingly or innocently, dresses in a provocative way and enters his field of view, it is as if his dilemma does not exist at all.

NOR IS A SENSE OF DILEMMA

LIMITED TO WOMEN FEIGNING GUILT or people needing toilets. No. Often, words and actions of others puzzle him. From day one, he finds this so of his co-workers, who adhere to their own culture, fostered, in part, by the corporation. On first meeting each day, everybody says "Hi Bill"– his first name is on a badge he wears. Everyone says "hi" to everyone. Although the intent is to create a milieu of welcome, he is off balance because, on his own, he seldom says hello. To strangers, most often, he sends a smile or nod. That he cannot read badges of co-workers increases his discomfort. His eyes are multi-focal due to multiple surgeries for myopia. He sees well enough to drive and watch TV, but letters and edges are not sharp and clear, so, he keeps asking their name, so he may say, "Hello" too. Follow-up conversations are a bit discomforting.

These conversations introduce a culture beyond that promulgated by store policy. It is a culture of the employees themselves, and unlike banter with customers, this culture provides few opportunities to be creative. He sees these conversations as ritual, not for communication, but to take the speaker from this moment to the next. After "Hello," when the maintenance man asks, "How are you?" the most frequent response is,

"Same shit, different day." as the other acknowledges him and returns to a task at hand. His own tasks drive him, so he bends to the norm and moves on. When he is not pressed to move on, he looks for different types of conversation —more personal and revealing. One day, as he sweeps through the produce section, he has time to start a conversation with Saloman, a produce man, by saying,

"¿Que es su nombre?"

"Saloman."

"Hola Saloman. ¿Como esta?"

"Bien, y tu, ¿como estas? Bill."

Now he can use the familiar personal pronoun and practice Spanish with Saloman, y por eso, contesta

"Estoy bien, pero hace muchos años que he trabajado tanto. Y tu, ¿cuantos años trabajas en esta tienda?"

"Veinte años." And switching to English, "How is it that you find the work so hard?"

"Because before I started this job, I did no physical work in 30 years, a long time to sit at a desk."

And that is how Saloman and the maintenance man started talking to each other in ways more personal and revealing of themselves. It is how produce became his favorite section to sweep. They speak some Spanish. They speak some English. As men, they slip into a ritual of men and talk about caracteristicas de las mujeres que pasan por la tienda (por alguna razon hablan de estas mujeres sola en español). The maintenance man understands this ritual exists everywhere. He joins without misgiving. He harbors no ill-intent toward women, believing women, like men, also talk about the opposite sex in ritual ways. Should the sexes talk so? He thinks one ought to be honest in such conversations, or not speak at all. He thinks each sex ought to respect the other.

At the start of a sweep when he pushes the broom out of the back and makes a left onto the store floor, he passes butter and yogurt, and meets Leon, a Chicano who speaks no Spanish. Over several days, the maintenance man learns Leon works full-time at a local hospital and nearly so at the store, and is having a hard time getting the managers to adjust his schedule so he can continue to work both jobs. The maintenance man sees that Leon is unhappy. When Leon says,

"I do not know what to do. I ask them to fix my schedule, but nothing changes."

The maintenance man, happy and secure in his finances, cannot be coerced financially, as seems to be the case for Leon. Yet, he remembers a time, years earlier, when he was fired for choosing to go to a parade instead of work. Trying to not be pushy, he asks Leon,

"Who is in charge of your life?"

"Me" Leon replies.

"Exactly" affirms the maintenance man,

"And what do you want?"

"A life outside of work."

Now that they are talking about what the butter and yogurt man wants, the maintenance man feels free to assert, "In that case, take control of your life. Try to get what you want. The store managers will not do it for you."

"I know, but...."

"No, it is up to you. Which job is most important to you?"

"The hospital."

"Then do what is best for you."

"Yeah."

They return to their respective tasks -- the maintenance man happy he is without financial concerns. He is not surprised some weeks later to learn Leon no longer works at the store, and thinks he would like to see him again to find out how his choice turned out, but he only ever knew Leon's first name.

TALKING WITH THE BUTTER
AND YOGURT MAN PROMPTED

THE MAINTENANCE MAN TO REMEMBER that when he was 28 years old, he was fired because he did what he wanted rather than what the boss wanted. The comedy of his dismissal transpired in a mobile home factory in Tampa. Building a mobile home convinced him to never live in one – a conviction formed after one week of screwing aluminum sheet metal siding onto two-by-two wood frames in Bay 3 of the factory. In that place,

Construction proceeds in stages: first, roll a steel undercarriage into Bay 1 and bolt rough flooring to it; next, move the carriage to Bay 2 and install framing, electric harness, and two-inch insulation bats, as well as finished flooring and cabinetry; thereafter, slide the carriage into Bay 3 – where wage slaves install hurricane straps, a sheet steel roof, aluminum siding, and windows and, finally, pass the home to Bay 4 for bathroom fixtures, and furniture.

Once upon a time, the maintenance man knew how many screws secured aluminum siding to the framing of a double-wide. It was an exact number, lost to passing time and interference from many, more important, numbers like 340, 2900 or 9400 dollars. Yet,

Being new to Florida, out of work on arrival, he was happy for the work. There was not much to think about on the job, except: keep edges of the siding from slicing the skin of your fingers and palms! A few weeks passed just so. One morning, occupied with protecting his skin and screwing siding to the frame, he did not notice a line boss come up behind and announce to those in the bay,

"Anybody who skips work this afternoon to go to the Gasparilla Days parade is fired." The threat miffed the maintenance man, who responds with oppositional defiance to arbitrary authority, and who knew nothing about Gasparilla Days. By asking co-workers, he learned Gasparilla Days celebrates a pirate with a party, a parade, and events like Mardi Gras. He said to himself: "I have to see this." At lunch,

He clocked out and went home to ask Her to go with him to the parade. She said,

"No. I have to go to work." She worked at a department store: always on time and attendant to store policies. He told Her about the ultimatum. She said,

"Well, you better go back to work. We need the money." A statement that made him smile the smile he used to make Her smile. She did. Then She said,

"Go, you will anyway, but I'm going to work." She did. He did not want to see the parade without Her, but did not want to go back to work. No, he would not cave to authority. He just went walking with his dog Free in a nearby junkyard, where they found a mountain of one-foot-square, woven straw tiles, and he spent an hour or so carrying some back to their rented house to decorate their bedroom. The next day, he entered the mobile home factory, went to clock in, did not find his time card, and looked for the boss, to ask

"Where is my time card? I can't find it."

"Because you don't have a time card."

"Why?"

"Because you were warned."

"But I didn't go to the parade, or anything to do with Gasparilla Days." The boss spit out,

"I don't care. You're fired. You can pick up your check on payday. Now get out." then turned and walked away to harangue people who still worked there. That was that, so the maintenance man turned and walked out, thinking that not bowing to authority was a victory. It was not. They had to rely on Her department store clerk's part-time salary: She loathed financial insecurity. He loathed seeing Her anxious about money. It turned to victory not many days later when he got a job at a construction site where restauranteurs on Bayshore Drive were replacing their old building with a bigger, better one. He started as a laborer, worked up to carpenter, and earned decent wages. He loved it. He ate lunch in the old restaurant where they served the best sweet potato pie he ever had. It was a high time because

He was working, She was working, and money rolled in, covered their needs, and provided extra. They ate dinner out every night – their apartment had no kitchen. Their favorite restaurant was Alvarez in Ybor City where he ate bolichi or black bean soup with cheese and onions, and lots of Cuban bread. What a life!

The construction firm offered to send him through guild schools so he could become a construction superintendent for them. The day of this offer he said to the superintendent

"Wow! After I talk to my wife tonight, I will let you know."

"Good."

He went home, retold Her the conversation with the superintendent. She said,

"What do you want to do?"

"I am sure I'd like to do it."

"Okay." On that happy note, they went to bed. Around midnight, mid-sleep, the phone rang. It was Clive, their friend from graduate school, who said,

"The duplex next to ours is vacant. We could rent it for you if you would like to come to Arizona for a while. What do you think?"

"I think it's pretty late." After a brief discussion of time zone differences, the maintenance man said,

"We'll talk and call you back."

"Okay."

Two enticing offers in a single day. The maintenance man knew he must decide, but what and how?" On the one hand,

There was the prospect of a good career in construction, learning the trades involved, and building real things. His grandfather, father, uncle, and a brother, all tradesmen, would be proud. This choice involved at least two years in trade schools. It made sense – you had to know the trades for construct a building before you supervised construction. On the other hand,

There was the exciting prospect of moving on. No jobs, no goals, only a duplex in Arizona, and who knew what else. In the end, just two years out of graduate school, he did not mull it long. He told Her,

"I'm going to call Clive back."

"Okay." She knew they were heading to Arizona.

He called. He gave notice, thanked his boss for the offer, and two days after their last day of work, their Chevrolet Super Sport convertible -- packed with possessions, dog Free, and themselves -- carried them to Arizona. They made it. It was June. It was hot. After a time, he looked for work in construction, and was surprised when

He walked onto a site in a subdivision development and talked to the foreman. After he related his history in Florida, the foreman offered him a job as a carpenter's assistant. Ecstatic, he asked,

"When do I start?"

"Tomorrow."

"What time?"

"Five thirty."

"Really!?"

"Yup."

The next morning, the maintenance man got up at four, was on site before five thirty, and already felt nearly overwhelmed by the heat. His task was to carry two sheets of plywood to a carpenter on the roof. The latter rapidly fitted and nailed the plywood in place. Exhausted by seven thirty, he stumbled frequently as he navigated up the scaffolding with the plywood. On the first short break, the foreman came over and said,

"For the rest of the day, carry one sheet at a time and try to keep up with the carpenter."

"Okay." A feeling of defeat washed over him. In Arizona, in one day, he became an inferior construction worker. The heat of Arizona and the pace of work stripped away the illusion that he could work construction there. At the end of his first day, the maintenance man, through bone-tired ears, heard the foreman say,

"Take tomorrow off and rest. I will call you when I need you."

"Okay." He realized he had been fired – gently. He never felt such relief! He went home, went to bed at four p.m., did not wake until late the next morning. When he got up, his first thought was, "Now what?"

Returning to his thoughts about the butter and yogurt man, he hoped Leon was as happy as he was when he got fired at the mobile home factory and at the construction site in Arizona. Not the end of the world, being fired was a ritual that took him from one moment to the next. Perhaps, such rituals are good.

A Journey to Arizona

WHEN THEY LIVED IN FLORIDA, Bruce, husband of his cousin Lorraine, sold them a 1966, 427 cubic inch, Chevrolet, Super Sport convertible. Fast, powerful, and exuberant, they drove it everywhere, to eat, to St. Pete's beach, to Orlando, to Sunset Bridge down the coast, to deserted beaches along Tampa Bay so Free could run. They were happy to be away from their two-room, kitchen-less, apartment, away from visits by unwanted visitors – the huge roaches benignly called palmetto bugs– that drove Her to fury- filled murder using shoes, fly swatter, newspaper, or, if fast enough, a can of Raid from the bathroom.

So, when Clive invited them to come live in the duplex next door. He was for it, and so was She. Enthusiastically, She said

"Let's go tonight" but after saying it, realized arrangements were needed, then said,

"Let's go as soon as possible."

He called Clive back. They gave notice, got their last checks, packed clothes, Free, cooler, a few odds and ends into the Chevy, and left. It was the beginning of June. Florida, Alabama, Mississippi, Louisiana, and eastern Texas were hot and muggy as they drove in the Super Sport without air conditioning. She disregarded the muggy heat and drove from Florida to Texas. She smoked. She drank coffee. She stopped for gas. She stopped for coffee. She stopped to pee. As they crossed Texas, a hot, muggy climate changed to a hotter, dryer one, She succumbed to exhaustion and pulled the car off the highway, and said,

"You have to drive. I have to sleep."

"Okay," They got out to change seats. After he walked Free, he started to drive. She fell right to sleep. He did well for about an hour, cruising about 70 miles per hour on a four-lane highway, but soon was unable to keep his eyes open. Once or twice, he caught himself driving with eyes closed. He pulled off the road and put the seat back to rest. No sooner done than he heard,

"Why are we stopped?" in an aggravated tone.

"I was falling asleep"

"How long have you been driving? Where are we?" When She heard him say, "Still in Texas. About an hour." She spit out,

"I'll drive." She did, all the way to Arizona, fueled by smoking cigarettes and drinking coffee, with stops for gas, pee, and coffee. Once or twice, they came upon a thundershower. She slowed the car to stay in the cooler air under the storm, and once out, raced on.

When they arrived at Clive's duplex in the early evening, they all talked for a few minutes and then both went and fell asleep on a mattress put on the floor for them. They woke late the next bright, dry, morning, It felt like a preheated oven. When they entered the duplex, they did not see a stove, refrigerator, kitchen table, chairs, orange shag carpet, two bedrooms, or swamp cooler, but rather

Billions, or more, of German roaches on every surface, in every cranny. They were everywhere. The unwanted, nightly visits by a few, humungous, Florida, palmetto bugs morphed into a teeming, all-the-time-present, horde of disgusting, little, German roaches. Roaches lived in the toilet basin, the linings of the stove, and every part of the refrigerator. They came out from in and under cabinets, from in and under sinks in the kitchen and bathroom. They lived in sockets, switches, and a swamp cooler. She took it in, turned, fled the duplex, stopped outside the door, and sobbed. In the finest moment of his life, the maintenance man followed Her out, embraced Her, and said softly,

"Don't worry. I will fix this."

"How can you fix this?"

"I will kill them all and clean everything as well. You stay next door until I finish." She said nothing, but did just that. He went to the hardware store, bought roach bombs, massive amounts of malathion, cans of Raid, and dozens of roach traps. Then he began, known among a few fleeing survivors, the Roach Holocaust. He went into cattycorner rooms (kitchen and a bedroom), set off bombs, and left. Twenty- four hours later he returned to find billions of bodies. He swept up and filled a garbage bag with them. He moved the refrigerator and stove into the Arizona sun, sprayed them with Raid, closed them up, and left them to bake. He hoped the two appliances could be saved, but it was not to be. The spun glass insulation of both was almost completely gone and laced with bodies of the dead and of a photophobic scattering of living remnants of the horde. Back in the house he spent more time tearing out the orange shag rug, spraying more survivors, and taking out the dead. She came to assess the state of her new home, then left again. They talked. She needed more. He kept at it. He could not bear disappointment in Her eyes. More killing was the cure. Two days of spraying and sweeping killed another half a billion or so. Their home was free of visual sightings, but they were not free. It was an old duplex with many dark hiding places in which momma roaches laid egg sacks. Hundreds of roaches per sack – all impervious to bombs and poison until they emerged. The final steps of the Holocaust featured two lines of attack.

First, he painted malathion strips in crosshatch patterns covering the entire interior floor of the duplex, as well as around the interior perimeter of every room, and across each passage between rooms. Second, 15, 30, and 45 days after the first bombs, he set off bombs again, to kill newborn babies as they left hidden egg sacks. At the end of a week before the final bombing campaign, he simply cleaned the house, then they bought a bed, a stove, and refrigerator and moved into the dead zone that was their half of the duplex. Happily, roaches that entered thereafter, died quickly – killed by instant, furious, pinpoint, strikes with weapons stored at the ready in handy locations. Unhappily,

Their duplex presented another horror. The shower was constructed of 4-inch by 4-inch sky blue tile. They knew this because tile at head height and above, was sky blue, but from head height down was covered by living slime in shades that turned from moldy gray-green at eye level to dark, gray-green at stomach level, and on to coal black from the knee level down. It was another disgusting feature about which he said,

"I will fix it, too." And She smiled a sweet smile (an amalgam of forgiveness, love, and resignation) then said,

"Okay you booby" which She had called him before. It Her affectionate nickname for him. and signaled that the crisis of Her well-being about their home was over. Although he knew the crisis of Her well-being was over, the living black mass remained. He donned rubber gloves. First, he tried to use Comet and elbow grease. Marginal progress. Next, he tried liquid cleaners of one sort or another. The same luck. He could not get through the slime to the tile. Finally, he bought a pack of double-edged razor blades. He scrapped each tile. When he reached tile on a patch of shower, he would use Comet to clean it a bit better. After he did this for the entire shower, he repeated the operation again. After two days of iterations of razors and Comet, he was ready for Her to inspect and decide IF it was good enough for Her. She found spots needing attention. He addressed them and grew happy the moment She approved. He was proud of what he had done – another fine moment.

The wisdom of moving to Arizona, dubious at the beginning of a long hot summer, never entered their thoughts. They were 28 years old. They did it, and, once there, created a home – a two-bedroom, roach-free, duplex apartment, well-lit by windows in every room, with a nice grass yard between units, and open fields nearby where he and Free walked and ran. As his Cajun friend Malcolm would say, "Thank you, Sweet Baby Jesus!"

Invoking Jesus's name, PROMPTED HIM TO RECALL

───────────────

THE TIME HE AND SHE talked about Christmas. They preferred a personal form of religion (try to live by the golden-rule) that led them to respect Christmas, but not so much the social aspects of the holiday that crept in and remained. Once,

On Her way past him to the post office, after She had finished writing personal notes, signing, addressing, and stamping a stack of Christmas cards, She asked "When exactly did I agree to do all the Christmas chores?" in a tone that caused him to think, "This is important to Her." When he thought "important", he paused. What to say? In the set of persons important to him, She was most important, so he considered his choices.

He considered a factual answer like "In 1982 you asked if I wanted to address the cards and I said 'no thanks'." Even if he recalled facts correctly, he was slow to voice an answer, whereas, She generated them quickly and was certain to have the last fact. He had his bad memory for facts, talked too slow, and failed to share the chores all those years. He skipped a factual answer.

He might have tried, "Why didn't you say something? I would have helped." On other occasions he recalled how swiftly Her disdain followed this answer. As a grown man, he knew no one is well-received for volunteering for work already done. And She would likely say "Is it also my job to say the Christmas cards need to be signed, addressed, stamped, and mailed?" thus providing more evidence of the validity of Her first question. He skipped that response. Next,

26

He thought about listing all he did for Christmas. Stringing lights occurred to him, but was a poor choice –sometimes he got them up, sometimes he did not. In one two-year stretch the lights were up right after Thanksgiving because he put them up in time the first year, then left them up all the second year. He forgot to take them down. Unfortunately, he could not think of another chore he did. If he said the lights, She would say the cards, then add finding, wrapping, and mailing presents, as well as dragging him to get a tree. Still,

Because he did the lights, he might have adopted a lawyer-like position and attack the "all" part of Her original question. From time to time, he had taken this approach. He would find a small flaw and pound away at it. Discussions in which he did so always ended badly with feelings hurt all around, so he did not do this about the cards. It was not in the Christmas spirit at all. Rejecting these approaches,

He almost said the right thing, "Are there chores left for me do (careful not to say "Her chores")?" This would have required him to do the Christmas chores that remained. So, he imagined making a case for a simple exchange of gifts among loved ones, either after Christmas Eve dinner or before Christmas breakfast. He imagined saying, "When did Christmas turn into such a production", then he imagined Her saying, "What do you know about Christmas productions". Instead of any of these things.

In a sincere voice, he did say, "Gee, I don't remember." And treated Her well the entire week before Christmas, because with time left to shop, he loved the wacky presents She found for him in commercial America. The thought, "Sometime this week I have to get the lights up," occurred just before he thought James Thurber made a living drawing cartoons and writing plays about a war between men and women. The maintenance man doubted it was war – rather an endless series of playful skirmishes. War is avoided if we use diplomacy. Diplomacy is a choice of the words we use. The best advice the maintenance man ever heard about choice was spoken by the knight in **Indiana Jones and the Last Crusade.** Charged with keeping the Holy Grail safe for all Christmases, the knight said, "Choose wisely." The maintenance man thought that was good advice for the holiday, or any other time.

HIS FIRST IMPORTANT
CHOICE HAPPENED

IN HIGH SCHOOL, HE HID uncertainty with flippant or blunt speech. Despite doing so, he made two fast friends. First was K who lived five houses down the block in their lower-middle class subdivision in the town where his dad Bill brought his wife Isabelle and two sons from New York to Illinois, after a two and a half-year separation. Second was Ray whom he met in sixth grade.

K had a free spirit, immune to barbs of the maintenance man, while Ray was a wise ass and hurled insults right back. With K, he went fishing, traipsed forests, and explored the Des Moines river. With Ray he played complex cand and board games. Between his 11th and 16th birthday, his second and third brothers, Rick, and Tom, were born.

The maintenance man had yet to make an adult choice. He made a few bad choices. He stole fishing lures from Shank's Hardware, got caught, and barred from the store – although neither police nor family learned of the theft – due to an owner, who sat him down and had a man-to-man talk. He stole tasty cantaloupes from a garden in the flood plain across the river that was the back border of their property. He, K, and a third hooligan stretched a string across the highway that ran down a wooded hill toward the river. On the string they hung newspapers so a driver of a car speeding down the hill would see a white wall loom up in front of them. In a nearby hiding spot they heard a car speed down the hill, slam on the breaks, and screech to a stop. Frightened by the intensity and urgency of the sound, they fled, away along the river. As he ran, he concluded the prank was not right, and resolved not to do such things again. However,

The resolve to do better did not lead to being less a wise ass or less blunt. He did some thinking about choices he was making. Some, not much. There was no epiphany so he continued as before, just a bit more mindful of consequences of events that might turn out badly. Because his friends talked about it, he thought about what to do after high school. A school acquaintance, Neal, intended to join the army. Because his father served in the Army Reserves and respected all services, the maintenance man agreed to join up with Neal. Yet, at the end of his junior year, Ray and two other friends talked about colleges they planned to attend, and argued about the merits of each school. Envy grew in the maintenance man's mind. College seemed exotic. He knew nothing about college -- not admission, not quality, not cost. He asked his dad. Having never attended,

His father provided no helpful details about getting into or financing college, or about quality of colleges. What he knew, he summarized in a single sentence: "Son, go to college, get a degree, and you will always be able to find work." Yikes! Jobs!? He was not sure, but he felt he crossed an invisible boundary that separated childhood from something closer to adulthood. Bedeviled trying to resolve the army versus college choice, he went to a counselor who just kept asking over and over, in different ways,

"What do you want to do?"

"I don't know." Et cetera. So, he asked his mom. She said,

"Son, whatever you choose to do, I will love you."

Great! Put it all back on him. Try to make him feel good at the same time. Good moms do. As a last resort, he went to one other adult, a physics teacher whom he respected. Mr. Heart, it turned out, had attended a small work-study school with low tuition. Mr. Heart got a degree, then he got a job – just as his father had advised. That is why,

In the space of a few months, the maintenance man applied to Mr. Heart's college, had an interview, received an acceptance letter, and information on costs. He learned a little over $1000 covered tuition, room, board (20 meals a week), and books for a year. Money for snacks, entertainment, and gambling was extra. He chose to go, then told Neal he would not to join the Army. He felt he let Neal down, but could not say how, except it had to do with having given his word. He learned about his school, participated in discussions about schools with Ray and the others, and, as he did, saw less of Neal.

There was the matter of $1000 to pay for tuition, room, board, and books, as well as money for snacks, entertainment, and gambling. His parents lived paycheck to paycheck, juggling installments on two cars, a house, appliances, and other fixtures of middle class living. They had no savings. When he talked with his parents, they said they would help if they could, but $1000 was beyond their means. He went to a bank in town and obtained a student loan for the cost of the first year, and, in time, he came to appreciate what his parents did do for him. When he was at college,

His mother, Isabelle, wrote from time to time. Sometimes a letter arrived with a box of snacks. sometimes in an envelope with a five-dollar bill. His father, Bill, co-signed the loan, and, via a friend, Willard, arranged for the maintenance man to have a full-time job the summer after his sophomore year. By taking time off work,

His father packed a small U-Haul and drove him to college – a trip made several times in the following four years. At the end of the first trip, just as he was about to leave, his father handed the maintenance man a check for $60 and said,

"Son, I wish it could be more, but it's all I can afford."

"That's okay Dad. I'll get by." To himself, "but how?"

With a "See you at Thanksgiving" his father left him, and he was alone for the first time in his life. And he remained alone for several minutes, hints of searching questions emerged in the recess of his mind, until rituals of the college swept him up: a tour with a welcome committee; orientation talks with a few faculty and administrators; exploration and arrangement of their room with his roommate; orientation picnic; and so on…. And from then on,

He was always, simply, a welcomed, loved, guest in his parents' home. He was 17 years old.

SOME CHOICES ARE NOT CHOICES

I F OPTIONS ARE FIXED, HOW is it a choice? During high school, he worked as a gardener on an estate, a dishwasher, a busboy, and a clerk in a pro-shop at a nine-hole golf course. He learned he could stay or leave these jobs, but not change them. So it was at college, where he worked on a crew that built an administration building. Students working as carpenters, electricians, masons, plumbers, and unskilled laborers comprised the crew. Absent skills, the maintenance man waited for the superintendent, a permanent staff member of the college, to fill the skill positions with students who possessed relevant experience. He was assigned to Doug, a sophomore who served as foreman, and who told him what to do. They became friends. Nevertheless, he felt like the worst player in a group waiting to be picked for a game of pick-up ball. Nevertheless,

The superintendent needed grunts to haul bricks, blocks, sand, cement mix, lime, pipes, lumber, and wire to the skilled workers. Other grunts mixed and delivered mortar. Some delivered messages. The superintendent delegated running messages because his deformed leg limited how much, how far, and how fast he walked. The maintenance man worked as a grunt until mid-year, at which time, students were permitted to apply to the work council for a transfer to a new job. He did, and started an odyssey through a variety of jobs -- janitor, pots and pans scrubber, and counter server in the student union. For him, the jobs at college were all the same – menial but necessary, done by people making their way toward a better life, toward something that required them to use their brains, and, for which they thought they were being trained. He liked every job. He saw that his work as a janitor in college and in Willard's high-rise apartment building prepared him to be a supermarket maintenance man later in life, whereas a major in mathematics and courses in psychology did not. He did not believe training the mind was better than training the body. Unskilled work permitted his mind to think about whatever he wanted, whenever he wanted – without rules.

THE MAINTENANCE MAN'S DILEMMA

D ID NOT END WHEN HE left the grocery store. After he left, coworkers asked, "Why?" His answer was a lament: he loved the job he had to leave; he loved bantering with customers; he loved teasing people who needed a toilet, yet empathized when asked, "Will you unlock the bathroom door for me?" He loved the rituals of the store like he loved the rituals of his family. He loved losing 30 pounds of fat because the pace of work was so fast, and, he loved that his muscles firmed up. That his pay permitted him to gamble more, and that his mind could go wherever, whenever, were bonuses. So, when pain in his hips started and an old ankle problem returned, he was bothered. He went to the manager and, as tears filled his eyes, sobbed out the words,

"Angela, I think I have to quit" and sobbed again, "Sorry, I love this job. I do not want to leave." She asked,

"What's happened?" and he said,

"My hips hurt a lot after I leave work, and my ankle has started bothering me again."

"That's not good. Is there anything we can do?"

"I was thinking four four-hour days a week might work. I can try."

"Well talk to Karen, work out the schedule, and we'll see."

"Okay" he said and returned to work, relieved that he would work four days in a row, four hours each day, and that these would be followed by three days for his body to rest and recover. He thought it might work, and it did – for two weeks. After a third week of work,

All three of his days off were filled with pain. His left hip stung and bit him whenever he flexed his lower body. For the first time since starting the job, he called out sick, but he knew he had reached an end. His mind asked his body,

"Is there was a way to keep working and somehow diminish the pain." His body said,

"No. You can't do this anymore." He cried, because he knew age had brought him to a point where it could recover given sufficient time, but three rest days was not enough. He knew his days of physical work – except around his home – were over. He went to Angela once more and said,

"I have to leave."

With a concerned voice, she asked if he had seen a doctor. No, he had nor would not. She asked if he thought a different, more distributed schedule, or even fewer hours would help. He had thought about it, but did not think it would help. She accepted his leaving, and said,

"We will miss you. You are a good worker."

He knew this and voiced his affirmation, "Uh huh. I know" and went on his way.

What now? He wondered as he left. He considered options, and doing so, also reflected on past choices. What resolved these choices? As far as he knew, he had only and always made tactical, not strategic, choices about a way forward, with no thought of a further future. To himself, he seemed to be a man born without noble goals. Was he bad or evil for being so? Was it inexcusable to lack motivation that enabled others to say, with complete conviction, "I am going to be, for example, a doctor, a lawyer, an entrepreneur, a president." He thought not: but had no idea why he was the way he was.

BEFORE LATER CHOICES

IN COLLEGE, FROM THE START he faced the same question a high school counselor asked 15 months earlier,

"What do you want to do? his faculty advisor asked.

"I don't know."

"Lucky for you, first year is almost all basics, mathematics, English, chemistry, language, and social science. You can take some time, but you should decide on a major by Christmas."

"Christmas?"

"In order to choose an elective in your major in the spring."

"Oh, okay." For him, it was odd he had to choose a major by the end of the first fall in order to choose an elective in the spring. That advice was incomplete – as subsequent choices revealed. What did he know? Not much. What were his sources of information? People around him. Were they reliable? He did not know. They were new in his life. Barely a week in college, four months until his 18th birthday, and it seemed everyone, everything was pushing him to adulthood. In that state,

First, he chose to have fun. He found three reliable paths to fun: get a girl and make out; play intramural sports and shoot off your wise ass mouth; and, drink and/or play cards. In a small college, in a rural part of the Midwest, two of these three options were discouraged by in loco parentis. Not that he cared. During his first fall semester,

He drank and gambled. This consumed his free time. Being 17, on weekend nights, when he had money, he drank bootlegged vodka and orange soda, got sick and collapsed into his bed. When he had little money, he played pitch for a dime a game, plus a dime a set. His genes, having endowed him with math aptitude, served him well. As an intuitive player most of the time he earned money for snacks, or to buy his way into a Saturday night poker game – in which he often earned more spending money.

He tried out and made the college soccer team his first year. As a substitute he seldom played, and in a game, while in the 18-yard box, an opponent pushed him to the pitch, the ball rolled in front of him, and he thoughtlessly sent the ball toward his goalie with his hands. Infraction, penalty shot, score, and a loss followed. He never played in another game after the coach decided he was not an asset to the team. He had not connected with a girl yet, but

Sally, a junior, made him a project. She was as tall as he, attractive, slim, and, according to juniors and seniors, quite promiscuous. Their exact words were, "She's a slut." He did not find her so. They sat around and talked. She knew how things worked in school and town, and in these things, she helped him. She would sneak into his dorm room they would talk, then sneak out. Afraid of discovery, he never caressed her breasts. They neither made out nor made love. They did kiss. Later in life, what he remembered was someone saw her leave his room, reported him, and he received social probation. For a month, he had to remain in his dorm room during free time. His time with Sally falsely enhanced his sexual reputation, because on his own he could not go up to a girl and ask anything, particularly not for a date.

By the end of fall semester, he knew his high school study habits were inadequate. His grade-point average hovered between a D and a C, but he missed academic probation by a tenth of a point, so he carried on the same. He did learn

He could make what he thought was an adult decision. He learned this because by the end of his first semester, he chose a major – and, after that he chose an elective for Spring semester. During fall semester, Dr. H, his general chemistry professor, entertained students with stories about building the Bomb somewhere in New Mexico – he never revealed specifics – and experiences with Oppenheimer. That a large, knot, cyst, or tumor bulged out of the side of his neck made him enigmatic. His General Chemistry course – not Trigonometry and

Analytic Geometry, not English, not French, and not Social Science – captured enough of the maintenance man's interest that, yep, he chose chemistry as a major, and Analytic Chemistry as his elective. He was on his way. Where? Who knew?

TO BE A CHEMISTRY MAJOR

H E HAD TO TAKE CHEMISTRY courses -- at least 30 semester hours of chemistry courses and labs. His first advanced course, Analytic Chemistry, involved laboratory work; with exercises that required him to learn techniques to determine elements in an unknown compound. Titration, precise measurement of quantities, mixing knowns and unknowns, observing reactions, boiling off water, and weighing empty and finished crucibles comprised each exercise. This was new! And soon, he knew Analytic Chemistry was not for him. What to do? How to survive? An interesting question for which he had neither a wise- ass nor a wise answer. Lucky for him,

In the fall, he had met and became friends with Tom, a town student, who commuted to campus from his home a mile or two from college. Tom and the maintenance man shared three passions: cards –pitch, poker, bridge, and whist in that order -- played for cash with ferocious, tenacity that cowed opponents; making wise-ass remarks to classmates; and, doing anything but study. They took the same chemistry class, became lab partners, and shared an academic fate that depended on solving the exercises. In layman's term, each exercise became, "What the heck is this stuff?"

In fairness to the two, they tried the correct way. They made precise measurement of known and unknown compounds, mixed the known compounds with the unknown, titrated, weighed their crucibles empty, burned off unneeded water, weighed their crucibles after burn-off, made their decisions, and handed in findings. With three chances to succeed, they correctly completed simple, early problems. As complexity of the exercises grew, success slipped away. Tom suggested an alternative solution; use failures, two each were permitted, to narrow possibilities, then use the recommended technique for the final answer. It was awful analytic chemistry, but effective academic technique. Both got a B in the course. Less time spent on exercises meant more time playing cards in the student union, which was the spot

They met and made friends with Larry, the head of the student union and a work council member, who had keys, did books, scheduled workers, and ordered supplies for the union. He was in charge. He was a no-nonsense student, hard at work on a pre-medical major that involved hard science courses. As the maintenance man and Tom scammed analytic chemistry, Larry completed biochemistry exercises with precise, impeccable technique. He liked the two freshmen for their wise-ass ways, but could not be swayed from his path – pre-medical undergraduate study, medical school, intern, residency, doctor, practice, death. Along the way, a wife and family would be nice. In all ways,

Larry was a decent, responsible, adult. He encouraged them to stop their nonsense and get to work. Good advice, well meant! It reminded the maintenance man of his father passing on wisdom he knew would serve the maintenance man well. However, both he and Tom lacked a goal – like become a doctor – so they heard but ignored Larry's advice. What turned out to be important was the opportunity to watch Larry do biochemistry, without taking the course. It was like analytic chemistry using better smelling compounds. The maintenance man concluded chemistry was not for him.

Whew! Now what? After spring semester, he needed a new major again. Not to worry, he was 18 and starting to figure college out. Meanwhile,

Differential and integral calculus was the difficult course in his spring schedule. Not the differential, but the integral, due to idiosyncrasies of the instructor, Mr. VB, a fastidious bachelor who lived just off campus in an apartment crammed with plants, on whom he bestowed water and food with loving care. The maintenance man believed campus lore about Mr. VB: that he had been there forever; that he taught his courses at the same time in the same room year after year;

that in Integral Calculus he named every procedure, like integration by parts, after some former student, like Johnny from Sublette, who Mr. VB associated with the procedure; and that he threw erasers at anyone who dozed off in class. So it was,

At 1:00 p.m., Differential and Integral Calculus started in January each spring semester. In that part of the Midwest, January and February are cold and dark. Floor to ceiling windows made the room drafty and chilly. His energy was split between shivering and doing differential calculus. On the mid-semester final exam for differential, he earned a B. He did. For what occurred in integral calculus, he blamed Mr. VB. Although the maintenance man believes differential calculus makes more sense than integral calculus, there is an alternate explanation for what occurred.

At 1:00 p.m. in that part of the Midwest, in late March and early April, a meteorological miracle occurred with astonishing regularity. The air turned warm and fragrant with smells of new life as grass, plants, and trees grew out and turned green. The angle of the sun changed enough so the floor to ceiling windows in the classroom let the full wonder of a bright sun enter and warm the room. It was then that Mr. VB started integral calculus. This miracle contributed to his classroom performance, as did noontime meals.

The menus and food preparation were a work area under control of a third-party vendor. Students prepared food, but food service personnel told them what to cook and how to cook it. Monday through Saturday, breakfast and lunch were served cafeteria style, breakfast from 6 to 8 a.m., lunch from 11:30 a.m. to 1:00 p.m. On Sunday, brunch was from 9 a.m. to noon. A family style dinner was served every night at 5:30 p.m. Six students sat at each table, Miss the time, miss the meal. People seldom skipped meals. At lunch and dinner, it was possible to load up on milk, meat, potatoes, vegetables, rolls, and desert. Limits on how much he ate were self-imposed. He refused to eat green or lima beans, any kind of fritters, or fried eggs, No thank you.

At 1:00 p.m. in calculus class, the maintenance man was stuffed. For the first half of the semester lunch served him well, helped him shiver to keep warm, provided energy to devote to staying awake, and to study differential. After mid-semester, food, fate, and form turned against him. No matter how hard he tried, he failed to stay awake for an entire class. He kept expecting Mr. VB to sling an eraser at him, but that never happened. Farewell folklore. It did not help that he seldom studied outside of class. At the end of the semester, he failed the integral exam and earned a D in the course and a look of disdain from Mr. VB. His experiences with the two forms of calculus did not favor unbiased judgement, and he described the outcome by saying, "Well, at least it's done." Not one to ponder the future, he never saw coming what came in the first semester of his second year. How ironic! Still, he was happy he missed academic probation, doubtful he would ever have sex, and content to be heading home. He was $1000 in debt – payment delayed until he finished school -- a loan program loophole that influenced later choices about continuing his education.

THE SUMMER FOLLOWING FIRST YEAR

HE AND HIS BROTHER HERB worked nights in a box making factory. With an electric jackhammer, he stripped superfluous paper from 1000-sheet stacks of 3 by 5-foot paperboard printed and die cut with box designs. Then he stacked each column of trimmed boxes on a palette to send on for folding and gluing. Herb cleaned glue pots. They worked with men from Kentucky and Tennessee, who smoked, swore, worked the factory year-round, and adhered to mores the brothers did not understand. Those men were loud, profane, and prone to violence. At the end of shifts, he and Herb left quickly. On the last night of a work week, they drank a few beers on an interstate overpass before going home to bed. He earned and saved enough to pay for one semester, with a bit left over to spend. The rest he borrowed and increased his debt to $1500. As the summer drifted away, he knew

He had to choose a new major. A study of the catalog revealed that a mathematics major required the fewest semester hours. While his math and analytic skills were intuitive, not based on precision and procedure, there were no labs in mathematics. This left more time for cards, so, he chose mathematics as his new major.

On returning to school, he told his faculty advisor, who made it so, and, also suggested he retake differential and integral calculus to eliminate the D from his record. Oh brother! A bother, bearable, but a burden. Had he thought about that? Nope.

At the orientation picnic to welcome students, the maintenance man was struck dumb with desire on seeing Her, his second love, with beautiful gray-green eyes, a Mona Lisa countenance, and stunning shyness. It took him 55 years to appreciate that moment. Smile. Sob.

In the years between then and now, many times he said, "She saved my life." For Her obituary, he wrote "She was the keel and rudder that kept the good ships William and Kevin on course." because, despite some missteps, for Her, he kept his worst impulses at bay. But all that was later. In the weeks and months after meeting Her, he did everything he could to see Her as often as possible. On the day of the picnic, he managed to walk Her to Her dormitory, get Her name, and a vague commitment to see him again.

Mathematics was a matter apart. In the fall, he took a finite mathematics course and did okay. In the spring, it was differential and integral calculus, again. Déjà vu. Dark, cold, early Midwest weeks encouraged study (as did She) and another B in differential. Sunny, warm, late spring weeks, and a carb- packed lunches –produced unstoppable descents into sleep, and a fated, failed, integral exam. Another final D – for dummy. Increased disdain from Mr. VB. Thankfully, there was no room in his program for a third try. He went on to take advanced calculus, probability, statistics, differential equations, linear algebra, et cetera. For the eight mathematics courses, a total of 26 credit hours, his final GPA was just over a C.

With Her in his life, he began to study more, and gamble less, but not quit altogether. No, in loco parentis locked the women up at 11:00 every night but Tuesday when they were locked up at 9:00 p.m. – so they would be present for mandatory chapel Wednesday morning. He explored French (6 hours), took mandatory English (6), and Christianity and Western Civilization (3), but a Math major provided space in his course of study for other topics.

He filled that space with courses that interested him. He elected two years of German, a year of Russian, 30 hours of psychology with Dr. and Mrs. P, and three hours of philosophy with Dr. AD. At the end of his second spring semester, his GPA rose from 1.9 to 2.3. Studying with Her, a prerequisite to making out, helped his GPA and countered his failure in integral calculus. Each time he and Mr. VB crossed paths on campus, Mr. VB would look at him with a strange curious stare, tilt his head, utter "tut, tut, tut…," while wagging his head from side to side. In those encounters, Mr. VB never said what induced this attitude, but the maintenance man knew it was integral calculus. He had no clue if Mr. VB felt anything else on seeing him. A year and some months later, as a wiser, wise-ass, well along the path of his major, having taken the Graduate Record Examinations required of all upper-class students, the maintenance man and She were sitting outside the classroom building when

Mr. VB came up holding a GRE report in hand. There was that look, that "tut, tut, tut," that wag of his head and, after checking the report, the statement,

"What a shame! You could have been a scholar."

Mr. VB's lament surprised the maintenance man. He had never sensed the affection or concern that Mr. VB exhibited in that moment. Although he had heard the term scholar before, it was only in old literature or in contexts he did not apply to himself. So, he asked Mr. VB

"What's a scholar?"

"Someone who studies for their life's work." "Studies what?"

"Whatever they choose." He asked

"How do they do that?" which provoked a skeptical look, as if Mr. VB was asking himself, "Can this boy be so naïve?" but still managed to utter one more statement of fact for the dolt facing him. He said,

"By continuing studies in graduate school."

For the second time since coming to college, the maintenance man was struck dumb. You could stay in school and just study (not a great passion) whatever you wanted (a growing passion). He asked Mr. VB to affirm this. Mr. VB did with a nod, as he went on his way to water his plants. Before, counselors and his advisor bombarded him with the question, "What do you want to do in life?" Now, he wanted to bombard them with a single question, "Why didn't you point this out to me when I came for advice?" and with the follow-up "How do I do this?"

Being a scholar interested him. Being ready was another matter.

A CIRCUITOUS PATH TO
SCHOLARSHIP BEGAN

THE SUMMER AFTER SECOND YEAR, his Dad's friend Willard offered him a summer job as a janitor in the high-rise apartment building where he supervised maintenance. The $340 per month salary staggered him. He took the job, because his earnings would cover his third-year costs. To get to work, he took a 5:30 a.m. North Shore train to a Chicago elevated station, transferred to an elevated train to Addison Ave, then walked from the station to the Lake Shore Blvd high-rise. The commute was difficult. He occasionally fell asleep and missed the Addison Ave stop, then had to get off at Belmont, and walk back! But the work prepared him for maintenance, because

Being a janitor made him happy. He enjoyed sweeping the stairs. All alone in a stairwell, he thought about Her as he dumped sweeping compound on the 23rd floor landing, thought about Her as he swept the compound down the flights of stairs, until the compound was so dirty he had to sweep it up and put new compound down. He thought about Her all the way down. That summer his mind never wandered far from Her. The work also required

The maintenance man to clean ground floor windows, elevator interiors, and trash bins. Residents requested he carry bags from a ground floor grocery to their apartments, and called Willard to request all manner of fix-it jobs –some perfect for an unskilled summer employee. Those passed to him he did. He had responsibilities – catching trains on time and working well – but otherwise,

He was free. Not in nirvana. If asked, he might have said, "I am going in the right direction."

45

On the path, he still had to decide

WHAT TO DO? WITH CHOICE of a major settled, and with the arrival of a second math professor, Mr. C, who expanded the choice of courses, he never took another class from Mr. VB. With a firm hand, She transformed him from not studying to studying enough to satisfy Her criterion (firmly fixed in Her mind). His grades improved, not to impressive levels, likely because he still gambled regularly, and because, after women were locked up, as a first-generation child of TV, he found nightly reports about Viet Nam addictive. Most macabre and entrancing were the body counts printed or voiced over pictures of the dead. In November,

President Kennedy was shot. Lyndon Johnson became President. Viet Nam grew from an action to a conflict to a war. Ever greater numbers of young men were drafted and sent over. He felt no threat. He had a deferment – not called, not going. The assassination provoked sadness– at that time Kennedy was a romantic and tragic hero – but not as much in him as in his weeping and wailing classmates. The death did not affect his choices or perspective. In fact,

In a few days, his life was the same as before, and, aside from memorials, funeral, and what-next discussions in the student union, he returned to studying with Her, gambling, and following the war on TV. By the middle of the year, they both studied and made love – adjusting to student mores, but not in loco parentis.

Mores about sex, caused by students being campus bound (only a few commuting students had cars), were simple: (1) if weather was tolerable or good, take a blanket and walk to an isolated spot, spread

46

the blanket, engage in sex; (2) if weather was inclement, be the first to claim a classroom in a classroom building, engage in sex; and (3) if weather was inclement and all classrooms taken, at the risk of a year's social probation, go to your dormitory room, engage in sex. Four dorm rooms located in the gymnasium, one per corner, went to eight senior men. Seeing their smug, satisfied faces, one deduced they had sex on a regular basis. One of them, Eric, from Spain, was notorious. With an exotic, European, aura, and handsome face, he had sex with whomever was willing. As for classrooms, a piece of clothing hanging on the door knob outside a closed door signaled that persons inside were to be left alone.

The maintenance man knew nothing about homosexuals. There were no openly homosexual students. Most frequently heard was a simple pejorative, "So and so is queer because s/he does (some specific, peculiar behavior). Many years after, the maintenance man wondered if and how, among themselves, the homosexuals on campus talked. He neither pushed back nor spread prevailing opinions. He was too preoccupied with his own sexual issues, and

He was selfish, involved with Her. His emotions were roiling because of Her; and because, despite strong attachment to Her, other women remained desirable. He kept these feelings to himself. Feelings not so strong as those for Her, but stronger than expected. Clearly a view of love gained from years of watching movies, TV, and his parents, was somehow incomplete. How? He did not know. Why? He had no clue. What should he do? He lacked ideas. So,

The fall slid through winter into spring, through the cold part of spring into the warm, greening, nearly summer part of spring. They spent their free time together. On one of these days, sitting with Her on the balustrade of the stairsteps into the classroom building, Mr. VB came up and they had the dialog that contained the assessment that reverberated in his head for all the years that followed, "You could have been a scholar." That day he reacted to emotions he read in Mr. VB, not to the statement, which was like a time bomb with multiple charges on delay fuses that caused a charge to go off the next year, and the next, and the next, until there were no more years in which it was relevant. No, that day that statement by Mr. VB left him curious about continuing school, and

With Viet Nam growing into a war, with enlistments declining, with draftees increasing, and with talk of ending student deferments, going to graduate school grew from an interest io a desired path. He was not against the war. Until then, he simply was morbidly curious about its details. After his father had settled them in the house on the river, with stretches of forest on either bank, from 6th grade 10th grade, "guns" was a game he and his friends played constantly. A stream of war movies and series, TV staples, stoked a passion for "guns." To play "guns" in contrast to seeing the dead in gruesome poses on nightly news were different experiences. He knew which was real and which was not. It was not clear to him when the thought occurred, but one day between the day Mr. VB said he might have been a scholar and the first month of his fourth year, he thought he would die if he went to Viet Nam. Was he afraid? A little. Was it a premonition? If you do not go, you cannot know. Did he feel guilty? No. What was his plan, his goal? He had none, unless his desire to go see Her and entice or coax Her into having sex with him – which meant he had to study – was a goal. Probably not, because late in the spring of his third year and early in his fourth year

He spent hours each week talking with the psychologists Dr. and Mrs. P. The talks were expansive, but Dr. P inevitably talked about German culture; or derivatives thereof. He loved Wagner. He admired the Desert Fox for his courage facing Nazi fanaticism, for his devotion to duty, and for his strength in the decision to commit suicide to save his family. For Dr. P, MacArthur came close to Rommel. He played MacArthur's **Duty, Honor, Country** speech in each of his classes. After praising the virtues of these men, he turned his attention to bums, hoods, and nuts that he opined were taking over the country. Years after he left college, the maintenance man learned Dr. P, had received a diagnosis of colon cancer, went home one night, put Wagner on the record player, drank cognac, then took cyanide.

Mrs. P, devastated, went off and married a bloke from Australia. After that, the one time they talked, she expressed happiness (he sensed nervous anxiety). She never met with him again. For him, the sadness of never talking to them again exceeded the sadness at Dr. P's death. But before the sadness of Dr. P's death,

Mrs. P helped focus his choice. Thus, he went to talk to Dr. AD (who had left the small college for a larger one) about philosophy. Dr. AD said he thought the maintenance man lacked sufficient interest to make a study of philosophy his life's work. Believing this assessment accurate, the maintenance man thanked Dr. AD, returned to college, and turned his attention to psychology. In the end, he decided to attend graduate school and study psychology – a choice freely made. On making the choice, questions flooded his mind.

Could he be a scholar? Mr. VB doubted it – had he not implied as much? The maintenance man experienced both doubt and optimism. After lackluster high school performance and only somewhat improved performance in college, he believed he could survive graduate school. Doing so offered three benefits. First, he could defer student loan payments ($2900) until after graduate school. Second, he postponed decisions about a life's work to an indefinite, future time. Finally, he retained his deferment until the end of graduate school. Student deferments were still valid, despite political pressure to end them. How to pay for graduate school? More loans he supposed. Where should he go to graduate school? Who would admit him? He did not know. During the fall he sent applications to two schools, and visited a third. Both applications were rejected due to his poor grades (overall GPA = 2.56). He failed to meet the standards of these schools. He visited the university where he had taken a summer course in experimental psychology. An admissions advisor smiled and said, "That's good" when the maintenance man gave him his GRE scores, but said, "No way!" when he reported his overall GPA. He felt rejected and depressed, and spent the rest of fall semester, as well as winter break, wondering what to do. During the break, he drove into Chicago to see Her. When Her mom went to work, they made love.

Back at school, he headed to talk with Mrs. P. Maybe she had an idea. Outside her office, he noticed for the first time a bulletin board covered with graduate school posters and solicitations. One caught his eye because, unlike the others, it had a stack of tear-off, pre-addressed, postage paid, post cards. He took one, provided the requested contact information, GPA, and GRE scores, then dropped it in the mail. Later, he carefully read the poster. It described a new program in experimental psychology in a department enthusiastically (or desperately) seeking students. A week or two later, he received a letter that invited him to apply, accompanied by application forms. He applied. The department admitted him, on probation, to an experimental psychology program at a university in the middle of corn country. Best pf all, the department offered him an assistantship and tuition remission. Taking loans was unnecessary. Satisfied there was a next step in his life, he went all in for experimental psychology, and

He started to sense a rhythm to his life, although he could not put it into words. He was just past 21 years old.

HIS ANSWER

TO THE QUESTION, "WHAT DO you want to do"? became, "Study experimental psychology," but that was off in September after the coming summer. Right away, the truly critical question emerged: how could they be together if She was 370 miles southeast of him? He feared Her absence. With her, he felt sexually capable, without her not so much. She had helped him shed some doubt. He thought She thought they were better together than apart, so he asked Her to marry him and go with him to corn country. She said, "Yes," and joy replaced fear and doubt. New burdens arrived the moment they told their parents. How did distant September draw so close so quickly? Why were the mothers raising so many questions? How should he know? Nevertheless, he remained joyful despite lacking answers to questions they asked.

"Who was invited?"

"Where would it be?"

"Is there a reception?"

"What food will be served?" His answer to these was

"I don't know."

"Who will do the services? To this he answered,

"Father N" from the church they attended in the town near their school.

"Well, what kind of invitations?" "When will you get the rings?" "Where will you get the rings?" "Will you have an engagement ring?" they asked.

"I don't care." he said and when he saw She frowned, he tried to care, but managed only to keep participating.

"What about her dress?" they asked,

"What about Her dress?" he asked back.

Every question required an answer – not an inspired answer, not a noble answer, not an enlighten- (-ed, -ing) answer – just an answer that kept everything moving ahead. It was ritual – here we are now, tomorrow we will be further along.

"Who will be the groom's men and the bride's maids?" They answered,

"Some family, some friends."

The single, all-important question that reverberated in his mind, to which he knew his answer, was,

"Who will pay?" And to himself he replied,

"Not me. I have no money." He became calm when She said,

"Don't worry, my dad will pay for the wedding, the reception hall, and the food." Her father, Jim (the banished), provided for all but a dress which Her mother, Phyllis (the banisher), insisted on buying. He and She earned money for rings, and for a car they needed to get to corn country. The wedding was three days before they had to be at university. They split the three days, two for a honeymoon, and one for travel. As to the honeymoon, she asked,

"Will you make a reservation for us at the Pagoda Inn? I would like to see its inside." Her interest grew after She had seen the outside while passing in a car. He said,

"Sure." Then he forgot his promise. As it is with rituals,

Events kept moving. They reached the moment when bride and maids, and groom and men had their parties. At the end of his party, the maintenance man's response was,

"How weird!" They drank, but not much – none were heavy drinkers – drove around Chicago looking for something -- they -knew-not-what – and ended up at a church where Father N was staying, and had asked them to visit. Why not?

Father N had been kind when She and the maintenance man attended his church. He understood school policy about mandatory church attendance, yet overlooked late or missed attendance. So it came to pass,

Four 21-year-old men were greeted by middle-aged Father N and his middle-aged friend, another priest, who led them into the living quarters of the latter where all drank some wine and talked about the wedding. Somehow, talk drifted from expectations for the wedding night to sex between men. The question

"What's happening here!?" filled the maintenance man's mind. At some point, he asked, "Are you suggesting we have sex with you?" Father N's friend jumped on the question, "Uhuh. Are you interested?"

"No, not me."

One of the groom's men, T, wanted in talk about it, but the rest wanted to leave. T kept talking to Farther N's friend, while the rest moved toward the door. Father N talked. The maintenance man heard nothing. Five minutes later he remembered nothing of what Father N said. He remembered discomfort, embarrassment, saying good-bye, and thinking, "Will the service happen? Would Father N perform the service?" But the following day,

Father N came on time, carried an odor of heavy-drinking, yet performed well. No talk of the evening before. Between the end of the service and the trip to the reception hall, Father N and the maintenance man talked briefly.

"Thank you, Father."

"You're welcome. I was pleased you asked me. I wanted to do it, and it was an opportunity to visit an old friend."

"Are you coming to the reception?"

"No. I'm heading home." The maintenance man said,

"Well, I'll be seeing you" or something like that, but they never met again, and the maintenance man still has a memory of a kind man with human needs, although those needs spooked him on the eve of his wedding – it was the first homosexual advance he had experienced.

He failed to reserve a room at the Pagoda Inn and created the worst moment of their wedding day. She was disappointed. The magnitude of her disappointment surprised him. That he had forgotten and failed to keep his promise hurt the most. Seeing that pain, he felt ashamed. For him, a motel room was no big deal. For Her, it was more. Did anything eliminate that pain? No, never – it faded away over time.

From then on, he tried to keep his word, on not give it when he could not. The newlyweds spent the second day of their honeymoon at parents' homes, first packing his things, then Hers, then

They drove to the university in the middle of corn country where they gained access to the married student apartment for which they applied. For him, the choice of housing was more important than any choice of wedding preparation, It was their first home. They selected an apartment in a new complex, the best housing they would have for many years – a well-lit, second-floor apartment with two bedrooms, bath, kitchen, and living-room sitting on top of a hill overlooking the university. It was immaculate, freshly painted, bugless, with a laundry close by. They moved in, stowed their meager belongings, then turned their attention to money. Just then, they felt rich, because

They had nearly one thousand dollars in gifts given to Her, as well as a few hundred from summer earnings, and, best of all, 180 dollars a month assistantship income, of which 110 was deducted for the apartment and utilities, leaving 70 for everything else -- regular income like grown-ups. So, they made a list and went shopping, filled five grocery bags with goods, took them home and filled the refrigerator that came with the apartment. The next day he went to school to meet his academic advisor (Dr. WB), his assistantship supervisor (Dr. JW), the department chair (Dr. AM), and fellow students in experimental psychology (Gary, Glenn, Jim, Keith, and Larry). Sure enough,

Dr. WB asked, "What do you want to do?"

"I applied for experimental psychology."

"There are different fields of study in experimental psychology."

"Oh."

"For example, Skinner's behaviorism. Do you like working with rats or pigeons?"

"I never have."

"Maybe you'd be interested in human experimental psychology, for example, human learning and memory." As Dr. WB said this with more enthusiasm, which the maintenance man noted, he replied,

"Yes, I think I'd like to work with humans rather than rats or pigeons."

"Good! Because my specialty is human short-term memory. I think you belong in my group."

"Oh my god! A group!" he thought, "What is that all about?" He was not enthusiastic about joining, so he said

"Uh huh" and politely added, "I have to see Dr. JW soon." Minutes later, he was on his way across campus. Dr. JW called himself a methodologist (a what?) and showed interest in the mathematics major of the maintenance man. As he examined the transcript, Dr. JW asked

"What about these Ds in differential and integral calculus.?" whereupon the maintenance man told Dr. JW the story of differential and integral in the classroom with floor to ceiling windows, sitting in a warm classroom during a fragrant spring, full of a carbohydrate rich lunch, and unable to remain awake. Satisfied, Dr. JW asked,

"Have you ever programmed a computer?"

"No."

"Do you know any programming language? Fortran, for example?"

"No."

"Well, we'll start there because I want you to write a Fortran program to compute correlation coefficients for a 100 by 100 matrix of variables." Save Fortran, he knew what all those words meant, but he did not understand what Dr. JW wanted from him. He learned soon enough. Computers entered and occupied a central role in his life. He took computer (architecture and languages) and statistics courses to enable him to write the correlation program in exchange for the 180 dollars he took home each month. After he wrote the program, after he switched assistantships, computers remained a fixture in his life. The choice to go to graduate school to fulfill an ill-defined goal of becoming a scholar, because his undergraduate mathematics professor took a disdainful air toward him, and because he did not want to go to Viet Nam, had placed him in circumstances where his brash, sarcastic attitude seemed unsuited to success, yet, continued to work, although he learned to apply it with more care. He was 21 years old, surprised that haphazard study in school and college brought him this far. As for other motivations toward being a scholar, later in life,

He remembered

TWO EXPERIENCES HE LINKED WITH elementary school. Every day, he and a friend, Skippy, walked from post-war, temporary housing, occupied by veterans with families, across a prairie to school, and home again after. On the way home one spring day, they found a baby bird fallen from a tree, whimpering cheeps to an unseen mother. With thoughtless curiosity, he stepped on the tiny, featherless creature, crushed life from it, poked the remains, went on home, and enthusiastically told his mother about it.

Anger flashed across her face, followed immediately by a look of profound sadness. She sobbed as she spoke.

"Oh son, I am so disappointed." Surprised –his thoughtless, energetic, curiosity changed to remorse, unexplained guilt, and concern — by the power of her reaction, he blurted

"I'm sorry."

"We just don't kill things…"

"I didn't know."

"Son, I love you. But you will not to do that again!" Then she hugged him.

"OK." His guilt softened by her embrace. All his life, the memory of the baby bird, his mother's emotional reaction, her admonition, and her forgiving embrace lodged in his mind. This memory re- surfaced in early adolescence, affected his moral development, and became the raw material from which he constructed principals of behavior towards others.

A second experience shaped his life by opening paths to adulthood. One day in first grade, the teacher put a symbol on the blackboard

–S– and made a sound, doing the same with K, I, P (twice) and Y. She asked "What does that spell?" He knew instantly, shouted "Skippy." She said "Right! Now we will do your name." Wow!

Like that he read words. Ideas sprang from strings of words called sentences. Best of all, sentences became stories and ideas about the world. From the first, he loved letters, words, and stories. He never stopped reading. Beyond middle school, reading was a path into the minds of adults. Along the way,

The path went through pre- and adolescent literature – sports stories, thrillers, and magazines. From **True, The Man's Magazine** and **Argosy**, he acquired a distorted view of relations between men and women. His father read western stories, kept stacks of them in the house, and encouraged his son to read, which he did all through 8th, 9th, and 10th grades. From Zane Grey, Luke Short, and Louis L'Amour stories he absorbed the stated ethos of western heroes – no nonsense, honest, talk with friends, foes, and others. His view of relations between men and women was elaborated by stories of solitary, romantic, tough men aiding distressed, beautiful, curvaceous, women. Golly! How could he measure up? How to know? Without answers, in the second year of high school,

His interests shifted from westerns to nonfiction, particularly articles about space and missiles, and, also to science fiction which he devoured. A long list of authors whose works he read (Asimov, Bradbury, *Clarke*, Heinlein, Le Guin, Vonnegut, and Zelazny) expanded his view of relations among people. Heinlein stressed relations between heroes and heroines, and manners, twisting his perspective, while Vonnegut exuded a fatalistic, somehow optimistic, sense of life. Zelazny's **Lord of Light** inspired him to read about Zen Buddhism, Tao, altered states of consciousness, and mystical experiences. These readings filled his free time during the last two years of high school and into college, but there, because he had to work 15 hours a week, as well as read and study for classes, his reading for pleasure diminished. Then She came into and filled his life. So,

When they arrived in corn country, made the rounds of professors to whom he had to report, and *received* his assistantship and class assignments, he understood substantial reading, study, and work lay ahead. He had to master computer architecture, machine, assembler, and higher computer languages, as well as domains of psychology called learning and cognition, and psycholinguistics, not to mention statistics. All had to be learned to fit in and keep up with the "group" his advisor mentioned and introduced to him He knew

To get and stay on a scholar's path, he had to study in earnest. That was new. Not monk-like study, but earnest efforts to understand -- because the "group" talked about theories and constructs, and *explored* different views with respect to their validity. He held his own defending positions on this or that construct. He knew he had not reached a well-defined goal in life, but felt like he had pulled into a rest stop, an interlude, perhaps to build his mind, body, and soul. How do such interludes go?

THE REAL INTERLUDE

A LONG A SCHOLAR'S PATH ENABLED by (1) being a math major that caused Dr. JW to direct him to learn computer languages and architecture, and (2) studying psychology with Dr. and Mrs. P that led Dr. WB to guide him to study learning, human short-term memory, and psycholinguistics, meant he attended weekly meetings of the "group." After he "joined," the group consisted of Dr. WB, the maintenance man, Gary, Glenn, Jim, and Larry, a number perfect for three-on-three driveway basketball. Meetings had two parts, first, a mandatory hour of basketball, and second, an hour or hour-and-a-half of discussion with tongues loosened by beer and snacks. The group provided a way

Group members helped each other make headway to Goal One – a master's degree Dr. WB urged be completed by summer's end – thereafter to focus on the Prime Goal, a doctoral dissertation, which Dr. WB pressed them to complete within 4, or better, 3 years. A product of American research training, Dr. WB coveted students who completed doctorates in a timely way, published results, and, doing so, enhanced his reputation as a mentor. Theses, dissertations, and other empirical studies were pushed toward publication -- authors gained academic cachet by building vitae and social science citation rates. The more publications and citations the more likely an important academic position followed, thereby completing a never-ending, ouroborostic, circle. At best,

New to this path of scholarship, the maintenance man was ambivalent. To be sure, he volunteered for the path – which, to him, meant earnest study rather than a labored drive to publish. Yet, he could articulate no personal end goal. He liked to study, but linked no goal to study, other than to know more, and be a scholar (to show Mr. VB). Others in the group endorsed Dr; WB's professional goals, but the maintenance man reserved commitment during his first two years. He did not think about being a university professor. Fortunately,

He met Harold, who was ABD (All But Dissertation) from a university in Michigan, and who was the smartest person the maintenance man ever met, bar none. Harold loved to play cards. The maintenance man, Harold, other students, and faculty played a treacherous version of cutthroat hearts. With five, six, or seven players there was a blind of two, four, or three cards, respectively. The first person to receive a discarded heart also received the blind. It was a game charged with chaos and uncertainty!

Harold played deliberately, examined each round of discards before the hand was turned (making it unavailable). With just a few cards left to play, he would mentally review play, determine the cards that remained in play, and who had them. As he did, the game slowed to a stop, so much so that every regular, at one time or another, had said to him

"For fuck's sake Harold, play a card." He smiled or laughed and calmly replied

"I have a right to think about my next move -- I'm playing with my money." If he saw he was about to win a game with the right play, he became decisive and quickly played his last cards. If his play might permit another player to win -- ending the game, he searched for ways to prolong the game. These moments took forever. Harold routinely absorbed high levels of points rather than permit someone else to win, instead of cutting his losses. The maintenance man saw this was a significant shortcoming for a player.

Harold had been teaching at the university in corn country for a year when the maintenance man and he met. Four years later, still playing cards at lunch, as the maintenance man's dissertation neared completion, Harold was still ABD, but living under threat of termination. Harold often said God gave him an abundance of intelligence and analytic skill, a decent share of compulsiveness, but no motivation to complete tasks simply to have them done. This combination of traits is deadly to a career at a research university, and for Harold, particularly, because

On the one hand, although he had collected and analyzed his data, he could not finish the writing. He would write, rewrite, and rewrite again. God failed to help him or provide divine guidance because, in writing sessions, if he did not complete a section, the next time he sat to write he started anew. Also, he did not translate the threat of job loss into a drive to finish. On the other hand, the same traits and behaviors anchored a brilliant analytic mind that he applied in academic discussions. He drove Dr. WB mad when he used well established memory principles to effectively counter hypotheses and arguments developed from over-parameterized, cognitive models of short and long-term memory. Just before he finished his own dissertation, the maintenance man urged Harold to get done, and not risk losing his job. Harold replied,

"I am not worried. Something will come up."

"How can you be so sure.?"

"Because my advisor, Dr. Melton (the influential psychologist), will help me find something."

"Wouldn't you rather have the dissertation done."

"Sure, but...." Then he would smile or laugh robustly, and only at the very end, just before termination, did a bit of apprehension enter his demeanor, and, thankfully, for him, his wife, his two daughters, and his friends, that bit of apprehension drove him to finish and defend his dissertation – seven years after data collection. For the maintenance man,

The saga of Harold was illuminating. He was a brilliant man, worked to his own standards, risked a career to make his work just so, yet still trusted that life would work out. He sought no arbitrary goal, but worked to satisfy himself. A few years on, the maintenance man learned Harold landed a position at a small, upstate, New York university, where pressure to publish was muted, and excellent teachers were respected, prized, and honored, Harold finished his career as a professor treated so. Perfect!

One by one Keith, Jim, Gary, Glenn, and Larry found thesis topics, worked on them, and discussed them in "group," while the maintenance man had not. He worried he would not make the first summer deadline and did not. Near the end of his second fall semester, he read about the Von Restorff effect, developed a hypothesis how the effect would work in short-term memory, and designed an experiment to test his hypothesis. He collected and analyzed data, confirmed his conjecture, wrote, and defended his thesis by the end of the second year, then submitted a brief, journal article, and shortly after saw it published.

How about that! Two years after Mr. VB implied that he probably would not become a scholar; he was a published author with a master's degree – just like Mr. VB. In the first two years of graduate study, he gained competence in computer science and statistics. Members of the group turned to him with specific questions about both. Unlike now, comprehensive, accessible, statistical analysis programs did not exist. Statistical analyses were time-consuming and tedious tasks that involved using card punch machines to build data sets, to specify analyses, and to assemble god-forsaken, IBM- required, control cards that "ran" the IBM 360-65 computer that filled the ground floor of the computer science building.

It took hours to set up a run. The cards of a run often filled three-foot trays. Errors were terrors because, first you had to find them, then correct them, and finally get the tray back in the run queue for the next run, of which there were four a day. He spotted errors efficiently, knew tricks to increase keypunch productivity, and devoted enough time to each analysis to complete three runs a day. Having achieved analytic and computational proficiency, he finished the Fortran correlation matrix program Dr. JW had assigned.

His third summer, Dr. WB arranged for him to attend an NSF in gathering Gainesville, Florida with leaders in the field of psycholinguistics. The maintenance man had read works by all of them, and, from afar, had great respect for their intellects. Conversations with them led to more realistic appraisals of them, and of himself. By holding his own, he believed his capabilities matched theirs. For example, one big shot referred to work of a respected scholar as "intellectual necrophilia" because the basis of that work was traditional learning and memory theory, not the exciting, "new," linguistic approach of Chomsky. Thereafter, the maintenance man saw that big shot as a person with a mix of aptitudes, skills, and flaws, which helped him reset his appraisals of the others – no one got a free pass, each earned respect or disrespect. Two years of earnest study had increased his resilience and self-esteem. If only he had a goal, he would be on his way. When he returned from the meeting,

Dr. WB had a plan: he arranged a teaching assistantship – to teach the department's first seminar on psycholinguistics in the spring quarter. According to Dr. WB, the maintenance man knew more about psycholinguistics than anyone in the department. It was a given that he should teach it. The prospect of teaching fellow graduate students increased his apprehension, but teaching appealed to him more than continuing the grind of running analyses, dealing with keypunch machines, working with IBM job control language and error codes, and scheduling life around computer runs every six hours. He accepted the assistantship. His student ratings were above average, and his performance was judged acceptable by his teaching supervisor, the department chair, and Dr. WB. There were neither awards nor howls for his hide. A "well done" here and there felt good. He learned to organize academic information, present it clearly, and measure student progress. Teaching did not match his concept of a scholar, but "success" let him consider it part of a scholar's role. Nevertheless, for a time after the teaching assistantship, he could not eliminate a saying that ping-ponged through his mind: "Those that can, do. Those that cannot, teach."

As graduate training neared an end, in short order, Jim finished and went to a university in a civil war border state, Gary completed and went to a university along the Ohio River. Keith went to a school in Michigan. Glenn finished, and disappeared. Larry hit the jackpot with a *Psychological Bulletin* article and ended up at a Big Eight school. At the NSF meeting on psycholinguistics, the maintenance man met Dr. WB's friend Richard who posited an interesting theory about the structure of language in human conversation. The theory intrigued the maintenance man, and prompted a minor epiphany: the theory predicted what parts of conversations two speakers in a dialog would remember and which they would forget. His epiphany led directly to a dissertation study.

During the first two years of his four-year path to a Ph.D., She had completed a B.A. in modern languages. After that, She worked to supplement their income, and helped him complete his dissertation.

The study he designed required transcription of ½ hour conversations between pairs of people, She volunteered to transcribe them. Once recorded, she had 3 days to complete a transcription, for him to construct memory tests given a week later. The study's design included a schedule of recording and testing that permitted Her to complete the transcriptions – yeoman's work. The recordings, transcriptions, test construction, and data collection proceeded without a hitch, however, the results supported neither his hypotheses nor any part of the theory. What a disaster! There would be no publication. The defense would be a nightmare. Little chance of a job comparable to those of the other group members? He moped for a bit. The God-awful prospect of writing the dissertation depressed him. How many times would he have to describe the failure of HIS study to corroborate HIS hypothesis? Once was one time too many! In this state,

He arrived at the end of spring semester of his fourth year, at the end of assistantship support, with a remote possibility of being drafted (his birth date was number 305 in the first Selective Service draft lottery). He wanted to quit and move to Canada. From that moment, events moved fast. Dr. WB's friend left the university by the shallow Great Lake for a job at a Big 10 school, recommended the maintenance man for the opening, had him submit his vita, and arranged an interview. Talks with Harold and Dr. WB convinced the maintenance man he could defend his dissertation despite abysmal results. Most important, She said,

"Booby, will you do one thing for me?"

"What?"

"Stay here this summer and write your dissertation."

"Why?"

"It will be better if it's done before we go."

"But I cannot defend until the fall.

"If it is written, that will be okay. Will you do it for me?"

"Okay, but there are still some problems."

"Like what?"

"It has to be typed, the content and format approved, before it can be submitted for scheduling." She answered,

"I'll help." Then smiled the smile that She smiled to make him smile, and he did, and said

"Okay." And they did. He wrote longhand drafts. She typed them. He took typed sections to Dr. WB for content approval. By this process, they reached a final version to take to the library for format approval. By adhering to library guidance and correcting format errors, final, pre-defense, approval arrived. This all occurred in their fourth summer in corn country – two and a half months without income. They lived on the remnants of wedding gifts, money she saved working in a bread factory, and a MasterCard credit card. All summer they ate beef sandwiches at Lum's. The interview was arranged. He went. The department needed a person who could teach both psycholinguistics and research methods courses. He had the right skills. They offered the job at the end of the interview. He called Her. They talked a bit. She asked,

"Would you rather take the job or go to Canada now?"

"Well… taking the job would be better for us."

"Well take the job." He knew She preferred to stay in the states rather than endure financial and employment uncertainty in Canada. He accepted. He still had to defend the work he created, but he felt certain, a la Harold, that things would work out. He was 25 years old.

An interlude in smoke

In their second year at the university in corn country a college friend, John, transferred there and became a fixture in the local marijuana culture. John kept saying to them "smoke some dope, man." He and

She were ambivalent. The maintenance man overcame much hesitancy before he agreed to do it, because, at the time, he believed the marijuana-is-a-pathway-to-heroin propaganda of the government (still telling lies all these years later). Because John smoked regularly, did not take other drugs, behaved normally, and did okay in classes, the maintenance man finally said,

"Okay, come over Saturday and we'll smoke."

"I'll be there." This is how it went.

John came to the apartment with an ounce of what he described as

"This is good shit. You will be high in no time." He rolled a joint and John, he, and She smoked.

John asked, "Are you high?"

"How would I know?"

"You might feel tingling moving up your spine and on the back of your neck."

"Nope." So, John rolled another joint and they smoked it. John asked

"Are you high?"

"Nope." Déjà vu. This went on joint after joint. She said She felt something, smiled that smile to make him smile. He barely caught her smile because he felt anxious about not being high and paranoid about every unusual sound. She said She was tired and went to bed. John rolled a joint and he and the maintenance man smoked it. After the 16th joint, John admitted bewilderment,

"How can I be so high and you not?"

"I don't know."

"We have to stop. I must keep some to smoke until I can afford another bag."

"Okay." Muttering more of the same John left and the maintenance man went to bed. He laid there wondering what had happened, slowly breathed out to relax and go to sleep, when the universe cracked like a bullwhip – the sound so real: was it just an imaginary sound in his head? Everything became more vivid. His paranoia about sounds changed to a dream in which he woke up to see a thief standing over him with a knife that he plunged toward the maintenance man's chest. The intended victim woke for real – scared, marveled at things around him, and hungry. He was high. For the rest of his time at the university in corn country, She, he, and John found time to smoke dope.

Dope

Dope is doing dope
Dope is laughing hope
Dope is a downer mope.
Dope is the Buddha scope.
Dope is nothing -- dope.
Dope is nothing -- dope.
Nope, nope, and nope,
Dope is only dope.

The next year his brother Herb visited with a friend on their way to report for duty at a naval air station in Texas. The friend gave them a tab of Orange Sunshine, supposedly made by Owsley himself. A few weeks later the maintenance man, wrote a note to himself that said, "Relax. This is reality, you are on acid," then, self-guided, took the whole tab, had the complete experience, and laughed like crazy every time he read the note. Without moving, he went out of and came back into his mind, and discovered, on looking at every one that entered his field of vision, he possessed an intense attraction to women, each woman, all women, not just Her. He said nothing to Her. It was, and was not, sexual attraction. It was, and was not, respect.

Thinking it love, he immersed himself in this sense of love, but ignorant then how much trouble it would cause later. Only in late life did he understand that sense of love had accompanied him from an early age.

An interlude in Arkansas

In their third year in corn country, Doug called and invited them to attend the Mountain View Folk Festival in Arkansas. He said "Dottie and I are going to the Mountain View Folk Festival. Do you want to go?" They said,

"Sure."

They talked about the festival and agreed on a way to meet. Some days after, the couples left for Arkansas. The rendezvous in Arkansas occurred without a hitch. Doug led them to a park where they set up a six-person tent. They ate dinner, settled into sleeping bags for the night, lay there warm and comfortable, talked in the dark, heard a heavy rain start, and watched as water flooded the tent, as if there was no tent at all. Frantic attempts to divert the flow failed. They gave up, retreated to their cars to spend the night, woke with stiff, damp bodies and cranky minds, to a warm, cloudless day. Later

They drove to town, parked, and walked around the festival. Vendors sold a heap of folksy goods. Here and there, small groups were playing music. In some groups a musician played spoons or a man on a string to beat a rhythm. There were fiddlers and mandolin players. Many groups had someone that played the mountain dulcimer. The maintenance man loved its droning and modal, melodic sounds, so he decided to buy one, searched for a vendor, found young Lynn McSpadden, who made the best dulcimers in America, and ordered one. That night,

The four went to visit friends of Doug and Dottie, who lived in a nearby town and arranged a small party. Some partiers drank moonshine, asked if he wanted to try it. He did. Right out of the jug. Whoa! It was like olden times (he imagined) and way too strong for him. The weekend ended. The four said goodbye and went home. Two months later,

The dulcimer arrived. The maintenance man put it on his lap and played. As his life proceeded, off and on, he would sit and play – happily – but he lacked aptitude for keeping a beat, could not remember lyrics (other than a line or two of a song's beginning or chorus), and was reduced to listening when he played with talented musicians. Whatever his heritage, it was not music

An interlude in Chicago

Right from the start of fall semester of the fourth year, urgent political activity animated the campus, fueled by a war that began to intrude on interests of students with deferments and by TV coverage of the chaos at the Democratic convention in Chicago. There were marches. Students elected a hippie as president of student government. Conversations focused on the counterculture, but especially the trial of the Chicago Seven. Although he, She and John were more hippie than activist, he participated in an anti-war march. A co-marcher, a black woman, denigrated hippies (him) for marching, and left him with no taste for mass action. Although classified 1-A, the Selective Service never reached number 305, and his personal sense of urgency evaporated –he was against the war, but disillusioned by a movement whose participants disrespected one another. He considered moving to Canada. He never decided if he contemplated moving to Canada due to feelings about the war, due to a lack of motivation enhanced by smoking dope, or due to depression over his dissertation results – a bust he still had to write up and defend. So, he did not protest, he did not emigrate, he simply smoked dope, and continued along the path he was on. By then,

They were good friends with their neighbors, Clive, and his wife Jeredith. With some regularity, he, She, and they ate together played board games. He and She also babysat baby Lisa. Once he served as the gentile to whom Clive sold his worldly goods in an act of mechiras chametz.

Another time, on returning from a shopping trip to the grocery, Clive and Jeredith stopped to greet them on way into their apartment. Either he or She asked

"Where's baby Lisa?" Oops.

"We have to go back to the Fruit and Grocery," Clive and Jeredith had forgotten Baby Lisa, walked out of Ames Fruit and Grocery without her, and drove home.

"Okay. See you later." A bit later Clive was back with baby Lisa.

Years later neither Clive nor Jeredith remembered the incident, but he and She did because their friends' faces were an indescribable, inscrutable, humorous mix of how-did-this-happen, I-pray-she-is-still-there, and holy shit!

One evening She and Clive were talking about the trial of the Chicago Seven. As they talked, they decided they ought to go to the trial. Not wanting to be left out, the maintenance man said "Me too." Jeredith had to care for Lisa. The three got in Clive's car, drove to Chicago, found a spot by the courthouse, parked, entered that hall of justice, and came face to face with Chicago police doing crowd control –a crowd with the same idea: we must go to the trial. To go up to the courtroom, there was a line of people with passes (Who knew who or where from?). He and Clive were checked and sent packing. She just loitered nearby, drifted past the first line of security, and joined a group getting on an elevator heading up to the courtroom. They went outside and waited for Her, not knowing if She made it into the courtroom and not knowing what to do, just knowing not to ask police to check on Her status. About 30 minutes later,

She emerged from the courthouse, spotted them, and threw them a smile,

"I tried, but they checked passes again, and sent me down."

With the possibility of observing history past, they left the courthouse behind, went to the car, visited the Chicago Art Institute, drove home, and told their story to those left behind.

THE INTERLUDE IN CORN
COUNTRY ENDS

In their fourth year, at summer's end, after She convinced him to get past a desire to quit, his dissertation was complete with content and format approved and with copies ready to hand out to committee members. Of his committee, he only feared Dr. LW, the cigar-chomping, no-nonsense professor of statistics– who helped him formulate the linear model that specified the analysis of his study. After he completed a psychometrics course with Dr. LW, the maintenance man thought LW was the intellectual equal of Harold. During the defense,

Dr. LW asked the question the maintenance man feared most,

"Why did your study fail to provide evidence to support your hypothesis?" This question is at the heart of any failed study. He had had to think about this ever since the study failed. By the time of his oral examination, he had settled on an answer that satisfied himself, and that permitted him to sleep nights before the defense. He answered,

"There are critical points between the original idea (or theory) and the finished study. First, is the theory sound? This depends upon what is known a priori and on the judgment of the investigator. In my opinion, the theory is sound. Second, did the design of the study provide a means to test the hypothesis generated by the theory? As the theory relates to normal human conversations, and as I used a study that provided normal conversations free of interruptions or distractions, I believe the study did provide a means to test the hypothesis. In fact, failure to support the theory is itself evidence that the design was adequate. Third, are the analyses correct? I am confident there are no problems with the analyses as all sources of variance are identified and taken into accounted. Finally, were the methods used in the study, correct? I believe not. Specifically, I used recognition memory to measure memory for content.

Now, I believe a recall test would have been a sounder choice. Still a bit nervous,

The maintenance continued discussing the measurement issue, but in the back of his mind a sense of relaxation grew. As the defense concluded, they asked him wait outside the room. Feeling calm, he felt his defense was a fine moment in his life. Dr. WB called him back into the room, shook his hand, as did the others, and congratulations were sprinkled on him like water, like he was a plant ready to flower. Sitting in Dr. WB's office after,

His advisor told him that Dr. LW had said it was the best dissertation study and defense he had attended in the department. Even discounting the small number of defenses in the new program, the maintenance man let himself fill with pride. And to think, if not for Her....

THEY ARE OFF TO WORK

FOR TRANSPORTATION TO, IN AND around, and out of corn country, they wore out three successive cars. A reliable 1960 Chevrolet Impala carried them from his parent's house to the university. In their second year, after they smoked marijuana and became steady consumers, after they imitated many attributes of "hippies," Doug offered them a 1960 Volkswagen van -- the quintessential "hippy" vehicle. The Chevy needed new tires and mechanical work, so they jumped at the chance to switch cars. Although he and She thought the van showed solidarity with true hippies, truthfully, they were two middle-class, young, Americans flirting with the counter-culture. They sold the Chevy to buy the van, and, immediately began to pay its real price.

The van's underpowered engine just managed to reach minimum Interstate speed (45 MPH) on flat, straight, windless interstate. Hills or wind reduced its speed below minimum. More than once a cruiser rolled up beside them as the van struggled up a hill, and a loudspeaker blared,

"Get up to minimum speed or get off the highway!"

He would give the officer a friendly wave, and press the gas pedal down as far as possible, praying to make the crest in time to demonstrate he had made minimum speed. This was the van's third worst feature. The second worst feature surfaced each winter, when the tiny rear engine sent heated air to the cab via a metal conduit running under the body. On its journey through the conduit, heated air turned cold. Worse, when driven, winter winds transformed the cool cab into a frost filled box. Sealing the cab off from the empty back provided little respite. On long winter trips, a fatal (if not for the fact the van was drafty) catalytic camping heater helped keep the temperature high enough to keep frost off the windows, but that was as good as it got.

The worst feature also occurred in winter. To get the van to start after sitting overnight, they had to remove the battery, bring it into their apartment, and replace it when they needed to drive somewhere. In corn country winters, as winds blew down from Canada driving stinging bits of snow into their faces, and as hands and feet grew numb, reattaching the battery produced oily, dirty, frozen hands and forlorn frustration with the circumstance. He barely endured it, She not at all. After two winters, they sold the van and bought an Oldsmobile sedan with an automatic transmission that paused, shifting either up or down, between gears. The Oldsmobile carried them out of corn country and

It pulled a small U-Haul, filled with their meager belongings, to the city in the easternmost part of the Midwest, right on the banks of the shallow Great Lake. Every stop it was a tank of gas, a quart of oil, a bathroom trip and another cup of coffee. It was not long after arriving,

He made a left turn too slowly, and an oncoming car crashed into and totaled the Oldsmobile. After the Olds, their drives through life included, respectively, a Ford Econoline, a 56-passenger Blue Bell school bus, a Chevrolet Super Sport, a Ford pickup truck, and a beat-up Audi. They eventually grew tired of maintaining used cars, and, once work provided the means, started buying new cars -- purchases that did not happen until they were 34 years old. He had an emotional attachment to the Super Sport – essentially a gift from Bruce and Lorraine. His positive, hippie-focused, feelings for the VW van dimmed on the first trip on an interstate and disappeared during the first winter. Forever after, cars were simply transportation.

To get to work

THE OLDSMOBILE CARRIED THEM TO the city by the shallow Great Lake, then around the lake-level plain it sat upon, up the hill south to Cleveland Heights, and into Coventry, a neighborhood comprised of old Jews, junkies, and hippies. They knew instantly they wanted to live there. They parked and walked the three streets of the neighborhood, named after two English counties and a city. By chance or fate, they found a vacancy in a three-story building with seven apartments, moved in within 48 hours of arriving in the city, and, bone tired from carrying belongings up three flights, they ate their first meal – pastrami sandwiches and egg creams – at Irv's deli. The first week day after,

Work started with a round of greetings. In order, he met the secretary, the chair, professors, and students present. Most of the students were women. Uh oh. He had an office suite, inner office with desk et al, and a separate waiting area. What opulence! A big improvement over a dormitory room in college and a gang office in graduate school. With a salary eight times larger than his assistantship, how bad could life be? Not too bad, but he said to himself, "This is my first adult job."

In high school, he worked for spending money. In college, he worked to defray costs. In graduate school, assistantships formed part of his education. He never considered any of that work his work. In the city by the lake, he might work and remain in this suite until he retired, quit, was fired, or died. This might be his life. He was 25 years old, still lacked a life goal, but could not avoid the fact he had reached adulthood. He received good pay for an adult's job. Colleagues relied on him to participate in activities of the department. Students looked to him for information, training, and, perhaps, wisdom. He could not prevent anxiety from creeping into his mind. Consequently,

He spent the remaining days before classes preparing to teach research methods and psycholinguistics. As a graduate student teaching a seminar in psycholinguistics or a course in general psychology, he had learned more effort was required to prepare and organize a presentation than to simply acquire information from articles, books, or other scholarly works. This was most true for his first courses as a faculty member. His uncertainty stemmed from his anticipation of the range of questions students might ask. He firmly believed more study was the antidote: more study, increased knowledge, less uncertainty, less anxiety. During the first classes in each subject,

He vacillated between feeling prepared and feeling not so. His anxiety vacillated accordingly. Also, in class, nonacademic thoughts and feelings distracted his mind during pauses and momentary musings. Spontaneous thoughts, such as "What great eyes (breasts|hips|legs)!" or "What a beautiful smile!" occurred without prompting. Wherever, whenever, a young woman entered his field of vision, such thoughts followed. Early on, he put those thoughts aside, and in no way made them manifest in class, meetings, or his office. For him, their basis was biological, so, although their surfacing in public settings surprised him, he did not feel guilty. Biology was fundamental. He held to this view although the concept of gender identity was conflated with that of biological sex. He felt one might choose whatever identify they want, but doing so did not require others to do or see things the same. Boundaries exist between thoughts of one person and those of another, as well as between respective behaviors. Boundaries work in both directions.

As his first year on the job proceeded, a combination of anxiety and doubt snuffed all motivation to teach, so he resigned. Once again, he asked himself, "What now?" Once again, he had no answer. He was 26 years old, and, if not for drugs, his inability to answer so simple a question might have concerned him.

AT THE SAME TIME,

ALTHOUGH THE MAINTENANCE MAN STRUGGLED with anxiety and doubt, according to his students, he taught well. She found work at an insurance firm downtown, made friends there, one of whom liked to say "What's coming to you ain't going from you." For the maintenance man, this saying was a profound, simple to understand, message about life and death. When he asked himself, "What now?" and had no answer, he asked her. She was ready, because,

In the year since they arrived in the city by the shallow Great Lake, She had been resourceful and busy. Through the four years of graduate school, and the first part of that year, he had opened their joint checking account, wrote, and tracked checks (debit cards did not exist), and insured there were no overdrafts. With a larger salary for him and a salary for Her, they expanded spending. At the end of the month, a day or two, but not three, before the direct deposit of his salary, he kited checks – possible because it took three days for checks to pass through the clearing house and be debited against the account. He accounted for this in the check register by displaying negative balances in red ink. In his defense, he never had an overdraft. However, about three months after arriving, She saw the register, saw the red ink entries, and asked

"What are these?"

"Oh, the nominal balance is negative. But we don't have to worry because it takes three days for checks to clear."

"You can't do that."

"I have been."

"You cannot do that; it is not right. You must budget, keep a positive balance, and stop writing checks when there is no money in the account,"

He realized She was serious. He also realized that he did not want anything to do with keeping a budget, so in a flippant, offhand way he asked

"Do you want to keep the account(s)?" To which She immediately said,

"Yes!" He handed Her the checkbook. Fifty-five years later, after she died, he wrote checks and kept track of the account again, but by then debit cards and online access made checks, the checkbook, and a check register unnecessary. From the moment She took over, he noticed a change. Rather than buying something, first they talked about it viz a vis the budget and availability of funds. She never said a word, but six months after taking over, She handed him a receipt for a paid promissory note for his student loans. Somewhere a savings account existed with God knows what balance. He thought Her frugal, very frugal, never stingy. If there was a need, She paid for it, or saved and paid for it. They had a charge card but did not carry a balance. When family members needed financial help, She sent it. If he expressed a want for which current funds were absent, She saved for it. He got an allowance for lunch and small expenses at school. Simultaneously,

Living among the Jews, junkies, and hippies, marijuana and other drugs were readily bought. so Unlike corn country, a greater variety of drugs was available. They bought and used acid, hashish, mescaline, and peyote. At Irv's deli, opiate junkies nodded and said incomprehensible things. They chose to avoid real and synthetic opiates. They were under some influence a lot of the time. People asked him what this or that drug was like. He could never answer. He did say eating peyote buttons caused nausea before a good feeling came, but most of the time he said the drugs he had used made him feel good, or he was not afraid to use them. If someone wanted to use marijuana, mescaline, peyote, or hashish, he had nothing bad to say, save the warning about peyote.

She did not like parties and he did. She preferred to be alone, or with him. When there was a party, most of the time he attended alone. At parties with students, there were drugs, with faculty not. At one party with a small group of students, they all played a truth or dare striptease game that ended with him wearing only underwear. A little later, with all but the hostess gone, they had sex on a couch, then agreed not to say anything about it. Days later, with another student in her apartment, they had sex on her bed, and agreed to say nothing. He never said a thing about either encounter.

A time She was in Chicago visiting Phyllis, he permitted two young women walking through the neighborhood to stay in the apartment. There was no sex, but She came home early, found them in Her home, and made them leave. He knew She was deeply disappointed. He knew she did not believe that no sex occurred. She never said She forgave him, but She did not leave him. Over the remainder of the year, he kept his biological self to himself and Her. So,

At the end of the year when he resigned and asked himself, "What's next?" and had no answer, he asked Her. She asked back,

"Well, I have some money saved and I am working, so we can get by for a while. Do you have something in mind?"

In the neighborhood, there were couples with elementary school age children –totaling about 20 children. In conversations at Irv's deli and the sandwich bar in a drugstore up the hill, these parents talked about a free school a la Summerhill. He knew of Summerhill because Clive had tried university teaching, had been fired, then taught in a free school. Clive wrote optimistic letters about the school and its founder, Sheldon. When the maintenance man heard the parents talking, he intruded and expressed his interest. The parents acknowledged his interest but nothing seemed to come of it. So, when he heard Her say, "Do you have something in mind?" he responded with the only thing that came to mind,

"Some people in the neighborhood have talked about opening a free school." He liked the phrase "free school." After all, he named the dog she gave him that year "Free."

"Is there a job for you?"

"Not yet."

"Are you going to look into it?"

"I think I will" he said and felt his path move away from university teaching to teaching young minds letters, words, sentences, addition and subtraction, and science. Having loved learning to read and then reading everything he could, for a moment, he thought, "Perhaps this is my destiny." The parents hired him, and three weeks after they hired him, they fired him. The parents and other teachers liked him, but not his methods. His notion of a free school was too free for them, and their notion – contracts strictly enforced in a love-filled environment – was not free enough for him. He ended up on Her dole.

Next, he found a job as a blind piano tuner's driver and assistant. He discovered limits to his empathy for others. The driving and work were straightforward. He did minor repairs under Jack the tuner's guidance. All this was fine. What bothered was a constant stream of questions Jack asked to visualize scenes associated with intrusive, interesting, sounds. Answering exhausted him. Doing so while driving was dangerous. He quit, and went on the dole again.

Finally, he mowed lawns, the last work he did in the city by the shallow Great Lake. He had befriended a graduate student named Larry, who attended his research methods class. They smoked marijuana together, Larry quit school. Their friendship grew when they made a thousand egg rolls for a street festival on the street where Larry lived. After the maintenance man resigned, after his previous odd jobs, the two of them decided to start a lawn mowing business. They canvassed homes on the Heights, gathered clients until they had $160 a week in billables, bought brand-new Lawnboy mowers, and began mowing. They judged the $160 as adequate. It was enough to allow them to avoid working five days a week.

A lawn-mowing man
I hear warplanes in the hum of simple machines,
the din of nothingness called importance,
laughing, so little happiness, in living rooms.
I hear nothing
as the poet speaks his words.
Softy said.

Each work day, they smoked a joint, loaded the van with lawnmowers and trash bags, and headed out to mow. Lawns needed to be cut once a week. New to the business, they failed to account for many things that would have made the job more predictable, but their worst mistake was failing to account for rain, which washed out a day, or two, of mowing. Three problems accompanied rain: when rain stopped schedules were messed up; income was lost when a lawn could not be cut; and, wet heavy grass clogged lawnmowers and made trash bags weigh a ton. Even with the rain,

They made it through the summer.

Two experiences at the university by the shallow Great Lake

As a faculty member, the duty of shepherding Allen Ginsberg around campus before a reading fell to him as a new faculty. Allen wanted to eat breakfast, to talk with students, and to be prepare or rest before his reading. The maintenance man took him to the student union for breakfast where Allen gave detailed instructions to the counter man on the preparation of his eggs. With breakfast in hand, they went to a table where Allen ate his eggs, and talked in a New York city nonstop style with gathered students. After listening briefly, and by prior agreement, the maintenance man went off to work and Allen took care of himself. They did not see each other again.

Another time, he sat in the student union drinking Cokes and talking with students. A big man, in his late twenties or early thirties, came up to the table and asked a few questions. A student made a comment intended to send the man on his way, but he launched into a tirade about capitalists, fascists, and running dog lackeys. The maintenance man asked about alternatives to a capitalist society, and heard a flood of praise for Chairman Mao, communism, and the little red book. At the mention of "fascists," the mind of the maintenance man started working on a wise ass remark, as he asked how Chairman Mao and his colleagues handled dissent. Re-education or death was the earnest response.

The maintenance man leaned back in his chair and said, in an ironic tone,

"Except for the label, fascists and communists seem to behave the same."

On hearing the words "the same," the Maoist grabbed the sitting maintenance man's shoulder and pulled him backward onto the floor. Students jumped to their feet. Shouting ensued. The word "police" was uttered by one or two, The Maoist took off. Shaken, the maintenance man, got to his feet, returned the chair to upright, returned to his seat, and answered "okay" to questions about his well-being, Agitated by the incident, he headed home. Walking to his car, he spotted the Maoist following behind, not close enough to be a threat, but close enough to concern him." This guy is nuts" he said to himself. When he got to his car, he quickly got in, started it, and left in a direction opposite to his usual route home. As a further precaution, on a circuitous route home, he made one or two stops to check if he was followed. He never saw the Maoist again.

What had he learned? Having listened, he knew he did not need to sit at the feet of poets and hear them talk on and on. Having failed to listen closely enough to the Maoist, he resolved to listen carefully to what people were saying, and be more careful making wise-ass comments toward people in love with violent philosophies.

WANDERING WITH DOUG AND DOTTIE

AFTER HIS YEAR OF ODD jobs, he taught two summer courses for the department on an emergency basis. The professor who replaced him left without warning for a more prestigious job. Because the department had treated him well, he agreed to help them. Otherwise, their daily life involved eating dinner at Irv's deli, walking dog Free, and smoking dope. When Doug called and invited them to visit, they accepted. A visit presented opportunity to see families too. They drove to Chicago, visited family during the day, and Doug and Dottie at night. Each night they sat in a second-story, front room overlooking Halstead Avenue with a small group that got high, ate, and laughed a lot.

They talked about Ken Kesey, Timothy Leary, and Richard Alpert (Ram Das). They talked about counterculture. They talked about the Moody Blues and Grateful Dead, and the book, **Electric Kool-Aid Acid Test**, by Tom Wolfe. They talked about traveling around the country a la the Merry Pranksters, a notion of interest to the four of them. Conversation changed to mirthful, whimsical interrogation when someone, not at all interested in the notion, in the hope of switching topics, asked,

"Can you afford to do it? Doug answered

"Of course, we can."

"How do you know?" To which, both Doug and the maintenance man blurted

"It is self-evident!" as laughter gushed after their response, which provoked a stream of questions about how and where to live, et cetera

–rational concerns ordinary people have, to which, the two crazy men kept answering,

"Of course, we can – it is self-evident!" followed by gushers of laughter. Between these two, the notion of self-evidence was a bond that brought them as close to each other as they ever would be. Only later was it self-evident rational concerns existed, and self-evident solutions to rational concerns emerge haphazardly. Despite a confluence of views that night, once on the trip, it was clear they were traveling different paths. Doug quit graduate school for the trip, while the maintenance man, with PhD in hand, goalless, just carried on. A week after the visit, Doug called and asked them

"Do you want to make the trip we talked about when you were here?" He and She talked, decided they did, called back, and said,

"Yes."

"Good. I talked with my mother and step-father. We can go to Connecticut, buy a bus, and live with them while we build it out."

"Bus?"

"Yes, my step-father says a local school district is required to sell its used buses after a certain number of years of use, even if they remain in good shape. What's nice – a 56-passenger school bus costs $500. What do you say?"

"Let's do it!" So,

The bus trip started. Planning, such as it was, took over. Each couple created a pool of money. He and she sold off furniture, as well as their Ford van. They discussed how to live in a school bus – two couples, a dog, and a one-year-old infant boy. The two women laid out their needs, the two men set to work to make it so – that was how it was. They believed their money would last two years. It was not even close. The bus was cheap, but

After they got to Connecticut, they found everything cost more. In Connecticut, Doug's stepfather Ronnie bought the bus and drove it to an open space on his lot. They reimbursed Ronnie. It was share alike, except expenses for dog Free and baby David. In Doug's mother's house, Doug, Dottie, and David stayed in an upstairs bedroom. He, She, and dog Free were permitted to stay on a hide-a-bed in the basement –

Doug's mom, for fear of dirt and hair, prohibited Free all areas of the house except the basement. She also expected everyone to do chores while they lived there. Fair enough. He cleaned the bathroom, while She worked in the kitchen. Oh, how he cleaned! Mostly from spite he felt that Free was banished, but also to demonstrate a "hippy" could clean as well as anyone. With quarters arranged and chores assigned,

He and Doug transformed the school bus. First, they removed seats, carted them to a dump, then measured the length, width, and height of the interior. The interior design was made final: one bed in the front for Doug, Dottie, and David; a second bed in back for he, She, and Free. The center space had a kitchen, shelves, toilet. and shower. A table sat opposite the front bed; a storage area stood opposite the back bed. A curtain separated the back and front. The beds converted to daytime sofas. With no blueprint, they had their vision and the seat of their pants. With his experience in trades and having served as a foreman when they worked construction in college, Doug became the de facto foreman on the bus reconstruction. As at school, the maintenance man did grunt work – of which there was more than enough. For his part,

Doug spent a lot of time under the bus. He ran propane lines to the water heater, refrigerator, and stove. He ran water lines to the sink and shower. He ran waste water lines to a holding tank. Before installing propane lines, a perplexing issue arose: there was no room for the propane tank inside the bus– a lesson learned for lack of a plan. He, with a PhD, Doug, despite experience in the trades, She, and Dottie were all college graduates: should they be expected to think of everything? Especially a detail like where a propane tank should go? Ronnie said it had to be off the back, which led to,

"Off the back where? Mounted on brackets, or what?" After some thought Doug said,

"We must extend the back bumper and put a plate in the space between the bus and bumper. If we do that, the tank will sit down in a protected space." That was their best idea. It meant more time under the bus: remove bumper from frame, decide how far off the back to extend it, drill new holes in frame, and reattach the bumper. It was

God-awful, dirty work for Doug and Ronnie, while the maintenance man waited for tasks fit for a grunt.

In building out the interior of the bus, most of the work was new construction: measure and saw (or cut), nail and screw, drill and bolt, and measure again. They went to recreational vehicle dealers to buy a stove, a refrigerator, a portable chemical toilet, a sink, and fixtures for the sink and shower – all bought new. Level the refrigerator. Check that it worked properly. Each item drained funds originally earmarked for the road – more details the four college graduates did not discuss. "Not to worry," someone said, "Something will come up." Speaking of up,

When the maintenance man and Doug stood up in the bus at the spot where they intended to put the shower, they found they lacked almost a foot of clearance. This was a serious problem! They did not want to crouch to shower – not only uncomfortable but also presenting the danger of constant contact with the fragile sides. Of the two possible options, a hole in the floor seemed preferable to a hole in the roof. Both options required metal work. What to do? No one was optimistic about lowering the floor, nor about the plumbing required to drain waste water from a jerry-built floor. They needed something pre-built and plumbing ready. There was nothing like that at any recreational vehicle dealer. Yet, the moment they described out loud what was required, it was self-evident that

A kitchen sink was perfect. More precisely, a flat-bottom, porcelain-covered, cast-iron, single sink with a central drain was perfect. After efforts to find and price a new sink failed, they opted for a used sink, so, off they went to a Norwich junkyard and there, in a dusty corner crowded with a menagerie of discarded sinks piled all about, they found and bought the perfect sink. Then it was

Cut the floor, fit the sink. Perfect! Remove the sink, seal the edges, secure the sink, add standard plumbing fixtures. Voila! Their beautiful sunken shower only lacked the water. What a proud moment. With ironic self-praise, they described themselves as on the front line of the recycling movement. With the build out nearly done, they elected to do a test run, drove the bus onto the road, up and down hills, around corners, start, stop, run through the gears, and returned home to address what they discovered.

The bus was road worthy. The build out required fine tuning. Beds, closets, and cupboards required additional securing. Restraints were added to keep food, silverware, dishes, and pans in place. They tied or taped pipes to reduce rattles and rubs. Sensing the home stretch, they took another test run, during which a local policeman pulled them over, and said, in an ambiguous manner,

"You can't drive on Connecticut roads like that." With some concern Doug, as driver, asked

"Like what? officer."

"You can't drive a school bus painted like a school bus if it isn't a school bus."

"Other colors are fine?" he asked.

"As far as I know, yup."

Relieved, off they drove, added paint to a mental list of unanticipated costs, bought gallons of black paint (for the sides), white paint (for the roof), covered the yellow paint and school signage, and decided they were ready for the road. Where to? One more detail not covered during romantic, idealistic, talks about The Trip. They shared a single consensual goal: everyone wanted to be somewhere warm for the coming winter. Beyond that,

No one had a specific travel goal. They wanted to eat well, sleep safe at night, and have the money last as long as possible. They supported no cause, lacked interest in traditional tourist places to visit, and sought no significant personal milestones. The prevailing attitude turned out to be, as one of them put it, "As long as we're traveling, why don't we visit family and friends?" No one objected, but

The maintenance man knew by Her silence, She was not much, if at all, for the notion. Living in the bus already taxed Her ability to cope. Stopping to visit relatives and friends – many unknown to Her – might push Her past Her limit. Nevertheless, She stayed silent, and later told him She wanted him to have what he wanted, while he thought he wanted Her to have what She wanted. It was a theme they revisited many times in their lives. After she died, he finally appreciated how selfless and generous Her silence was. Who did they want to visit? Smitty and Millie on Long Island. Doctored at last, Harold and his wife J in the Finger Lakes region. Someone, forgotten now, in West Virginia. Lenny and Bee near Detroit. His and Her family around Chicago. Doug and Dottie's friends in that city. Dottie's family in St Louis. Bert and John in Arkansas. Finally, Bruce and Lorraine in Florida.

For the maintenance man, each visit was an instance of déjà vu: "Hello," and "Nice-to-meet-you "preceded "Oohs," and- "Ahs" as they showed the bus, on to "What-have-you-been-up-to?" " Let's-have-dinner," "Tell us about the trip," walk Free, back to the bus for bed, and on the road again after one or two nights.

dog Free

Me and dog Free go,
feet and claws clapping, clicking down
stairs, out for a walk.
For him, a celebration!
Summer's evening coolness
keeps Loving couples moving.
For them, a revelation!
Friends going by toss greetings,
and we return them.
For me, jubilation!

The bus spent many nights parked in someone's driveway or a nearby parking lot. Once they spent a night off a lonely road in the mountains of West Virginia. Near the end of the Trip, they spent a night on a deserted Florida beach. Between visits, stops in KOA's suited them – water and electric hook-ups, and the ability to empty the chemical toilet kept them near middle-class standards with which they were comfortable -- quite distinct from whatever class the Merry Pranksters experienced. And all the time,

Their pools of money drained away.

The maintenance man recalled five experiences from The Trip. First, the curtain separating front and back failed to stop sound, particularly, sounds of love-making or intra-couple conversations. He knew this constrained his and Her love-making. As the four never discussed it, he did not know how on Doug and Dottie were affected.

Second, when they stopped at his cousin Smitty's house in Long Island, he recalled how Smitty and Millie had blown like a gale into his grandmother Sarah's house on their return from Army service in Germany, and how he, at nine or ten years old, fell in love for the first time, with Millie, and how, now 28 years old, the same feeling came right back to him – being neither self-evident nor rational!

Third, passing through Indianapolis, Doug at the wheel, engaged in animated conversation with the maintenance man, WHAM, the bus plowed into a car stopped ahead of them. Before impact, Doug tried to stop, managed to slow the bus, but the mass of the bus carried too much momentum, and a collision occurred. An old guy got out and examined the rear of his car. Doug and the maintenance man did the same. The bus was unscathed. Surprisingly, so was the car. Doug asked the old guy,

"Do you want to call the police?" The old man said,

"That's not necessary."

"Are you sure? Maybe you should go to the hospital and have a doctor look at you."

"No, that is not necessary. The car seems fine."

"Are you sure?"

"Yep." They exchanged insurance information, and the old man left. It seemed a minor miracle. At least disaster had been dodged, so off they went. Two years later, the old man submitted a claim for a detached testicle he claimed the accident caused. In a real miracle, GEICO, the maintenance man's insurance company, settled without complaint, question, or change in rates. What the maintenance really wanted to know was exactly when that testicle detached.

Fourth, in St Louis, Dottie's sister's stepmother made a spaghetti dinner for them. Warm French bread with butter, noodles, and a sauce that smelled wonderful. He took his first bite, a big one, and gagged.

The sauce was so sweet he could not eat it. He struggled greatly to finish the meal, declined seconds, and learned you cannot rely on a single sense to determine something is good.

Fifth, on a remote Florida beach where they camped for a night, he, She, and Free walked across the idyllic beach toward the sea in bare feet. Free stopped, sat down, and started chewing his paws, as she yelled "Ouch!" and he felt sharp stabs in one foot then the other. All were victims of sand spurs, a seed pod God invented to keep riffraff off Florida beaches. No more bare feet on the beach. The next day, they drove south past hills of sea shells in Apalachicola to Tampa. During their stay in a KOA outside of Tampa, they needed money, not immediately, but soon, because

Their pools of money were nearing empty. Unwilling to engage in nefarious schemes to keep the bus rolling, the oft-used comment "Something will come up," changed to" Someone will have to work." Doug was adamant. He did not want to work. Dottie did not want to work, she wanted to care for her son. Interactions between them turned tense. At the same time, he and She were willing to work, but found it difficult to do so without a car. Whether any of them had jobs or not, they agreed they had to reduce expenses. While examining newspapers for work, they explored what houses cost to rent, and learned renting a house was cheaper than paying to park the bus in a KOA. They found and rented a house directly north of MacDill Air Force Base, divided it into their space, our space, and joint space. Soon after,

They visited his cousin Lorraine and her husband Bruce in St Petersburg, gave a tour of the bus, talked, had dinner, and described their financial condition and the need to work. Days later, Bruce offered to sell he and She his 1966 Chevrolet 427 cubic inch Super Sport convertible for three hundred dollars. Given Her frugality and ability to preserve funds for emergencies, they bought the car and expanded their choices for work. Despite wanting to care for her son, Dottie was the first to work – as a waitress. She was the next to find work – packing shrimp in a fish factory. She smelt like shrimp and hated it, so soon after, she found work as a sales clerk at a Dale Mabry mall. Dottie did not hide her unhappiness from Doug, so he went to work next, as an assembler of mobile homes in a factory. The maintenance man was last. He followed Doug into the mobile home factory. Soon after, Dottie quit waiting tables and cared for her son, leaving Doug unhappy that he had to do (work) what he said he did not want to do (work). Although

The bus was in the driveway ready to go, there was no talk of moving on. In fact, there was less and less talk altogether. With Doug the only one working, and with expenses greater than those of he and She, Doug wanted to move the bus to a cheap campground. With a car, and two salaries, he and She wanted to stay in the city. Dinners became difficult because he and She wanted to eat either fast food or Spanish food in Ybor City, while Doug and Dottie, to save money, chose to eat inexpensive, wholesome food at home. Diverging paths. For he and She, the bus Trip was over, not more than six months after it began.

The maintenance man got fired at the mobile home factory because he defied the bosses and left work, putatively, to attend the Gasparilla Days parade. Doug and Dottie proposed buying his and Her share of the bus, to take it over completely. He and She agreed to sell. They stayed in the house until the rent period ended. Doug got a good paying job as a statistical consultant at a local university, and he and Dottie moved the bus to a campground closer to the university on the north side of Tampa. He and She moved into a two-room apartment without a kitchen in central Tampa. He got a job on a construction site located on Bayshore Drive and worked his way up to carpenter from grunt.

In their small apartment in Tampa, he and She received a call from Clive. Their response to that call put he, She, and Free on the road to something new – Arizona – and back to something familiar as well -- school.

KNOWING DOUG

Aᴀ Doug ᴀɴᴅ Dᴏᴛᴛɪᴇ ᴛᴏᴏᴋ the bus, after he and She moved to their tiny, kitchen-less, apartment, Doug worked at the University of South Florida for a time, then floated into work with stained glass. He began with panels and later focused on making kaleidoscopes to sell at local craft shows. Dottie opened Windseye Fine Craft Gallery. In time, she helped Doug with kaleidoscope production and sold the scopes in her gallery. Doug adopted Windseye as a business name, and sales of the kaleidoscopes were strong, which enabled them move to an upscale neighborhood in New Port Richey. The more creative and original his kaleidoscope designs became, the greater their commercial success of Windseye. He shifted from craft shows to art shows, and to sales online when the internet came into existence. They moved to a quiet, wooded, area near a man-made lake, north of Little Rock, Arkansas. Windseye kaleidoscopes became world famous.

Visits between Arizona and Florida, then and Arkansas occurred over the years.

Doug believed he had been the victim of early abuse. Via therapy, he sought relief from this belief and the pain this belief caused. Participating in therapy continued throughout his life. He tested many varieties. His current therapy and its effects were a staple of conversations with the maintenance man – a pattern that prevailed until the last night of his last visit to Arkansas. On that night, near the end of a conversation, Doug said,

"I have been playing a role all my life." The maintenance man asked

"What do you mean?"

93

"I mean I have never been myself. I have always done and said what was expected of me."

"Always"

"Yes, all the time."

"Even when we are talking like now?"

"Yes."

"In this role playing, do you believe you act and say things different than your true self would do?"

"Yes, absolutely."

The maintenance man drew back from the picnic table where they sat. His mind formed an idea that he did not like. To dispel its unwanted consequences, he asked,

"Would you judge all that you have said throughout our friendship to be essentially untrue?"

"That's right."

"That our friendship and my view of you, based on your behaviors to this moment, were based on false communications."

"Yes."

"Can I trust what you are saying to me now?"

"I don't think so."

Stunned, the maintenance man sat back, drained of emotion, ill-at-ease, with nothing to say or ask. It was late, so he spoke about leaving early and getting to bed. He went to bed. In the morning, he left, and never visited Arkansas again, but continued to write and e-mail Doug.

Doug wrote long e-mails, focused on the nature and consequences of his therapy, each sent it to a list of many recipients, including the maintenance man, who first read them with curiosity, then later, after he recalled that last conversation, with uncertainty and confusion. His doubt caused him to ask that Doug take him off the list. He also offered to talk or exchange e-mails one-on-one. Doug removed him from the list, but there were no one-on-one conversations or e-mails. As the maintenance man thought about this, he concluded his request was responsible for an unspoken estrangement, which he felt, rightly or wrongly, was not his to resolve. Years passed in this state, and

When the maintenance began writing about his life, he wrote Doug two e-mails requesting details about the build-out of the school bus. The requests went unanswered, He concluded the estrangement was real. On a day he reviewed some old correspondence, he found letters from Doug, which he did not read again — due to the doubt created by that last conversation. There was no self-evident, correct thing to do. Finally, he mailed them to Doug with a note saying perhaps Doug would find them useful. A few weeks later,

He received an email from Dottie, who asked him to call. When he called, she told him that Doug had dementia. A sad understanding replaced his doubt. After hearing a description of the condition, his thoughts concentrated on his sense of the unspoken estrangement. Selfishly, he decided to resolve the matter — he did not want he or Doug to die without resolution, however the resolution unfolded. He decided to visit Doug and Dottie in North Carolina to see his friend of 61 years. When he called, Dottie warmly and enthusiastically supported his choice to visit. In the evening about a week later, their son Eric picked him up at the airport and primed him regarding his dad's condition. At the house, when they arrived,

His friend's bedtime was approaching, with just time for

"Hello."

"Hello." A hug, and,

"It's good to see you." And,

"True." Then Dottie and Eric prepared Doug and put him to bed. They guided him through getting settled for sleep with plain, simple directions to which the man responded with "yes" and "thank you." He fell asleep quickly. Dottie, her son Eric, and another son, David — visiting from Florida — talked about Doug's condition and Dottie's burdens and responsibilities. Somehow, with David, the maintenance man entered a discussion — that advanced toward argument —about whether people without problems existed. The maintenance man sensed a similarity to fruitless arguments he had had in the past, so he pulled himself from the discussion and turned his attention to Dottie, to whom he asked,

"Dottie, do you know that you are world famous?"

"What are you talking about?" she asked.

"Kaleidoscopes." To which David added

"You are famous in the world of kaleidoscopes. They are collector's items." And the maintenance man added,

"Your kaleidoscopes are all over the internet, and they sell for four times what you originally charged."

"I don't believe it." But Eric said

"It's true."

There was more conversation but the maintenance man was tired and his mind wandered. Shown his room and bathroom, he went to bed. The next morning, and for the following 10 hours, with a break now and then to go vape, He concentrated all his attention on the man who he had believed had been his best friend – until the night that belief was shattered. He decided to start talking about experiences they had shared in their youth, and brought up topics as they came to him. His goal was to elicit responses that were as complete and extended as his friend could manage. He asked

"Doug, do you remember working on the bus?"

"Yes."

"What do you remember about that?"

"I remember…" Doug started and then paused. The maintenance man waited. Doug looked at him and the maintenance man waited and held the gaze. He waited. He thought perhaps he should prompt his friend, instead he waited. And then,

"I remember working on it at my mother's house." The maintenance man smiled. Doug smiled. Dottie smiled. And so it went, one question and one answer at a time. Each question about a shared experience. Each answer labored into speech, most of the time complete and relevant. Each exchange requiring the patience to let the answer emerge. There was none of the fast-talking, flippant, ironic, speech of either the maintenance man or Doug of earlier times. The more they talked, the more joy the maintenance man experienced. After an hour or so, Doug appeared tired, distracted, prompting the maintenance man to ask,

"Doug, would you like to take a break, rest for a while, and talk again later?"

"Yes, I would." Came the immediate response.

"Okay, I will go for a walk and smoke. How long should we rest? A minute, several minutes, an hour, all day, forever?"

"For an hour."

"Okay, I will see you in an hour." Then he went for a walk and vaped while he walked. At the end of an hour, during which Dottie had moved Doug to his recliner, covered by a throw that depicted a huge watermelon, and called "the watermelon chair," the maintenance man came In from the back yard and said,

"I'm back!"

"Yes."

"Do you remember me?" "Yes."

"What's my name?"

"Bill." Dottie smiled, Doug smiled, the maintenance man smiled, then he got a dining room chair and put it right in front of Doug, and started again. He asked,

"Do you remember playing cards with Tom and Larry?"

"Yes."

"Where did that happen?"

"We played cards in the Den at school." "What was Tom like?"

Doug paused for a long time. He looked at the maintenance man, who looked back and held the gaze, until,

"He seemed unsure of himself." A description that did capture an essence of Tom.

They talked about Larry, they talked about the bus again, about the evening they smoked dope and the hilarious moment they experienced self-evidence. They talked about the time they walked through a cemetery in the Finger Lakes region, and experienced a "BOOM" of unknown origin. From time to time the maintenance man would go out for a vape, at which time he would say,

"I'll be right back" and get an

"Okay" in return. On a return, he said,

"I'm back" to his friend in the watermelon chair, who said,

"Good." And so it went, halting, labored, long pauses – sentence by sentence. Not the free-flowing conversations of old, nevertheless the maintenance man felt his old friend was present, despite a struggle to voice his thoughts. At one point, the maintenance man said

"I'm glad I came to see you" and heard

"Why did you come?" A rare, coming-from-within, question that day.

"I came because I had something to say to you." A second, mindful, question, that, when heard, filled the mind of the maintenance man with joy and hope

"What did you have to say?"

"I came to say I love you like a brother." Fighting tears, he felt the estrangement evaporate as he heard,

"Yes."

"Yes." And so, it continued until,

Dinnertime arrived. They used a mobile app to order Italian. They ate. For such an uplifting day, Doug's bed time came too early. When he was settled in bed, and asleep, Dottie and he talked while her sons played an online game. What kept reverberating in the maintenance man's head were the words,

"He has not talked so much in years. I am so happy. I am so happy you came."

"Today exceeded the hopes I had before arriving. It must be very hard for you."

"It's not so bad because Doug is always so sweet now. He helps as he can, he is polite and says 'Thank you,' a lot when I do something for him. I can't tell you how much that means to me."

"Still. it is a lot of work." Dottie's tone became philosophical when she said

"Yes, it is. I did not expect this would happen at this stage of life, but I accept it, and that he is so pleasant is a blessing. The most difficult thing is when he falls. I cannot lift him by myself. Thank goodness, Eric is only 15 minutes away. Recently, I had to ask the neighbors to help, but I manage."

He smiled. At that moment, a thought filled his mind, so he said,

"You know Dottie I must apologize."

"Why."

"After all these years, it has just occurred to me that I was never as good a friend to you as I was to Doug."

"Well, I believe friendships made young are stronger than those that follow, and you knew Doug a long time before we met."

"I suppose so, but now I want you to know I love you too."

That night, like after all good nights, he had a sound and peaceful sleep, woke early on Sunday, showered, had coffee and juice, and decided to talk about the present with Doug. He sat down with his friend, and watched Doug eat his breakfast. With deliberate precision, for each bite Doug lowered his spoon into a dish of applesauce, raised it to his mouth, and swallowed. He wiped his mouth with a napkin. Then he repeated the same actions with a plate of scrambled eggs and bite-size pieces of ham. Only a need to chew these foods, which he did thoroughly, altered the process. For the maintenance man, a single word entered his mind – dignity. His friend maintained his dignity. That thought gave him hope for a day like the one before. It was not to be.

When the maintenance man asked of Doug a question or made a statement to provoke an independent, complete thought, Doug responded with "Yes," "No," "True," "Maybe," "I do not know," "It's possible," or a limited number of other one or two-word replies. When asked what he was thinking, Doug most often said

"Not much."

Occasionally, a moment like those of the day before occurred, but overall, no, and sadness grew inside the maintenance man. In the afternoon, he changed approach. He started,

"Doug. Would you like to play a game?" "Yes."

"I will say something and you need to finish it, okay?"

"Okay."

"Okay, ready?"

"Yes."

The maintenance man said "Doug sees...." And waited ...longer than pauses of the day before "the couch."

"Doug knows...."

The answers were less than the maintenance man hoped, but he continued for a while longer, then stopped. They had leftover Italian for dinner. They watched television until it was time for bed. On the way into the bedroom the maintenance man stood in front of Doug and said,

"Can I give you a hug?"

"Sure."

They hugged and the maintenance man stepped back and said,

"I love you like a brother man. Can you say that to me?"

"I love you like a brother." That was enough for the maintenance man, but he added

"I am leaving before you wake up in the morning. So, this is goodbye."

"Okay."

Dottie put Doug to bed. For a few minutes the maintenance man and she sat down in the living room and talked. The maintenance man told her how Saturday he had been so happy, and how sad he felt today. He added,

"if I ever come back, I do not think my friend will be here – one way or another." She nodded and thanked him for coming and helping. They did not say much else. After some getting up and down, and after a vape,

They met in the kitchen and the maintenance man asked

"Can I give you a hug?"

"I would like a hug." They did, and he said,

"I have something to tell you." He hoped he could express the thought without tears.

"Okay."

"If you become depressed, or if you feel overwhelmed, or if a great sadness comes, I want you to call me. I will do whatever is possible for me to do as soon as I can do it. Okay?"

"Okay."

Having done what he had come to do, and having said what he had to say, he went to bed. He slept poorly and woke 30 minutes before his four-a.m. alarm. He showered, had juice, and packed. He gathered his bed linens and towels and placed them on the washer. It was dark and raining as he waited for his 4:40 Uber to the airport. He went outside and stood under a six-inch eave at the front of the house, just enough to keep him dry. The Uber came and he went home.

A year later, Doug died. It was the maintenance man's 79th year.

LOOKING FOR WORK IN ARIZONA

AFTER CLIVE CALLED, AFTER THEY drove from Florida to Arizona, after they killed billions of roaches in the duplex Clive rented for them, after they made the duplex livable, they had no money. Within days, She became a file clerk at an insurance office. The state employment agency sent him to a site where he got a job as a carpenter's assistant. On day one, as the heat grew ferocious, he failed to reliably carry the required two sheets of plywood to the roofers. His body was not ready to work construction in Arizona's summer. The foreman let him go. Was it a mistake to leave Florida where a company had offered to send him through trade schools? Like many choices, there was no going back –until they had cash to do so. Right then, they were stuck, and with her salary insufficient, he had to find something. His friends Clive and Jeredith had divorced. Jeredith had gone east to Toronto, then west to Vancouver with baby Lisa. She got a Ph.D. and became a professor and poet. In Arizona, Clive married Gayle and they lived in a duplex. After obtaining his Ph.D., Clive taught mathematics at the former teacher's college by the big, dry river. The duplexes were blocks from the college. Clive was sensible and astute, traits that he inherited or learned from his sensible and astute parents. After he was fired by the University, with money earned teaching, he bought a run-down, trailer park with a dozen spaces on one or two acres of land near South Mountain. The park generated some income, but no profit – as a landlord he was too soft-hearted – for when a tenant said they did not have the rent, he said, "Take your time." They did. With the college so close, the maintenance man thought that

The former teacher's college, now a large university, might provide a position his skills matched.

What were his ambitions? He did not think about teaching or research, instead he thought of a quarter or half-time position in the computer center consulting on statistical problems. Having worked with Dr. LW on the complex ANOVA model for his dissertation, and having taught statistics and research methods at the university by the shallow Great Lake, he had confidence in those skills. With a tactical goal defined, he told Her his plan. Having observed his anxiety about teaching, She asked if he believed it was an acceptable alternative to Florida. He said "Yes," so She concurred. After a night's sleep, after breakfast the next morning, after putting on some comfortable clothes, he advanced on the university like Patton on the Nazis. Where to start? Not that he knew, because, previously,

His visit and interview for the only academic job he ever pursued had been arranged by a friend of Dr. WB. No matter, he wanted to consult on statistics in the computer center, so he headed there. He walked into the computer center office, and asked the secretary to see the director. She said,

"Wait here, I'll see if he is available." A moment later, she returned "Max will see you." And waved him to the door of Max's office.

Introductions. The maintenance man described his academic training and experience, then the type of position he sought. Max said

"Our consultants do not do that kind of work. They work on architecture and engineering issues."

"Oh. Okay. Thanks for seeing me." Good-bye pleasantries. He stood up and started to leave when Max said

"I just thought of something. In the education building, Dr. GH is director of testing services. He has people who do the type of consulting you want. You might try there."

"Thanks very much!" It was a lead that matched his goal. He walked a half mile across a desiccated desert masquerading as a campus, in search of Dr. GH who might hold his future in his hands. He found the testing services, entered, and walked up to a counter where, an attractive, friendly, short, somewhat round, young woman, Elmo, said

"Can I help you?"

"I'd like to see Dr. GH."

"Hold on, I'll see if he can see you." She walked out from behind the counter, past him to an office behind him on his left. His eyes followed her the whole way as she simply looked into the office, did not say a word, and walked back behind the counter.

"He will see you now. Right in there." She waved toward the spot she had just left.

He walked into the office and met Dr. GH. As with Max, he described his skills and the type of position he sought. Dr. GH listened with interest, and when the maintenance man was done, said

"We have four positions like you described, and two are vacant..." His words trailed into a pause while the maintenance man's mind bubbled with anticipatory happiness. GH continued "...however, these positions are reserved for graduate students who specialize in measurement, statistics, and research methodology in our department. Would you be interested in applying?"

"I have a PhD and have been a graduate student...." His words trailed off into a pause as flashes of happiness darkened and disappeared, and continued, "...and of one thing I am certain. I am not interested in being a student again."

Good-bye pleasantries. He was about to leave the office when GH said,

"You know, one of our professors died recently. He taught statistics. The department needs a person to teach his courses. I do not know what the plans are for replacing him, but you might go across the hall and talk to Dr. KVW, chair of the department."

"Thanks very much." Enthusiasm muted, he resolved to follow the lead, crossed the hall, and asked the secretary, boss of the office, to see Dr. KVW. In a sergeant's tone, she said

"He is attending meetings elsewhere, and returns after lunch. You can try back then." She offered no appointment. He wondered if it was his appearance, or if it was just her way, but responded,

"Okay. I will be back after lunch." He left the office and went to get something to eat, which gave him time to muse about his appearance, and the effect it might have on his prospects. His hair was down to his shoulders. He wore a white, t-shirt, bell-bottom jeans, and leather sandals. As his initial quest had been for a part-time position, he had not given any thought to dress. Now, he wondered if it would be better to walk home and change, or just carry on. It might or might not have been the thought of traipsing back and forth across the desert, but he decided to finish his meal, kill a little time, and return, as is, to the department office. So, he did.

The streak of getting in to see heads of departments ran hot because when he returned after lunch, Dr. KVW was in, and met him immediately. For a third time, he described his skills and the type of position he sought. Dr. KVW listened with care and interest. When he finished, KVW said

"How extraordinary. You say you obtained your degree from the university in corn country."

"Right. I graduated three years ago."

"Dr. GH told you we had a professor die suddenly." "Yes, he did."

"Did he tell you anything about him?"

"No."

"Well, his name was John K and he graduated from the same university you did, four years ago."

"John K!? The former Jesuit?" He uttered these questions stunned by the magnitude of the coincidence – John K had been an amiable acquaintance of the maintenance man in graduate school, had come to this school in the desert, had the same academic background, and had died just after the maintenance man arrived in the desert. Whacked silly, he thought "If this is chance, all things are possible." Dr. KVW said,

"Yes." KVW recognized the magnitude of the coincidence as well. "How truly extraordinary!"

There was little else to say. The maintenance man thought Dr. KVW had made a positive appraisal of him – a thought reinforced when KVW said.

"I think you should meet with students and faculty who are around this summer."

"Okay."

"Would you be willing to present a symposium on a statistics or methodology topic of your choice?"

"Today?" With a whimsical chuckle, Dr. KVW answered,

"No, not today, say in a week or two when we can arrange a date and have people here."

"I could do that."

"Good. Come back in two days and we will set everything up." He never mentioned t-shirt, bell- bottoms, sandals, or long hair. Good-bye pleasantries. He left for home, crossed the scorching desert, walked into their pleasant little duplex, waited for her to get off work, and, just as she walked in the door, blurted out

"You will never guess what happened today." He said -- grinning like the Cheshire Cat.

"You got a job."

"What the…"

"It's all over your face, booby."

He told her the whole story and when he got to the part about giving a symposium, she asked

"Will you be ready in two weeks?"

"I think so. First, I need a topic."

As always, she said, "Let me know if there is anything I can do."

"I can't think of anything right now."

Two days later, he returned, in more professional clothes, to Dr. KVW's office and they fixed a date for the symposium – two weeks hence. Good-byes, departure, the walk home across the desert, and an exhausted collapse into a chair where he pondered, with no little anxiety, what topic to prepare for the symposium. "I'll think about it tomorrow" he said to himself, then went to bed and fell asleep from the exhaustion of walking back and forth across the desert. When tomorrow came, he reminisced about the genial gruffness of Dr. LW, chomping away on an unlit cigar, saying his skills with variance components of random, mixed, and fixed statistical models were just part of a bag of tricks.

The maintenance man chose to discuss variance components, and spent most of his time before the symposium reviewing the topic and preparing what he believed was a coherent presentation with enough detail to demonstrate competence, but not so much as to alienate mathematically challenged persons. The date came, his presentation took about 40 minutes, attending faculty asked a few topical questions, and then KVW opened the session to more general questions by faculty and students; who, it turns out, had more interest in why he left the university by the shallow Great Lake, and why and what he did after. He talked about the bus trip for more than half of the next 60 minutes. They loved him. Dr. KVW said he would be in touch, and,

He called a few days later and offered a one-year, visiting assistant professor's position -- steady full-time work that enabled Her to quit the insurance company. Hallelujah! Back in the money! Always, She worried about finances, but let herself relax for a time after he signed a contract to teach beginning and intermediate statistics in the coming fall and spring semesters. Two significant events happened during that year. First, the department advertised for a permanent person for the position – Dr. KVW, who he forever after called Keith, encouraged him to apply. He did. The department hired someone else. Second, a short, intense, man walked into his office early in the fall semester and announced,

"Hi, I am RWK., call me Ray. I teach learning, and train graduate students to do research."

"Nice to meet you." Next, the maintenance man recalled Ray asking,

"What do you think about research?" Without thinking, and with a touch of flippancy, he answered

"Not much." To which Ray responded by standing up, saying

"See you" and leaving. It was the last time he and Ray talked for two years.

As the year ended, he and She made plans to move on. They talked about California and the coast. Keith came to him and informed him that: Dr. GH was taking a sabbatical; the department and testing service needed a temporary replacement; one of GH's students who had been slated for the position took a more lucrative position at the last minute; and, at this late date, a replacement was needed. Then Keith asked,

"Would you be willing to serve as acting director of testing services and teach his courses, too?"

He knew he had to talk to Her about it, so he said he would give his answer the following day. He and She talked, and being herself, Her primary concern was "Is it okay with you?" It was. The next day he took the job. Doing so created a new opportunity. With each academic contract, he opted to spread his nine-month academic salary over 12 months. With the acting director job secure for the coming fall, they had a whole summer free with salary. What to do, where to go? She had an idea.

"Let's go to Mexico." They did.

Her major was foreign languages, and as She spoke Spanish fluently, he thought there would be no problems with language. They flew Aero Mexico to Distrito Federal (D.F.). She directed the taxi driver take them to their downtown hotel. That She was shy, introverted, and ill-at-ease with new people and situations created a circumstance in which She preferred he take charge. Despite Her superior skill, he took the lead, while She provided a crash course in Spanish. In D.F., he learned numbers, directions, "Donde esta…?" "Como se dice…?" and other useful phrases. He managed to get them to Los Piramides de Teotihuacan, the floating gardens of Xochimilco, the cathedral, museums, and the jai alai fronton. He ordered and they ate in fine restaurants and at street vendors. The first word he learned on his own, "cinecero," She did not know. An ashtray was essential for smoking after meals. Positive experiences, but

Although the climate was perfect in D.F., his senses were overwhelmed. People were everywhere. From their top-floor hotel room, he saw people living in lean-tos on roofs of nearby buildings. On the streets, mothers with babies, swarms of children, and down-and-out individuals drew very near and beseeched them for money. Vendors pushed products and shouted prices. Fast and heavy traffic followed rules he did not know, making him uncertain about crossing streets or taking taxis. All the time in D.F. he was unsettled, not unhappy, by how close the lives of so many were to his, and surprised by how much he needed the respite of their hotel room. He was also surprised that

He was happy to get back home to the scorching desert. His perspective on the heat had changed. His perspective on teaching changed too. When he taught at the university by the shallow Great Lake, his students were primarily women seeking master's degrees in professions in the speech and hearing sciences. They sought no special expertise in statistics or research methods. Many feared mathematics. Teaching such students was a lot like being a guardian: make sure they know and can do the basics, and steer them around emotional struggles their fear caused. More than anything, he wanted these first students to like him. Teaching basic and intermediate statistics at the university by the dry river bed was different. Most of his students pursued PhDs, either in a domain of psychology or in statistics, measurement, and research methodology. Most were intelligent, unafraid to ask questions. To prepare, he studied the topics anew, in earnest, with singular attention to rationales and assumptions. In other words, he prepared, not by new learning, but by overlearning what he already knew. From these students, he preferred to receive respect rather than affection. His emotional reaction to teaching was mixed, uncertain, and depended on specific incidents, good and bad, as they occurred in classes. He could not say teaching was his life's work, but had no alternative in mind because the path to trade school and construction superintendent faded as the year passed and She continued to need to be financially secure. It was the case

She never told him what path to take. Instead, She supported each choice he made, and likely lived in a state unsettled by his lack of clear goals, and what that meant for jobs and salary. She feared having no money because, for one, it took away Her ability to make Her own choices. Once he made a choice, She was with him, only asking him to affirm it was truly his choice, not Her need, that determined it. So, it was when they talked about the acting director's position. So, it was when they returned from D.F., and he acted as director of the testing service, and prepared to teach Dr. GH's courses. And so it was, when his preparations for those courses delivered another jolt.

Dr. GH taught an advanced statistics and a special techniques course, the former each semester and the latter in the fall semester. Before GH left on sabbatical, he gave the maintenance man a full set of materials for advanced statistics and the syllabus for special topics. After examining these materials,

Anxiety filled his mind. He was a wreck. Advanced statistics covered topics he studied but never taught, so teaching would be a chore – requiring time to review assumptions, rationales, and methods. However, the true obstacle to emotional calm was special topics, a 15-topic anthology of infrequently used, advanced methods, of which he had studied or was conversant with three. Fifteen topics in 15 weeks, one a week, 12 new to him, the remaining three not among his strengths. There was no way out. The contract was signed. He was in it for a year. Thank God for Elmo!

Classified as a secretary, Elmo was the heart, head, and hands of the testing service. All faculty received identical, respectful, service when they brought examinations for scoring. She administered national standardized tests and adhered exactly to examination protocols. He and Elmo talked. By the end of the talk, she understood his anxiety, its cause, and found a way to help. She said,

"Do not worry about the testing service, I will take care of it. If you are needed, I will let you know. Take care of your classes." He wanted to cry, but only managed to mumble "Thanks…" before heading off to the library to collect books and journal articles about the first few special topics. For the rest of that semester, he carried special topics materials everywhere, to take advantage of any opportunity to study. That semester,

The special topics class was on Tuesday morning, and the advanced statistics class on Tuesday and Thursday afternoon. Before the semester began, he had time to prepare a single presentation for special topics and review about a third of the material for the statistics class. After the first week of instruction, his schedule never varied until the semester ended. After the topics class he would gather the materials for the next week and, until Sunday morning, read them during every spare moment everywhere he went. From Sunday morning until Tuesday morning, he prepared a presentation and handouts. Here and there, he would devote time to review for the advanced statistics class. He lived in dread of inadequate knowledge, poor preparation, or the possibility his students lacked respect for his efforts, and thoughts of giving up occurred more than once. The one thing he knew with certainty: he had never studied so long or hard to master so many topics in so short a time. By the spring semester, he felt he achieved the status Mr. VB doubted he would. For better or worse, he was a scholar.

In the spring semester, the work load eased, Dr. GH returned and resigned as director. Keith, having become a good friend, encouraged him to apply. He did. The department hired someone else. At the end of spring, he and She prepared to move on – they thought the west coast called, and planned to travel there. A new dean was hired for the college. In one of his first acts, he approved a longstanding request by Keith and Dr. GH to add an associate director position to the testing services. Keith argued on his behalf, came to him, and asked,

"Are you be interested in being associate director of the testing services?" He and She talked. Having observed his dreadful emotional state during the preceding fall, She expressed skepticism. He explained he would never have to teach the topics course again, and having gone through what he did, that he was academically and emotionally stronger, He assured Her he would be alright. She relented. He accepted the position. He was content -- their financial position was secure. He was not happy or joyous, simply relieved, still not certain this was his path in life. Uncertainty seemed a permanent facet of life, but in his third year at the former teacher's college, he had a permanent, tenure-track position as an assistant professor and a half-time administrative appointment as associate director of the testing service.

Somewhere in his mind, the melody, and a lyric from a song by the Grateful Dead drifted through his mind, sung by his mind's voice, "When life looks like easy street, there is danger at your door[2]."

THE CHOICE THAT MADE
HIS PATH PERMANENT

D R. MF REPLACED KEITH AS chair. Where Keith was circumspect, prone to long questions, answers, and statements, all delivered softly, Dr. MF was direct, wry, terse, and spoke in a matter-of-fact manner. Before Keith stepped down, the year the maintenance man taught special topics and the following year as well –when his doubts about teaching were strongest – he and Keith talked during walks around campus. He revealed his doubts, and Keith, a careful listener, described his own feelings about teaching – he too had had doubts early – then shared his judgment of the maintenance man's value, based on informal feedback from students and professors. These talks reduced doubt, fortified resolve, and encouraged him to continue. MF was another matter, because

She struck at the heart of issues. As a tenure track professor, the maintenance man submitted performance review papers. These reviews had meaning. Consistently inadequate or bad reviews were the principal cause for terminating untenured faculty. The third-year review was critical – as it described explicitly what must be improved to earn tenure in the fifth year. Dr, MF delivered his review. He saw her coming. Her face was firmly fixed on business. Once again, his inner ears heard that lyric from **Uncle John's Band**.

She came into the testing service and walked up to him. Her manner reminded him of his own. She started,

"Let's talk in your office."

"Okay." They went in, he first, she behind, pushing the door closed. She never sat down, just simply asked,

"Bill, do you like it here?" He knew she wanted a yes or a no answer, skip nuance, skip wise-ass, so he said,

"Yes." And sealed his fate.

"Your performance review is complete." She handed him a sheet of paper, "Read this." Typed on the paper, formally addressed to him, were the words:

"If you expect to earn promotion and tenure you have to publish significantly more."

"Do you have any questions?" Another yes-no question, to which he said,

"No." There it was. Exactly. To continue, he had to do what he never thought much about doing. "Good. You should know, ratings and reviews of your teaching were fine." Then she left.

Since his dissertation, he had conducted no research. About that time, one of Ray's students asked for his dissertation, read it, then suggested they conduct a similar study, a knock-off of the dissertation using different measures of memory – those that he claimed might be were more appropriate during his defense. Use of human subjects required elaborate review – thanks to recent federal guidelines. The student said "No problem, I'll talk to Ray," went off, then returned, and said everything was set. The maintenance man said he wanted to talk to Ray – he did not think the human subjects review could be done so quickly. Off he went, to talk Ray about human subjects' guidelines, getting the study reviewed, and the source of subjects for the study. A hint of a puzzled frown flashed across Ray's face before he smiled and assured the maintenance man everything was fine, then escorted him out. The replication of his dissertation never occurred. They did not talk to each other for the next 11 years.

To address his research shortfall, over the next two years, he chose to work on expedient topics which included; equivalence of scores among different standard tests, university admission issues, and computerized testing. Access to data in the testing service made these studies possible. Tenure insured job security because a tenured professor is terminated for one of two reasons, either moral turpitude or financial exigency. Moral turpitude is bad behavior like running a whore house, never meeting classes, or coercing sex with students. Financial exigency occurs when a university cannot or will not financially support a department and its faculty. Because administrators are political beasts and control financial decisions, financial exigency enables chicanery by unscrupulous administrators.

While he worked to attain tenure, he fell in love for the third time in his life. JB, who was several years younger and a few inches shorter; had wide hips and shoulders, a trim body, medium breasts; and looked out from an Englishwoman's face and eyes. What eyes – flashing beacons that beckoned him to come in and meet her soul. Eyes, eyes, ayes! On his way in, without doubt, they loved each other. They loved each other on the floor of her living room. They loved each other in the back seat of the Super Sport. She was wife to a student who had taken his course. The affair was brief, furtive: she had two children and feared retribution by her husband; he dreaded causing Her disappointment and pain.

Dread grappled with new love. His oath to Her remained ever present. The newly known body of JB, her loving gaze, and her new scents intensified the struggle. It was not a case of what next, rather what is best – for him, for Her, and for his new love. In the end, his oath outweighed all else. He told JB he had to tell his wife. JB told her husband, who divorced her. Each got one child. He told Her and She became angry, deeply disappointed, and sad. As She cried, She said,

"I thought we would only love each other for all our lives." He answered

"I do love you. I never stopped. I chose both to tell you and to stay with you, if you still want that."

"Leave me alone." And

From then on, even after she indicated she would stay with him, even after, a long time later, she again smiled that smile that made him smile, her eyes never again expressed only love. There was love, but also traces of disappointment and distrust. He told Her he would not have sexual intercourse with other women. He did not. The rest of Her life he kept that promise. He endured the change in Her eyes, as well as Her mix of feelings toward him. He walked a fine line between promises to Her and the warmth and attraction he felt toward women, warmth that remained, that colored his behaviors, some sexual. By the time he received tenure, the affair was over, he lived with the qualified grace She granted him, and as for work, in the five years of review for promotion and tenure, fortified by the assurances from Keith,

Self-confidence replaced doubt about teaching. The work he published to earn promotion and tenure failed to excite him, but he appreciated that he conducted and pursued it to publication. Thus, with research capabilities fortified by promotion (i.e., his peers judged him competent), he developed an interest in having his own thematic program of research – a gold standard among academics. To foster a program of research, one: (1) developed an idea (theory and hypotheses); (2) suggested studies; (3) completed them; (4) analyzed data and published findings; then, (5) modified the idea as needed to develop further studies. He only lacked a topic of interest. Which topic? It turned out that choice depended on others, because

As he taught statistics, measurement, and research design, not substantive topics like learning or development, and as his dissertation was a substantive bust, Dr. Morris O, entered his life. Morris was intelligent, a bit of a New York smart-ass, and a scientist who pursued his interests with determination. He had, in his mid-twenties achieved recognition for work on risk taking by older adults. They met when Morris asked the maintenance man to appraise an analysis he chose for a study, as well as to obtain help conducting the analysis. This interaction had two outcomes. First, that study closed the book on risk taking – Morris closed it. Second, they enjoyed working with each other, and decided to find a topic to research together.

Morris had a friend, Dr. LKG, a professor at an elite university back east. LKG was respected and well known in gerontology – a driven academic – who had an interest in happiness. She suggested that a meta-analysis of research on happiness among the elderly was needed. Morris told the maintenance man. The topic had strong potential to support a program of research because, as a topic, happiness provided endless possible studies of interest. It was a plus for him that meta-analysis was a new and interesting methodology. They agreed to take on the project. LKG estimated about 50 studies had been conducted on the topic so the meta-analysis might take a year from start to finish. As for her estimate,

They found reasons to change it. First, "happiness" had to be defined. They settled on the phrase subjective well-being because it covered topics that included: self-ratings of happiness, mood (positive and negative), optimism, satisfaction, subjective well-being itself, and other terms indicating a positive disposition towards one's life. Next, searches of the literature, using the broader set of terms, led to more than 800 published papers, not the 50 suggested by LKG. On a first review, many papers were rejected because they had no empirical findings (meta-analysis combines empirical findings), but after these were culled, nearly six hundred papers remained. For these, a codebook was created that described the process of extracting findings and study characteristics (e.g., type of study, type of subjects, etc.). Once there was a codebook, each study had to be read and coded. Finally, coded information had to be entered into the computer and analyzed. Given their assessment of what was required, Morris and the maintenance man found, half in jest, that "This will take forever" was a better estimate, Hence, they recruited two junior collaborators. From start to finish, the project took seven years, resulted in more than 25 publications, saw Morris and the maintenance man take sabbaticals. One collaborator graduated. She took a job as an assistant dean. The other completed his dissertation on religion and subjective well-being despite suffering chronic cystic fibrosis.

The maintenance man spent his sabbatical year at a great university on the southside of a big city hard by the middle Great Lake. There he met Dr. LH, an expert on meta-analysis, and they published an article together. He took a course from a respected methodologist, Dr. RDB. Experiences with these two cemented his confidence in his skill (solving problems with known statistical techniques), as well as acceptance of what he did not do (create new statistical techniques).

Prior to the sabbatical, he lamented not studying mathematics with greater rigor. During the sabbatical, for the first time he realized how much more effective and influential he might have been had he done so. Yet, he never again thought less of himself for choices made in adolescence. He knew he was a productive and helpful person. Knowing this satisfied him. Having established a program of research, he was content to call himself a scholar. From then, when a belittling thought occurred, he thought about Eric Hoffer, a full-time longshoreman who published books on philosophy. Somehow, thinking of Hoffer helped him accept his own peculiar, meandering path. He never again regretted not pursuing mathematics rigorously in high school and college. Regarding LH,

The maintenance man remembered him with fondness not for their scholarly discussions and collaboration but for an experience that occurred when they were together in New York for a publisher's meeting to plan a book on meta-analysis on which LH was principal editor. After a long day of work discussions, dinner, and drinks, he and LH wondered through the hotel, ended up on the mezzanine outside a hall in which a packed, animated wedding reception was in full swing. They claimed affiliation with the bride, entered, had a few drinks, did a bit of dancing, embellished their back story with the guests, said their goodbyes, and retired to their rooms.

INTO AND OUT OF ADMINISTRATION

IN THE FIRST FOUR YEARS of review for promotion, his position required him to work with the Director of Testing Services, Dr. DK, a brilliant, cunning, prevaricator. Their interactions went poorly, so they stayed out of each other's way. DK was interested in modernizing the testing service and expanding its products. He succeeded. He modified test result reports to include new, useful, statistics on tests, integrated test information across multiple tests in a class, and eased scoring and interpretation burdens on professors. His research focused on development of order analysis, a method of rank-ordering item information in tests. Trained as a clinical psychologist in the People's Republic of Czechoslovakia, he found a U.S. citizen, married her, moved to the States, returned to university, studied methodology, obtained U.S. citizenship, then divorced his wife. Growing up in a communist regime made him paranoid about and obsequious toward persons he perceived as more powerful. He habitually said that which avoided confrontation with such people. For the maintenance man,

DK's behavior reached a nadir after he modified policies to accept, score, administer, and return classroom tests, and required staff to adhere to and enforce those policies. Most of the burden fell on Elmo, who scrupulously applied the policies until the day an obnoxious professor disputed the rules, demanded special treatment, and became loud and disruptive. Elmo held fast. The professor insisted on seeing the Director. She escorted him to DK's office. When the two men came out, DK told Elmo she was wrong. He ordered her to do what the professor wanted, and not behave that way again.,

DK evaded a conflict his policies caused, the spoiled professor got what he wanted, and Elmo was embarrassed, helpless, and angry. Not long after, she left the testing services to move to Seattle. On seeing Elmo treated so, the maintenance man felt both intense anger and a sense of helplessness. DK was in charge, and disrespect of Elmo was not an actionable offense. The maintenance man stayed as associate director for four years, but a steady stream of incidents in which DK evaded responsibility for his actions led the maintenance man to resign. When he made that decision,

He thought himself quite clever. He believed that after he resigned the half-time administrative appointment, he would be in the unique position of having a ½-time academic appointment, with tenure. Better than what he had sought when he first walked on campus, but the Dean said "No. Be a full-time professor or, literally, take a hike." Absent long-term goals, accepting the full-time position seemed preferable to looking for something new. He did not know or consider that choosing the full-time position would carry him to the end of his career. No, just then, he was a full-time, tenured associate professor, 34 years old.

No kidding, Kevin

ALL THE TIME LIVING IN corn country, being by the shallow Great Lake, tripping in the bus, enduring the scorching desert in the duplex, they made love, but She did not get pregnant. When they reached their early thirties – about the time he accepted a permanent position – he fretted, wanted to act. Her view was more serene, as She said,

"It will happen if it's meant to be." He pushed for more. She helped.

They tried mapping Her ovulation with temperature charts, and targeted intercourse to the most likely moments of ovulation. They tried alternate positions. Neither of them liked the clinical nature of these efforts. Her opinion was still

"It will happen if it's meant to be." He pushed even more, which led to a doctor, which led to medical examinations of them both and the testing of his sperm. What a process! A nurse led him from the lobby to a little room. As it was known he was there for a sperm test, it was remarkable how they skated around the act he was to perform. When she handed him the little cup she said

"You know what this is for, right?"

"Yes."

"When you are through put the cup there" as she pointed to a cubby with doors on each side of the wall."

"Okay."

"Relax, take your time, no hurry. If you need some help, there are materials to look at over there" as she pointed to a nearby drawer. Finally,

"When you are done let the desk know, and you can leave."

"Okay." She left. He masturbated into the cup. After ejaculation, he put the cup in the cubby and closed the door. Before he left the little room, he checked the drawer. Sure enough, pornography – softcore, hardcore, heterosexual, homosexual, whatever-a-penis-desired. Oh, the advances of modern medicine. He left the little room, nodded to the desk nurse, and went home.

Meanwhile, She underwent her own examination, but never described it to him. Days later they met the doctor again. He looked at the maintenance man and said, drily, clinically,

"Your sperm count is okay. Although they are slow swimmers, they are adequate to achieve impregnation."

On hearing the word "slow" he feared that he would next hear "… it's your fault you can't get pregnant," but on hearing "adequate" he relaxed with an amused thought ("my sperms' behavior mirrors my own"). Then the doctor turned to Her, and like auto mechanic doing sheet metal work with a mallet, pounded out

"You have endometriosis, and a relatively large cyst. These prevent impregnation. No sperm, no matter how mobile, reach the egg. The best course of action is surgery." Bang, bang, bang, bang, bang…. Then the "good doctor" asked

"Would you like to schedule surgery?" The maintenance man thought "Fuck you" but said

"We will have to think it over, talk about it, and let you know." They left the office. She was more quiet than usual. They did not talk about it on the drive home, just remained quiet. For him, having the surgery struck him as taking a huge chance. For him, being quiet permitted serious thought about what came next. So, he thought, and left her to do the same. It occurred to him that even with surgery, a pregnancy was uncertain. He called the doctor who confirmed that the probability of getting pregnant was low, and advised that removing the endometriosis and cyst was a prudent act. A lot to think about: his desire to have and experience raising a child, the risks of surgery to remove dysfunctional parts, the risks of not removing the dysfunctional parts, and the actual change in probability of having their own child. At the end of his thinking, he told her

"I do not want a child so badly that I would force you to have the surgery." She smiled at that, and said "Okay." In the end, She decided to have the surgery for health reasons, as the cyst, and its size, concerned Her. When She told him, he accepted Her decision. He did not think about surgery, risks, or having or not having a baby. He only thought about her mother-fucking, hillbilly, step-father, Hop, who routinely abused her preadolescent uterus and who – the maintenance man believed – was responsible for its state. All he thought was "Fuck you Hop! Rot in hell!" "Fuck you Hop! Rot in hell!" "Fuck you Hop! Rot in hell!" And then returned attention to Her, and to Her well-being, for there was much to do.

Before surgery, She paid all the bills and put their finances in order. She did not fear death, rather preferred that he not mess with Her finances. Fine by him. She ensured there was food in the house. She gathered everything She needed for a week's stay in the hospital per their guidance, including a forbidden pack of cigarettes. Papers were signed giving doctors immunity for decisions (based on expert judgment?) made during surgery. She entered surgery with a uterus, a cyst, and endometriosis, and exited two hour later without endometriosis, a cyst, or a uterus. The doctor told him the surgery went fine and, in his opinion, he had to remove the uterus. No uterus, no child of their own. Not for all time.

The surgeon's decision to remove the uterus triggered an episode of depression in Her. She agreed to surgery for Her health and to increase chances to have a child – an act of love for him. He wanted a child more than She, because She, not he, doubted She would be a good mother. The surgery made moot fertility tests, temperature plots, urgent sex at fertile times, and a plan to raise their own child. Emerging from anesthesia, She said first,

"Where are my cigarettes?" and next

"When can I go home?" and in these matters he was no help because staff had taken Her cigarettes away before She was in surgery. There was no smoking in the hospital, and She had not been released to go home.

In fact, staff said She would be there a full week. She was unhappy he would|could|should not help Her with Her requests|demands. He smiled. She was unhappy because She could not do what She wanted to do. She was unhappy the surgeon removed Her uterus, but not as unhappy as being unable to smoke immediately. The next visit he had a pack of Tareytons, Her favorite, but on going to Her room, found She was not there. In near panic (Was there an emergency?!), he went to the nurse's station, and they told him

"She is walking around here someplace. We cannot keep Her in bed." Typical, he thought. He never could make Her do something She did not want to do, nor prevent Her from doing what She wanted to do. Off he went in search of Her, and found Her in a small interior courtyard where patients could get outside. She saw him, and asked,

"Did you bring my cigarettes?" He nodded, smiled, and handed Her the pack, which She took, took out a cigarette, and lit, resourcefully, with a lighter She managed to hide someplace, then returned the lighter and pack to the same hiding place. He had to ask,

"Why aren't you in bed?"

"I kept asking them what I had to do to go home?" "And they said you had to get out of bed?"

"Yes. I must be able to walk on my own, I must eat and keep meals down, and I must poop. She never used the word "shit." I have not stopped walking since they told me. And I eat everything they give me. Even the orange juice. I am waiting to poop."

The next day She pooped, and the day after that She was home. She accepted that She could not have Her own child. What She could not accept was that the surgeon removed Her uterus without ever having mentioned that specific possibility, but rather relied on the non-specific language of an informed consent form to cover his ass. There was no evidence to dispute the surgeon's judgment. In the end, Her attitude hardened to seeing doctors as little as possible, and to never again rely on their judgment. There would be no more informed consents that gave carte blanche to doctors. As to the maintenance man, he preferred never to go to a doctor at all. As to Her depression,

She worked past it, accepted the consequences, and focused on crafts, business, and Her life-long fight against depression ("Rot in hell, Hop!"). He continued to hope to raise a child. It took time before their thoughts turned to adoption. He was first, because he wanted to have a child. She was content to be with him, and said so. Yet, She loved him, and from that love, benefits emerged. Uncertain and anxious, he asked

"Would you adopt and raise a child with me." It was how they faced issues: give the other a choice to do or not. She paused, thought, and sat still for a long moment. He prepared to hear "No" – because saying "Yes" was as great a burden on Her as raising Her own child. She regarded him, with clear eyes and a serious, firm, face revealing deep thought, and said, in a voice absent frivolity or emotion,

"Yes." Jubilation filled his mind, and

At 34 years old, they began their adoption journey, absent knowledge of adoption, or the journey. They began at the state agency. Fill out forms for everything. Forms that asked about your genealogical history, your medical history, your social and criminal history. Interviews, inspections, etc. all part of a bureaucratic process to ensure you possessed parental potential. The questions, discussions, and interviews honed his idea of the child he wanted -- a newborn as much like him as possible. Selfish, but honest. Only to be approved. Only to have a case worker tell them, matter-of-factly, the likelihood was small that the state would place a newborn white baby with them. Then to be told there were many older, non-white children if he would accept one. In that moment, the agency became a dead end. Selfish, he said no thank you. Other options? Private adoptions, private agencies, religious organizations. On they went.

Their friends Clive and Gayle were in the process of adoption via a lawyer. After talking with them, he and She decided against a lawyer. For them, involving lawyers seemed to be all about money. They considered a surrogate – to ensure propagation of his DNA – but that also struck them as buying a baby. They talked, weighed pros and cons, and rejected surrogacy. The journey continued. After more phone calls, some visits, and a stroke of luck, they ended in an office of Catholic Family Services, a God-blessed agency -- if one exists. They

124

were within two years of turning 40 when they talked to the Catholic Family Services social worker. They said,

"We cannot have a child of our own." The social worker responded, "The agency only works with infertile couples." He said,

"We want a newborn, Caucasian baby." The worker answered,

"Catholic Family Services only deals with newborns and believes in matching characteristics of the baby with those of the parents," They said,

"We turn 40 in two years. Does that disqualify us?" She smiled and informed them,

"No. Once we accept you, we work with you until we place a child with you."

He asked "How long will it take?" She answered,

"We can start today. There is a lot to be done., but the agency only works with as many couples as they believe they can place babies with within a year." She asked,

"Are we accepted?" The social worker said,

"Accepted, yes. Approved, not yet." They smiled at each other. The social worker went on,

"Are you ready to start?"

"We are. "

The journey continued. Forms, histories, meetings with other parents-to-be, interviews, house visits all proceeded and preceded, by 4 months, their approval.

When she informed them of the approval, the social worker asked,

"Is the baby's room ready?" to which he answered,

"We are working on it" to which she said in a matter-of-fact tone,

"Better get it done soon. Often a baby comes unexpectedly. It is not like, wait 9 months, then the baby comes. It is more like, here is a baby. Whose is it?"

They created a nursery in a room off the kitchen that had served as their bedroom. Doing so required them to build an addition on the house. The addition -- two bedrooms and a bathroom -- doubled the square footage of their tiny home. Time passed. They finished the addition. He fretted and wondered. Time passed. They finished the nursery. Time passed. Through it all they waited. Eight days before Christmas, just before their 40th birthdays, the social worker called and asked,

"Are you ready?" What a question!

"Yes!"

"I think we have a newborn for you. Would you like to come and visit him?" Such a question. How do you answer such a question? Fighting tears, emotions cracking his voice, he just said

"Yes. When can we come?" They arranged a time the following day.

What a day! First the case worker took them to her office and described the newborn's mother's background, conditions the mother had placed on the adoption (no interactions with the child until his 18th birthday), and the possibility the baby suffered from fetal alcohol exposure. They took it all in.

Then the social worker asked. "Do you still want to see him?"

"Yes." And they proceeded to the agency's nursery where a small, dark-haired, boy lay asleep, stomach down, in a crib. The case worker picked him up and handed him to Her. She cradled the baby and smiled, then handed him the baby. He smiled and cradled the tiny boy. The first thing he saw was the boy's dark brown eyes, then a scabbed abrasion on his nose about a half-inch in diameter.

"What's this?" He asked the case worker.

"He has been active and agitated since delivery. When he is on his stomach, he moves his head back and forth, and that is how he got the sore on his nose."

"Ahh..." He loved the child the moment he held him, scab, its cause, and possible implications of fetal alcohol syndrome notwithstanding. All he saw was a beautiful baby boy -- exactly what he wanted to see. The next thing he heard was the social worker asking,

"What do you think? Is this your baby?"

They looked at each other and said, "Yes. Can we take him home?"

"Tomorrow. There are some things that need doing. A few papers, you know..."

"Of course."

They went home. On the way, they bought some baby formula. Bottles, sterilizer, blankets, some clothes, a crib, a car seat, and a myriad of other infant-care items already sat in the nursery –waiting for this moment. The next day, backing out of the driveway to go to the agency, they had to stop, return home, and get the car seat – a poignant indicator of how life was about to change.

No name struck them as self-evident. They considered names from: lists of names, suggestions from friends and family, and their own ideas – all discussed and rejected. Finally, they did a traditional thing. The boy's middle names came from Her father (James) and his grandfather (Martin). They chose Kevin as a given name. It was acceptable, not illuminating. They gathered Kevin James Martin up, placed him carefully in his car seat, and went home. At home, alone with a baby, as every parent knows, life changed. There was no more time spent on the question, "What next?" Although the question did not go away, there was little time to ponder, list options, or make a choice. Not only did he not think about the question, but also, he did not think about not thinking about it – he had entered the years of trying to raise a decent, caring, human being, and She was his companion through it all.

He was 13 days short of his 40th birthday. She 19 days short of Hers. Kevin was nine days old.

ABOUT KEVIN

THEY BECAME A TENTATIVE FAMILY (final adoption occurred a year later [state law requires birth parents have a year to change their minds] in a judge's office where they swore oaths and the judge decreed: "Now and forever you are a family.") At the final hearing, no one mentioned the work to come. It was unnecessary. During the year they waited for final adoption, they had experienced it in full.

He rose early, and fed the baby in the morning. She stayed up late, and fed him after midnight. They shared other feeding times, except, She did them while he was at the university. He cleaned and sterilized the bottles, and made formula and filled bottles. They changed diapers, bathed the baby, loved, and attended to him. She and he were tired most of the time. In short order,

Kevin was on the move. He climbed before he walked. Pots, pans, and dishes kept on low, open, shelves had to be moved above his reach. It was as if a flood swept through the house and washed away everything below three feet. He learned to climb out of his crib and be on the move. Most excursions led to their bed. They would pull him up, cuddle him, and fall back asleep. He walked, talked, and rode a two-wheel bike, without training wheels, by two years old. When toilet training was complete, the maintenance man took his son to university to attend a campus preschool. At day's end and weekends, Kevin spent his time outdoors on their two-acre property in South Phoenix. When the maintenance man's parents parked their travel trailer on the property, they doted on Kevin, and one summer took him to New Mexico for two weeks to give the parents a break.

A little after the boy learned to talk the maintenance man asked him

"Who does daddy love?" and Kevin answered

"Me." To which the maintenance man asked

"Who loves daddy?" to which Kevin said

"Me." To which the maintenance man said

"That's right!"

This litany was a regular feature three or more times a week from that first time until Kevin was eight or nine years of age. Performing filled the mind of the maintenance man with joy.

On a down side, his son loved miniature cars and trucks and wanted to play "Hot Wheels" with his dad. Alas, it was a game created by a child, comprised of unclear, malleable, rules, at the end of which, cars and trucks always smashed into each other. The game bored the maintenance man beyond tears. He would play a bit, then search for other entertainment for his son. Often, he created tasks that took him out of the game. After boredom and abandonment of the game, guilt followed – but he could not sustain interest in smashing toy cars together.

The maintenance man also experienced guilt the two times he slapped his son's hands, told Her about the incidents, and had to listen to Her say,

"Don't ever do that again!" The first incident occurred when the boy started to put a knife in an electrical socket. The maintenance man instantly slapped the boy's hand and knife away, shouting

"No. No. No." Soon after, all the sockets without something plugged in were plugged with plastic guards.

The second incident occurred as the maintenance man and his son drove to university. Kevin did not want to go. He grabbed the wheel, jerked it to turn the car around. The maintenance man slapped his hand off the wheel, shouting,

"No. No. No." He tried to follow the shouts with a quieter explanation, but his son would not have it. Surprised, pouting, he ignored his father by turning away. The maintenance man felt more guilt at his son's reaction than his wife's,

"Don't ever do that again!"

At four years of age, Kevin and his dad spent summer days at an Olympic-sized public pool. The maintenance man taught him the crawl stroke, and within three weeks – by successive approximations – had him swimming the length of the pool, a skill required before swimmers could use the diving boards. After he proved to an unbelieving supervisor that he met the swimming criterion, Kevin used the diving board constantly.

As Kevin approached kindergarten age, they chose to move to a neighborhood close to university, because harassment of white children was common in South Phoenix public schools. They rented a home with a pool and spent the summer living near, in, and around the pool. The maintenance man helped Her learn to float, swim, and overcome a life-long fear of water. It was their best summer in the desert. While there, they searched for a home near university.

Looking was the easy part. Many houses fit the geographic criterion – within a mile or two of the university – yet, after they toured a house, trying to choose tortured them. Either he found one that met his needs and She pointed out why it did not meet Hers, or vice versa. In the end, a five-bedroom, ranch-style, semi-custom, home on College Avenue, a mile-and-a-half south of the university met their needs and wants (save the absence of a pool). They bought it anyway, moved in, and became, at 47 years old, individual property owners for the first time. Soon after, they learned the: plumbing, roof, water heater, garbage disposal, exterior paint, inefficient windows, as well as a stream of other house parts needed attention, repair, or replacement. Addressing these problems exhausted them more than caring for Kevin. In some ways it was also more disruptive, because differences about money surfaced with each problem. Meanwhile,

Kevin attended public school -- a mismatch that only ended when he graduated from high school. He had a mind of his own and behaved so. From the start, he resisted academic work. The lessons he took from grade school were based on statements from his first and third-grade teachers. The former routinely said, "Children don't like math," and the latter posted a sign that said, "An error is no terror."

Kevin acted out the consequences of these views. He refused to do math. He resisted inducements to study. He would say, "I don't like math," or "An error is no terror." He refused to practice multiplication tables with the maintenance man, who, by the end of hours and hours of trying all manner of ways to encourage, induce, or coerce his son to study – each without success – accepted with sadness that his son would not have a career based on academic skills. He loved his son. What could he do? Only accept him for what he was – a hard lesson for one who had drifted through public school and college, minimally applied himself in graduate school, and only transformed himself into a scholar in the second year of work at a university. A difficult lesson for the maintenance man and a release from study for his boy: each had his own path to travel. The latter's path led

Kevin to start drinking in middle school, hang out with like-minded youth, excel at skateboarding, explore the ventilation system of his high school, experience the wrath of zero-tolerance administrators, and finish high school in an alternate school where district administrators dumped adolescents who resisted or rebelled, or simply did not thrive in regular high school. "An error is no terror." Drinking led to two DUI's, and a criminal trespass conviction. After a combined 30 days of incarceration in county jail, Kevin decided he did not want to return to jail. At home,

He and the maintenance man argued about keeping a clean room, about respecting Her, and about drinking. On different occasions when angry, Kevin punched holes in walls and his door. His father fixed the walls but not the door. The hole in the door allowed someone on the outside to reach in and unlock it. During a physical confrontation that ended with them wrestling on the floor, Kevin claimed abuse and wanted to call the police. The maintenance man obliged. The police came, talked with each separately, and left without further action. That was the last physical clash between them. Verbal clashes about drinking, cleanliness, and showing respect went on. These troubles were balanced by good traits because

His son had a big warm heart toward friends. He was loyal to friends, and respected girls and boys equally. He shared what money he had, and his possessions, unselfishly. Some friends were selfish, and took advantage. He accepted and tolerated their overreach, to the point of denying his own needs. For this trait alone, the maintenance man loved his son with all his heart, and continued to search for a path to adulthood for him. And because

Kevin possessed no trace of competitiveness. Going for the win, as opposed to the fun, of a game or activity, was not part of his sense of self. He was content to bike and skate by himself. He participated in youth sports. In a youth basketball league, during games, he ran as fast as he could from one end to the other. As he reached the free throw line, he executed a baseball slide, and ended up on his backside with the other nine kids circling, passing, and shooting around him. If he got up and got a rebound, he would pass the ball off and speed to the other end to repeat the act. The coach did not like it. Players did not like it. Parents did not like it. His father was good naturedly apoplectic. Kevin did not care, was relegated to substitute status, but persisted in how he got fun from the game. As he grew up, behaviors reflecting his disinterest in winning emerged in soccer and lacrosse. And because

Prospects of money and fame failed to ignite achievement motivation, or a competitive fire, or diminish his warmth towards friends, it took a long time for the maintenance man to fully accept his son as he was. But he did. What better choice? Not force.

Only playing video games did Kevin exhibit a sense of competition. Whether playing alone or in multi-player games, that a computer, not a person, mediated his acts permitted him to kill, maim, stomp, obliterate, and crush opponent(s) – even friends. The maintenance man tried, once or twice, to compete with his son in **Grand Theft Auto**, but he did not like the game itself, did not play well, and foreswore video games ever after. Instead, he tried improve his understanding of his son by taking him on trips to exotic places. To this end, they made three distinct trips during Kevin's adolescence. For the first trip

He and the boy traveled to Arkansas to visit Doug and Dottie. At the time, Doug and Dottie's oldest son David lived elsewhere on his own, and their youngest son Eric lived at home. For the maintenance man, four memories captured the essence of the trip. First,

On the way to and from Arkansas, they stopped at Balmorhea State Park, famous for a humongous, spring-fed, swimming pool, as well as two streams harboring two species of endangered pupfish. At the elbow of the L-shaped pool was a lagoon deep enough to practice scuba diving. One leg of the L inclined from a shallow end to a deeper end like ordinary pools. The other leg was very deep and populated by large fish. The two streams trickled out from the swimming pool and appeared to never be more than a foot deep. As they walked along the stream and stooped down here and there, they could see the endangered fish in their limited world. Second, in Arkansas,

Watching Kevin struggle, take several headers, and then successfully water-ski on Greer's Ferry Lake filled the maintenance man with pride. That Kevin managed to get and stay up during the first few tries reminded the maintenance man of two-year old Kevin who mastered a two-wheel bike in his first lesson on the bike. What a sense of balance! Third,

There were the chiggers. Who knew? Not desert dwellers. Before taking precautions (prescribed by their hosts after an early encounter), walking in the woods led to itching bumps – mostly located at sock lines. A dab of nail polish on each bump turned out to be an effective antidote. Changes to how one wore one's shoes, socks, and pants prevented recurrences. Staying on a road that weaved through the woods and connected the community to the main highway eliminated the threat altogether. However, the existence of chiggers dissuaded them from ever considering Arkansas as a potential home. A benefit of the desert – to weigh against costs, like summer heat, is a paucity of nasty insects. Finally,

It was the trip on which Doug dropped his bomb about role-playing and truthfulness during the years he and the maintenance man had been friends. Only years later, did he make a journey – filled with poignant emotion – to see and talk with Doug. The second exotic trip involved

The maintenance man, his father, and Kevin drove and ferried to Alaska in his Dad's Ford van. On their meandering journey, they avoided Interstates where possible. Their path from the desert took them through the Joshua Tree National Forest, over the Hoover Dam, through Las Vegas, through mine country and a long, lonely, valley in north-central Nevada, then into eastern Oregon, where they had a surprise encounter with a beautiful waterfall in the middle of that dry country. They turned west to reach Highway 101 on the coast where they turned north, spent a night at the summer home of friends in Yachats, Oregon. From Yachats, they headed up the coast to Port Angeles and took a ferry to Victoria, Vancouver Island. As none had an interest in historic buildings and other such monuments,

They got onto Highway 1 out of Victoria and proceeded north to Nanaimo. To the maintenance man, it seemed as if hippy remnants of the 1960's all wound up in Nanaimo. At a Nanaimo casino, in which a strange form of blackjack was played, the maintenance man found no luck. After one night, they took Highway 19 to Port Hardy and caught an overnight British Columbia ferry to Prince Rupert. From the deck of the ferry, they watched dolphin and killer whales skirt the ship, dart across the bow, and exuded a sense of great enjoyment of life. They were the first big animals seen since the trip began. "Wow!"

"Look at them go!" And

"Wow!" Was all they managed to say. Their cabin was another matter, and

"Woh…" was the extent of their emotional reaction as they eyed the two bunk beds and chair, as the thought – one night sleeping in a chair will not be that bad – ran through the maintenance man's head. Because the cabin on the next ferry, going north from Prince Rupert to Skagway, had similar accommodations, he had to modify that thought. Oh well, three nights sleeping in a chair is not so bad. Asi es la vida. The route of the second ferry, called the Inside Passage, coursed between the mainland and a string of islands on the ocean side of the passage, to Ketchikan, then Juneau, and Skagway. The Inside Passage supplied two remarkable phenomena. First, the islands on the ocean side were often covered by heavy clouds that hovered over them. From the water to an altitude of 50-100 feet the air was as clear as any sunny day, but from there on up, thick, cumulous, clouds, a combination of white and dark colors, signaled rain that never came. Second, as the ship plowed north, water in the center of the Passage was dark and green, but on the mainland side about 60 to 100 feet landward, the water had a light brown and muddy hue. There was no mixing. It was as if God had drawn a line in the water and said, "Stick to your side," and the waters obeyed. Astonishing! During a stop in Ketchikan, someone pointed out the proposed location for the bridge to nowhere – famous for its status as a federal budget earmark that was never funded. In Juneau, they had time to take the car off the ferry and drive into town for a meal. After eating, with time on their hands, they drove out of Juneau and not long after just ran out of road – no dirt or gravel roads, no paths, just nothing but the natural world, something never encountered driving out of lower-48 cities and towns. In Skagway, they stopped for gas and a snack. That the town was geared to tourism did not interest them, and they soon headed east for Yukon territory and later south toward Stewart, British Columbia. The road south had both paved and gravel roads. While the environment seemed untouched by man, they saw no game animals, but on a stop along an unpaved section where they got out to have a snack and stretch their legs, a tiny flock of black birds with white shoulders spotted the granola snacks, turned brave, and flew right up to the visitors. Recalling a similar incident on the Pacific Crest Trail, the maintenance man put some granola in his hand and stretched it out. In short order, a bird fearlessly came and landed on his hand to take a bite. Kevin duplicated the action and experienced the same result. Wonderful!

On the journey east and south they stopped by a stream and saw big fish in the water. Real big fish! They pulled out their fishing gear and tried to lure one. The maintenance man failed, but Kevin hooked a salmon, nearly two feet long, fat, and heavy. After he hauled it in and held it up, he removed the lure and released the fish. Joy filled the heart of the maintenance man on his son's behalf, as catching a salmon had been one of Kevin's goals for the trip. Further attempts failed, so they moved on.

When they reached Stewart, they bought gas and asked a local about bears, who replied

"If you want to see bears, go to Hyder." They did. There, it took less than a minute to go from one end of Hyder to the other. No bears. They turned around and stopped to ask a person about bears. That person directed them to a spit of a road, running along the course of a river, that ended in a cleared-out spot, where a few parked cars sat. They got out of the van and started to walk. A ranger approached.

After pleasantries, they asked about bears. The ranger said "Follow me" and started walking along a levee with water on either side. They followed. He stopped. They stopped. He pointed. They looked, and not 40 feet ahead a huge bear was on the bank of the levee, tearing the skin off a salmon, and eating the fat covering the flesh of the fish. A little further on, two smaller bears were mimicking the larger one. The ranger said,

"That is a mother and her two cubs. Do not go any further." Was there ever a more unnecessary instruction? There were more bears further along the levee, and now and then a bear would descend from the woods on the side opposite and go down the bank. All the bears mimicked mama bear's behavior, tearing off the skin of fish that teemed in the water, eating the fat, and leaving the flesh to rot. They asked the ranger about it, and he replied

"The bears only want to add fat for hibernation."

"And the rest of the fish?" Grandpa asked.

"The birds…" It was only then that an image of uncounted white birds consuming or carrying off parts of the dead fish became a primary focus.

They had seen enough. For his part, out of concern for the safety of his son, his father, and himself, the maintenance man turned back towards the car. The ranger did the same. After a few steps, the ranger said

"Stop!"

"What is it?"

"A male." He pointed down the levee along the opposite side to a spot about 100 yards down river where a male bear, appearing to be nine feet tall, stood on his hind legs looking in their direction. The ranger commanded

"Stay still!"

Okay by them. The bear dropped onto four legs and moved off at a right angle to their path to the car. At the ranger's signal, they quickly moved on to the van." Phews" and "Wows!" filled the silence of the van. Wild life not one of them had ever seen before, or since.

They retraced their route to Stewart and then followed Highway 37 on its path mostly south and east to pass through Jaspar and Banff National Parks. In those parks, they encountered hikers, moose, mountain goats, some small unidentified critters, and smaller bears – exciting to see. But the bears of Hyder? Woh, those bears! Amused with a thought that popped into his mind, the maintenance man asked,

"How do those bears survive without mobile phones?" and saw a look of strained tolerance pass across his son's face.

Coming out of the Canadian Rockies onto the great prairie of Alberta heading toward Calgary, they talked about home. Everyone was ready to head back. So, they did. Grandpa and dad took turns at the wheel. They abandoned back roads, and put the petal down hard. Mileposts flew by, especially in Montana. In what seemed like just a few hours they were across Montana, flew through Idaho potato country, and entered Utah. They took a detour to bounce on top of the water of the Great Salt Lake, then returned to their route and pace. They were soon home where they received Her relieved, gentle, happy welcome. As for the third trip,

An odyssey with origins before Kevin was born, when Sarah's talks of Ireland and the tales he read about its heroes, history, and revolution sparked a desire to go there. Sarah's death and his son's high school graduation reignited his desire to go, and he thought – if he went to Ireland, he must travel on to Spain. Hence, he asked his son if a trip to Ireland and Spain was a good gift for him after graduation. His son answered,

"Uhuh." Planning began in earnest when his brother Rick visited and the maintenance man asked him if he wanted to go. Rick answered

"Uhuh. I will go to Ireland, but not to Spain." He asked his brothers Herb and Tom, but they could not. He asked Her. She chose to stay home. Instead, She said that she held him, irresponsible as he was, completely, undeniably, irrevocably, responsible for the well-being of Her son. On this topic, Her last words were

"Do you understand?" To which, he replied

"Uhuh."

They rented a car in Ireland and circumnavigated the island by driving: through Northern Ireland along the north coast to Port Rush; next across to Donegal; then down the west coast to Sligo and Dromore West, the birthplace of Sarah. From Dromore West it was on to Galway, the Cliffs of Moher, and the Ring of Kerry; east to Cork and Cobh; and, finally, back north to Dublin. They did so, but the maintenance man's memory of that wonderful island was indelibly overprinted by experiences not involving geography or natural beauty. He mostly remembered the night after they arrived in Dromore West and checked into a b and b. Filled with anticipation – this was the birthplace of Sarah – he arranged, via the proprietor, to meet a man to take them to the Scott family farm as well as introduce surviving locals who had known the family – all now dead or in America. That settled,

The proprietor told them that the only place to have dinner was down the driveway and across the road – close but closing soon. They rushed over for a roast chicken dinner. Roast chicken with baked potatoes, mashed potatoes, French-fried potatoes, potato salad, and potato chips. All those potatoes made him think of Her with a smile – because potatoes, in any style, were Her favorite food – and with wistfulness because She was not there to revel in it. After dinner, they investigated the pub next door, a dreary place with a couple of pool tables and no patrons, and returned to the b and b. The most memorable part of the night occurred as the two brothers prepared for bed. Kevin decided he wanted to go to the pub. Father and son discussed the matter, and they reached agreement: Kevin could go to the pub on his own, and would return no later than 1:30 a.m. Off he went. The maintenance man could not sleep, kept checking the clock, and when 1:30 came and went, became angry. He got up, walked to the pub, and found his son playing pool and drinking beer. They argued. Inebriated, Kevin sullenly left the bar with his father. Just after they crossed the road, Kevin took off running down the road, jumped into a thicket of bushes, and disappeared. The maintenance man followed, did not find his son, called out in the cool, dark, quiet night, but received no reply. What to do? His wife's words bellowed in his mind. In that moment,

He rejected both involving the Garda and traipsing alone through unfamiliar countryside to look for a drunk teenager. He settled on going back to bed where he slept off-and-on the rest of the night. When he woke, his son was out cold in bed. Relieved, but still angry, he went for breakfast and returned to wake Kevin, which he accomplished in a brusque and unhappy way. They spent that day at the Scott farm, visiting the locals, and touring points of interest. The day passed in an ordinary, pleasant, way –absent revelations or illumination – separately experienced by a far-off, fuming, father, a sullen, solitary, son, and a baffled, bemused, brother who steadfastly concentrated on the immediate surroundings. For the three of them,

Emotions were an odd mixture of tension between father and son, detachment on the part of the brother, and a subdued wonder evoked by the sights, sounds, and people of the island. When asked at one or another time after the trip, each of them said

"I'm glad we went."

The remaining days in Ireland they spent hopping from one b and b to another, and stopping in Cobh to investigate if Sarah had emigrated from Ireland there. She did not. A year later he found out she had left for America from Liverpool. They finished the tour in Dublin, first with a dinner at MacDonalds, and later with drinks in a hotel bar alive with Irish music and people singing emotion laden songs. The last morning, after a visit to the duty-free shop, Rick took his flight to America. Later that day, father and son flew to Spain. In Madrid, a first stop was El Corte Ingles to buy a phone, for Kevin to be in touch with his girlfriend Misha. Over succeeding days, from Madrid to Donostia to Cadiz, Kevin regularly called her and they talked – a lot. The maintenance man regularly returned to Vodaphone for more minutes.

In Donostia, his friend Nekane and her family hosted the Americans with proud Basque hospitality. While the maintenance man appreciated their efforts, he sensed discomfort and withdrawal in

Kevin, which he ascribed to Kevin's desire to go home – sparked and enhanced by calls to Misha. Attempts to interest Kevin in immediate surroundings met with little success, as did attempts to determine a reason for the withdrawal. On their bus trip to Cadiz, and during the first days in Cadiz, the withdrawal intensified, so much so that Kevin refused to go to the introductory Spanish classes he had agreed to attend while the maintenance man attended his own classes. A few days of this behavior – and an evening when he had to extract a mildly inebriated Kevin from a bar – pushed the maintenance man to press his son for an explanation. He learned that Misha had ended the relationship. Simply put, Kevin's heart was broken.

An acre's worth of sadness

-

There goes my crunchy-gaited son
in unrequited autumn love.
Piling leaves and picking twigs,
burning them
till an acre's worth of sadness done.

Disconsolate at the news, the maintenance man set aside language classes and his other interests, to try to lift his son's spirits, which led him to ask

"What do you want to do?"

"I want to go home."

"We cannot because we are locked into the date of our return tickets, and I cannot afford the cost of changing them. Is there anything else?"

"Like what?"

"I don't know, but we could start by my stopping classes, and finding something to do together."

"Okay, but what could we do?"

"Let me think about it for a bit." So, he did, and later, he asked "Would you like to go to Sevilla and visit a bodega?"

"What's that?"

"It's a place where they make wine." "Okay."

They informed the language school they were done taking classes, took the train to Sevilla, where they walked to the bodega that produced the sherry known as Tio Pepe, subjected themselves to a tour, and ended the afternoon in a tasting room, where the bodega provided each person a small bottle of Tio Pepe. They sat alone at a table next to two couples from Great Britain. One of these four recognized their American accent and started making comments about Americans -- intended to send them up in a good-natured way, but the maintenance man reflected the intent of each comment with a send-up of his own. Soon the six were sitting around the same table drinking their Tio Pepe and getting inebriated. Somehow the conversation turned to opinions about drinking, specifically, his dim view towards Kevin's drinking. All four Brits hammered him for his puritanical views, urged him to lighten up on his son, and united around the theme that drinking was a reasonable pastime for the young. A glance at the bemused smile of his son confirmed this alternate view of drinking firmly embedded itself with the notions "Children don't like math" and "An error is no terror." Still, his son was smiling, and some smiles are worth cherishing. On the train back to Cadiz, he asked,

"Would you like to do some more sightseeing?"

"Okay. Where?" Having had the time to think, he said

"We could go to Gibraltar – they speak English there -- or we could go to the Alhambra – one of the most beautiful buildings in the world. What do you think?"

"Gibraltar." The next day they went there by bus, and learned

The Spanish people view Gibraltar as part of Spain – a view demonstrated in a petty way on arrival. When they left the bus in La Linea de la Concepción, they encountered long, long, lines of people waiting to pass the border – Spanish authorities slow-walked the entry of Spanish workers – those that provided services to residents of Gibraltar. The border guards instructed tourists to bypass the lines, whereby they walked into throngs of vendors and tour guides speaking an English patois. The maintenance man and his son negotiated a 50-euro trip around and to the summit of the Rock – a hangout for a troop of panhandling Barbary apes – one of whom willingly sat on the shoulders of Kevin and, after, those of his father –in exchange for a few grapes and several slices of orange. Back in La Linea, hunger overcame them and they went to a Chinese restaurant. The waitress surprised the maintenance man when she said,

"Will you marry me and take me to America?" To which he replied

"I am already married." Which caused her to turn to Kevin and ask

"Will you marry me and take me to America?" To which he replied

"No, I do not want to get married right now."

They never knew if she was serious or teasing, but She brought their meals and left them alone. They ate, went to the register, paid the bill, and left. Did she ever get to America? Another unanswered question. They returned to Cadiz to catch the next-day, night-coach through Madrid to Barcelona. From the Sants station in Barcelona, they took the metro to the station nearest the College of Pharmacy on El Diagonal where his friend Juana had arranged a room. Over the next few days and nights, they went to dinner with Juana and her family, visited La Sagrada Familia, El Parque Guell, the Hard Rock Café for a cheeseburger, a super mall, and took a tour bus around the city. To divert his son's attention from the breakup, the maintenance man took him to France on a regional train. That train arrived at Port Bou, the last town in Spain, just a few kilometers over the hill from Cerbere, France. They remained seated until the conductor said to get off.

"But we are going to Cerbere."

"This train does not go to Cerbere."

Ohoh. "Can we get a train to Cerbere here." "Yes, in an hour."

An hour later they boarded another train and got off two minutes later in Cerbere. They left the empty station, walked down a dirty street to a small tunnel under the tracks, climbed steps up to a street, and saw a derelict, art deco hotel dead ahead. They walked toward the hotel not having seen a soul since leaving the station. On a nearby corner, on a concrete and tile fence, a cat watched us. Kevin went over, and the cat did not move, and stayed still while Kevin petted him. From there, they headed down the hill through the houses until they reached a road that went around a bay bordered by Cerbere proper. They walked toward the beach where a small group of people – the first seen -- played in the water.

The group contained an older British couple living in France being visited by their son and his family from Australia. The maintenance man talked with them for a half hour while Kevin explored the beach. When the family said good-bye and headed inland for an afternoon meal, the maintenance man walked over to the shops along the road. All closed. He walked to a nearby plaza and looked at the shops there – all closed. he spotted a dilapidated café and went in for a coffee. The proprietress told him that the town was closed for the day. Everyone was inland for a festival. What were the odds?

He went back to Kevin who seemed to be doing okay playing in the water, picking up stones, and doodling around on the beach. After a while they went back to the station. It was still deserted. Worse, the schedule revealed there was no train from Cerbere to Barcelona. What gives? He called a cab, but the dispatcher said the cabs did not cross the border. Now what? No planes, no trains, no cabs, no car. They started walking. The road ran to the end of the bay, switched back, and went over the hill some distance to Port Bou. They had about an hour until the next train left Port Bou. As they walked, an occasional car went by, which provided a scale by which to measure the trip to the top of the hill. The maintenance man judged that they would not make the train if they walked the whole way, so he started to hitchhike. His son looked at him as if he was crazy.

The fifth car that passed picked them up. The driver was Spanish, an employee of RENFRE who worked in the train yards in Cerbere, and he drove them the entire 12 kilometers up and over the hill, past the abandoned border post that prevented cabs from crossing, and into Port Bou, just 9 minutes before the train left. They ran up the hill to the station. His heart pumped fast, his legs burnt, and his lungs ached, but they boarded the train back to Barcelona on time. When the train stopped at Plaza de Cataluña before Sants, they decided to get off and have one last cheeseburger at the Hard Rock Café. After one last-night sleep in Spain, they headed home. Once home, the odyssey in Ireland and Spain inspired the maintenance man to write a detailed, first-person, present-tense, account of the trip, available as a free PDF on the web page Themaintenancesdilemma.com. After this trip,

She, the maintenance man, and Kevin endured a trying period in their lives. Kevin continued to drink, spent most of his time in his room, and played video games all night. He worked part-time, making, and delivering pizza. And kept his bedroom, across the hall from their own, in a state that failed utterly to be clean. He had two DUI's for which he spent 15 days in the county jail. There were two visits to emergency rooms for alcohol poisoning. Once, as he walked home from a local bar, the police picked him up – as a suspect in a burglary – and had him stand in the street while they drove the offended party by for identification. He was not the burglar. Girl friends came and stayed in his room. They had noisy sex, sometimes waking the maintenance man in the early hours. Most of the girls tried and failed to have him clean his room, and, not long after, left him. The parents were flummoxed. They could not agree on what to do. Each loved Kevin in their own way. Each had ideas about what to do. They could not agree on a single strategy. It was a time during which three persons lived separate lives in the same house; he at the university, She in her crafts and business, and Kevin in his room. He and She reached the end of their patience and set a firm date for him to leave. Then,

They worried about his ability to survive. They loved him. He frustrated them. They talked about what they could do to ease him into the world outside without their resources. They finally agreed on one thing: if he did not have to worry about rent, he might be able to work the rest out by himself. They agreed to buy him a home of his own. They wondered if Kevin would accept the offer, so they asked him,

"If we buy you your own home, would that be good for you?" " Yes."

"And you'd be responsible for helping decide where and what to buy?"

"Yes!"

"And pay your own bills?"

"Yes."

"And you understand the limit on what we can spend?"

"Yes."

By the deadline, they purchased a four-bedroom townhouse, Kevin moved all his furnishings into it, and left all his garbage behind. After two days in his own home, he found a job working in the kitchen of a dinner theater. His parents were stunned. Why hadn't they booted him earlier? One or the other of them always offered him another chance. In Kevin's 36th year,

He had a stroke that destroyed a majority of his cerebellum. Late one night his roommates called and said they were taking him to the emergency room: he was behaving in strange and incoherent ways. He and She met the roommates and Kevin in the emergency room parking lot, helped Kevin into the hospital -- he needed to be held up by both arms -- and waited for information from the staff. Attending physicians wasted no time. They had Kevin transported to Barrow's neurological unit and told his parents that they should go there for further information on their son's conditions. When they called Barrow's, they were informed of strict Covid protocols which severely limited the time and number of visits and visitors, as well as the mask requirements. The morning after,

They were at Barrow's as early as permitted. During that visit, they learned that Kevin had suffered a major stroke but death was not imminent. In his room, they saw their son unconscious, pale, hooked to monitors and medical devices, and heard the doctors describe – in technical and obscure language – what course of actions had been initiated. They left, relieved that their son was alive, but apprehensive about his recovery and future. Across the next few days,

Kevin was conscious when they visited, but not rational. He was able to talk, but what he talked about did not match the reality of his situation. He hallucinated and described his hallucinations as if they were real, for example: his nurse and her drug-dealing boyfriend distributed drugs to patients. When the police realized what was happening, they came to the hospital to arrest the criminals. The couple took off through the halls with a phalanx of police in pursuit.

Alarms were ringing everywhere. The noise was so loud that Kevin reported he was jolted from a sound sleep, and saw the nurse running down the hall with the police behind. The hallucinations stopped in a matter of days, but real, serious, and persistent, consequences of the stroke remained. Kevin suffered: double vision; numbness in his right arm, hand, and leg; vertigo and associated nausea; and an arhythmic heartbeat. Less than a week after his admission to Barrow's, he was transferred to a rehabilitation hospital. There,

He began a long, slow recovery. Twice daily rehabilitation session brought his vision and gait to near normal. The double vision gradually disappeared. However, he continued to suffer numbness in his limbs, and vertigo when he stood too long. After two weeks at the rehabilitation hospital, he was released for home care which included twice a week visits with physical therapists, and selection of and visits with a primary care physician. The maintenance man assumed responsibility for making and getting him to appointments, checking with him often when he was at home, and overseeing his financial affairs. A year after the stroke, Kevin was able to work part-time and resumed his position as a cook at the dinner theater.

His recovery of so much of his previous capabilities buoyed his parents. However, his ability to make and execute plans, never strong before his stroke, was unchanged by the stroke. This source of concern continued, but did not increase. If anything, they were relieved that he resumed nearly all aspects of his previous life, and even managed to reduce, but not eliminate drinking, the behavior the neurologists identified as a likely cause of his stroke.

After She died, father and son eased into a better relation, able to call and talk to each other without anger, disappointment, or guilt, simply two people who knew each other well and cared.

HE EXPERIENCES ADMINISTRATION
AND TAKES AFFIRMATIVE ACTION

BEFORE BEING PROMOTED TO ASSOCIATE professor, he mastered his course offerings, worked hard with Morris, and improved his vita to be among the best in the college. After promotion, in a conversation with Tom, a friend and college gossip, Tom suggested he compare his salary with others in the college. The maintenance man asked,

"How do I do that?" Tom replied

"The state budget for the university is available in the library."

"So?"

"So, the dollar value of every line item, including each professor listed by name, organized by college and department is in the budget." In a matter of hours, the maintenance man had studied the salaries of faculty in his college. A detailed comparison of departments and faculty provoked feelings he did not like. His blood simmered, because

His department, despite being most productive in research studies and publications, was the lowest paid in the college. Further, the highest paid full professors in his department were the lowest paid in the college. That he was in the middle of the distribution of salaries in his department was about right. What angered him the most was the discrepancy between his salary and that of a male Hispanic hired that year. Once on a tenure-track, the maintenance man received performance reviews for each of the five years before the promotion decision. Most assistant professors work hard during this five-year period of review. By contrast, the dean hired this Hispanic male – not close to promotion at his previous institution – as a tenured associate professor – without review. For the maintenance man, it was salt in the wound that the Hispanic was offered a salary $9400 (35%) higher than his own. That his new Honda Accord cost $9400 was the salt that deepened his resentment

Affirmative action? Not as affirmative action was originally defined: among equally qualified candidates, first offer the position to a person in a protected class. This was not affirmative actions, but academic chicanery, and possibly fraud. He blamed the dean, a man who lacked common sense and possessed instincts of a hack. Because of his resentment, his support for affirmative action waned, but did not disappear. It disappeared completely after another dubious hire.

Some might say (some probably did), "Stop whining, white boy." Had he heard that he would have said,

"I may whine, but past discrimination, claimed but not substantiated, does not justify financial injustice." His anger deepened further when Ray, then chair of the department, handed him a memo, written by the dean, recommending faculty salary adjustments to the provost. Smiling slyly, Ray asked,

"What do you think of this?"

It was a list of faculty members, mostly women and minorities, but including himself and a few other white males, paired with a suggested increase, and followed by a short rationale. Some names were next to amounts of $500 and $1000, a few went as high as $5000. As rationale, many names were followed by "protected class, market adjustment." Next to his name zero dollars. "Unable to estimate." was the listed rationale. He read it in front of Ray, and blurted,

"I think this is a pile of shit."

Ray smiled like a hillbilly who just loosed a pack of dogs after a coon. Heaven, help the coon! Unless stopped, dogs tear a coon apart. In his own hunt, the maintenance man used something less messy, but deadlier. He used plain-to-see, easy-to-understand, analyses of salary data. The dean died an administrator's death. It was one time the maintenance man's motive was both strong and singularly about money. He put all his analyses in a report, and, heeding advice from a friend, sent it through channels. First, to Ray, who, after setting off the maintenance man's wrath, doubted the effort would pay off, yet sent it to the dean, who denied the suggested adjustment. The maintenance man appealed to the provost, a sleazy little fellow, who foisted his appeal on Elmer G, associate provost, a long-time, honorable long-time employee of the university, who was passed over for promotion to provost by the carpetbagging, sleazy, little fellow.

Elmer called him in to talk, and asked him to explain the report and its implications: his report countered every excuse the dean offered in defense of his adjustments. EG smiled the smile of a person foreseeing obtaining a little revenge of his own, but just said, in a professional voice,

"I'm going to have my office do some analysis of your data and I will be back in touch."

"Okay" confident that his years of work to master statistical technique had made his report unassailable. So, he left Elmer's office and went to see Ray. They had a smoke. He told everything to Ray, who now thought and said the maintenance man was on to something. One could see wheels turning in Ray's head. If this worked for the maintenance man, with a dubious past and checkered beginning at the university, it might work for others, like a wheel-chair bound, female, professor of developmental psychology, who had the lowest salary of all tenured full professors in the college.

They only had to wait for a response.

A day later, a staff researcher in the Office of Institutional Studies called the maintenance man and asked for guidance on an analysis of salary data. After a question or two, the maintenance man knew the researcher sought advice on how to analyze the data in his report. He simply said

"Hold off on doing anything. I am going to call Elmer. I think we can resolve this without further analyses." With a relieved tone, the staffer quickly said.

"Okay." And the maintenance man called Elmer immediately after to ask,

"Elmer, your man in Institutional Studies just called me to advise him on how to analyze the data in my report. Do you think this has gone far enough."

"Yes, I do. Will you come over in an hour, We will talk again?"

"I'll be there." He went and told Ray, who said

"I'll be damned. You beat them."

"Yep." Smiling like the man whose dog treed a coon and got a nice bite out his ass as well. An hour later,

He sat across from Elmer, who seemed to be relieved not to be in conflict with him, and still with a hint of smile of a man getting a measure of his own revenge – at the expense of a sleazy, little, fellow. Before Elmer even spoke, the maintenance man knew that the provost had caved, that Elmer got some satisfaction from it, and that something was coming. Elmer started with,

"I have been authorized to offer you up to a $3000 adjustment."

"That's all he'll let you offer me?"

"That's right."

"Between you and I, if you were in charge, might you have offered more?"

"Mm hmm." With an affirmative nod.

"Well, I'll take the $3000, and thank you personally Elmer."

Elmer became a friend, and a poker playing partner for another 20 years. Had he pressed, he felt certain he would have gotten more money, but, fuck, it was only money, and talking to the sleazy, little, fellow would leave him with a grimy, oily, shit all over his soul feeling. When Ray heard the news, he decided to act, took the maintenance man's report, and started a list of faculty members in the department with justifiable cases. The maintenance man, who happily basked in that fine moment, had showed him the way.

While the maintenance man settled down, content with a victory, and happy with more money to spend each month, Ray began total conflict with the dean. His words (those of a Regent's professor) carried weight. When he demanded the sleazy, little, fellow dismiss the dean, the little fellow assented, but exacted a heavy price – Ray agreed to act as dean while a search for a new one occurred.

A bad dean went! Long live the good (acting) dean!

The effect of these political acts on the life of the maintenance man was profound. As soon as Ray agreed to be dean for a year, he wanted a person he trusted as chair of the department, and he settled on the maintenance man. The faculty, save the maintenance man, concurred. Recalling the testing service, the last thing the maintenance man wanted was more administration, so he declined. Ray began his campaign. Faculty told him the department had taken care of him (aside from two searches in which they hired others), and now it was his duty|obligation|responsibility to take care of the department. He resisted. To celebrate becoming dean, Ray hosted a party.

Guests included department faculty, a coterie of Ray's academic allies, some of his advanced students, and MF, former chair, and current vice president of student affairs. The party disguised a devious plan: all night long, subsets of persons, found their way to the maintenance man, flattered him, "You are one of the smartest professors in the college;" tried to pump him up, "Your statistics courses are the best;" or gave a variation of a call to arms, "In these dangerous times, you must defend us. As a tenured member of the faculty, you have a responsibility." They kept giving him drinks. Just before midnight, he was sitting outside on one side of a picnic bench, alone, facing, on the side opposite, Ray, Jim, a faculty member, two students, Ray's wife and former student, and Alex, former student, and his wife. All were drinking. He looked across the table. He saw their heads nodding up and down in unison, bodies rocking, as they chanted, "Only you can do it. It must be you." "Only you can do it. It must be you." "Only you can do it. It must be you." He felt seasick watching their heads bob up and down, and at the end, he said he would do it. Their joy preceded a concerted efforts to make him sober.

By the beginning of the next work week, everyone knew he was chair of the department. At home, She had reservations, but accepted his decision. Unlike efforts to teach well or conduct research, academic preparations were unnecessary, yet, because he spoke for 15 other faculty,

He had to change – first his physical appearance. A shaggy beard became trimmed and stayed so. Hair, once shoulder length, matched that of a modern business man – not too long, neck hair line razor trimmed. Next, his wardrobe: jeans, casual short and long sleeve t-shirts, sandals, and sneakers changed to suits, sport coats, ties, black socks, dress pants, dress shirts, and dress shoes. He retained one item to remind himself he had taken on a role for the sake of others: a Grateful Dead t-shirt became a regular undershirt on work days. To himself and to very close friends, he reported,

"Every day is Halloween." Nevertheless, an inescapable, descent into the dull, gray, purgatory of administration proceeded. The new chair and acting dean worked out a process by which he, as chair, forwarded the names of underpaid persons, as identified by his report, and accompanied by a referral for a salary increase. One by one, Ray set an amount, and forwarded it to the little fellow for approval. It worked again…and again… and again. When all that could be adjusted were, the dean assigned him to oversee a committee to stop a proposal that local school boards, rather than college faculty, control the curriculum of the teacher preparation programs. A local school superintendent with political ambition pushed the proposal, and Ray would have none of it, He told the maintenance man to make it so. Using university and Board of Regent policies about curriculum change, they stopped the proposal. With a mouth full of mutters, the superintendent gave up, and left, his head of golden hair on fire.

The year of the good dean continued. The department got a fair share of microcomputer funds that let the maintenance man place computers in the hands of productive faculty. Spring semester, the search for a new dean settled on a new candidate. Controlled by the little fellow, the hire turned into an affirmative action coup for the university – she was the first black dean at a state university. As a former department chair at a back-east, purportedly elite, university, she wanted to take charge, and no one, especially an obdurate white man who taught statistics, was going to stop her. She had an agenda (set by a sleazy, little fellow [who later married her]): reorganize eight departments into three divisions. The good year was the maintenance man's first, last, and only year as chair. The good dean prepared to leave for Italy on sabbatical and return home via travel around the world. Ray's thoughts were filled with visions of Rome when he stopped by to chat,

"Bill, I have arranged for you to be division director while I am gone. Please do this for the good of our faculty and other good people in the college. I am asking as a friend."

"Okay, Ray."

What other answer could he give after being called friend for the first time. So, he became division director – not because he was a faculty choice but because a good dean bartered with a new dean. In exchange for not opposing her, she accepted Ray's recommendation that the maintenance man be acting division director. A salary increase came with the position and moved his salary above a comfortable level. At home, when he told Her, She warned him,

"You may use up the extra money rapidly when you deal with Her all the time."

"You're right... but I have to try... for the good of all."

"Mmm...mmm... and for the good of you? What?"

"When Ray gets back, I can quit if it goes badly." He kept wearing that Grateful Dead t-shirt, but he kept hearing that damn lyric,

The new dean and acting director had their first taste of each other's style and personality at an administrative retreat attended by the dean, her associate deans, division directors and staff or faculty responsible for important units in the college -- in all, about 10 people. The retreat was all about doing things her way. At one point, he asked,

"What if performance data suggest another alternative is more effective?" The new dean said,

"That is not important. What I want is what is important." No other person raised an objection to this statement. Oh Oh! He tried once more,

"Are you saying we should ignore evidence as we proceed?" With a bit of "watch out!" in her eyes, she answered,

"I'm saying I am the dean, I am in charge, and we will do it my way." Right there, he spent half of his pay raise. And said no more. Having his own history of being in people's face about issues, he sensed she would spiral into genuine anger – no need to incite that in a retreat intended to develop working relations. However, later at a sit-down dinner at a huge round table, she did two things that sealed his opinion of her.

First, she started and continued to berate the server. They were the only party in the restaurant, and she the only server – drinks, making salads, delivering salads and entrees, were her responsibility. The dean started by saying to the woman, "I am paying for good service."

The waitress tried to explain the staffing shortfall.

"I don't care about your problems, I paid for good food and service, and I expect it."

The waitress realized her circumstance – she must have dealt with obnoxious people in the past because she did no more explaining. She slipped into a quiet mode of behavior and just said,

"Yes mam" or "No mam" or "Right away" or "As quick as I can" and kept doing her job. The new dean persisted in voicing fault with her service. The maintenance man witnessed firsthand the most disrespectful performances by a person in authority he had ever seen -- matched only by the cowardly behavior of a director of the testing service when he threw Elno under the bus to appease an obnoxious faculty member. After they finished desert, during a lull in conversation, the new dean reached for a serving dish filled mints and chocolates.

She picked up the dish, moved it close to her place, reached down for her purse, opened it in her lap, grasped the plate again, and dumped everything into the purse, as she said,

"I paid for this; I'm taking it."

He was not about to say the college, not she, paid for it. He was embarrassed, and anxious to get to his room, away from her, so he got up, and in the softest, calmest voice he could muster said,

"Another busy day tomorrow, so I'll say 'good night, everyone'" then left without waiting for feigned pleasantries. These were not his people. The coming year looked as if it would be more a black hole than gray purgatory. He sensed he needed all his strength and perseverance. Asi es la vida!

There were regular administrative council meetings. She did not take his council. Before classes began, she tried to impose heavier teaching loads on everyone except a few pets, like two hires from

Colorado who got special treats. He tried to explain how more classes dilute student-faculty ratios, a measure used to justify the number of faculty lines, and work against classes with small enrollments – for advanced students – an issue that arises often in programs with internships and other specialized courses. They argued.

When fall semester started, arguments about spring schedule started. She tried to command faculty to conduct research relevant to education. They argued -- what was educationally relevant – his meta-analysis work on subjective well-being was not. These arguments regularly ended when she said,

"I'm the dean. I'm in charge. We will do it my way." If he was feeling particularly flippant, to have the last word, he would answer with,

"Yes, you are..." letting it trail off as if something unexpected or undesirable was about to be said. Eventually, he adopted a cold formal manner of speaking with her: no more feigned greetings. If she captured him in the breeze way to say something, he listened. If he decided she was not looking for a reply he would say,

"I have a meeting (or a class) soon, so I have to go now."

In an administrative council meeting near the end of the fall semester, after an exasperating exchange with him, she looked directly at him and, with disdain in her voice, said, "Bill, you have to lighten up." Stunned, simmering, he just looked at her, eye to eye. All sorts of nasty retorts came to mind, but he suppressed them, looked right at her, still impelled to respond, then remembered something before he answered,

"I need to lighten up? Hmmm.... Of course, you are right." He took off his suit jacket. He took off his tie. He took off his dress shirt. He pulled his Grateful Dead t-shirt out of his pants, and pulled it over his belt and loops, and sat down, whereupon he deadpanned,

"There, I have lightened up." She uttered not another word about his demeanor. Right! But the conflict did not end. Searches for permanent directors in the three divisions were underway. As part of his administrative duties, he sent the same memo to each faculty member in his division. The memo stated the specifics of the position, all the required qualifications of candidates, and, at the bottom the memo, the sentence, "All division faculty are encouraged to apply." Only he applied. The same thing happened in the other two divisions. Acting division directors became appointed, permanent, directors. He lasted two weeks. Off in the office of the sleazy little fellow wheels turned: the university affirmative action officer, at the behest of the little fellow found: "the search was inappropriately conducted with respect to affirmative action." He, the acting director, had not reached out to potential minority and women candidates to specifically encourage them to apply. Back from sabbatical, Ray and he talked.

Ray said the dean wanted her own person. There was nothing to be done. She got what she wanted. It turned out Dr. GH, former director of university testing, agreed to serve. He was a good German of Prussian persuasion – he followed her orders to the letter.

In an act of defiance, the angry maintenance man conducted a survey of college faculty opinions about governance of his college (i.e., the dean). That he published the findings in the city paper incensed her. She complained to the acting provost, who replaced the little fellow after he became president of a school of alternate medical training. The acting provost, a tall, bland, man from engineering, called him in and asked,

"What do you want?"

"I want you to fire her."

"That will not happen."

"Why not?"

"It would not be good for the reputation of the university."

"Because she is a black woman, I suppose." Thinking 'affirmative action crap' as he waited for a response that never came. Instead,

"Is there something else we can do?"

"Yes, get me out of that college."

"I cannot do that unilaterally, but if you find a department that will take you, I will support a transfer."

He was no distinguished professor. His words lacked the weight of Ray. He was not deterred. He looked for a new home. He, Ray, and Morris tried to transfer to Psychology. The faculty in Psychology accepted Morris and spurned Ray and the maintenance man. Ray bunkered in, stopped trying to change departments, but explored offers in Australia and New Zealand. The maintenance man applied for jobs as department chair at two different universities in the Midwest, earned interviews, but was not chosen. Thereafter, he looked for a new department. He knew that

Graduate students from a department specializing in exercise science, sport psychology, and physical and wellness education routinely took his three-course sequence in statistics. He went to the chair of that department. The chair said he was interested. With that information he went to the dean of the liberal arts college. The dean was interested – that the maintenance man had helped him many years earlier with analyses helped the maintenance man now. There were just two hurdles left – GH, the Prussian, and his dean. True to his new respect for rules and proper procedure, GH rubber stamped his transfer request, and passed it on to his higher authority. It turns out she was livid, beside herself with ill-feeling toward him for conducting the survey of college faculty and publishing the findings in the newspaper. She hated the maintenance man. She would let him go in a heartbeat, except he was on a tenure-track, line-item in the state budget – which she could not bear to let go. There she was, stuck between hate for him and greed for the line.

Someone in higher administration, possibly MF, suggested he be allowed to transfer and his line be called a snap-back line – which meant if he left the university, the line would go back to its original college. It was malarky, but the dean bought it. He moved to a new department. He taught his courses. He and Ray developed a joint research program that meant he had to go to Ray's bunker regularly. On the way in and out, at times, he encountered her. Because any day spent interacting with her qualified as a "worst day of my life," he never said a thing to her. Not even "thanks" or "bye-bye." And so, the hate of a cruel dean for the maintenance man enabled him to transfer to the wilderness of a storage room converted to an office in the old men's gymnasium in a department of kinesiology in a college of liberal arts where he continued to teach the same courses with different labels.

Later, after she fled to be provost at an urban university in Chicago, the snap left the line. In time, the faculty at that university drove their new provost out. She finished her career as provost, living in a big house on a bluff overlooking a small university on the plains of Nebraska. Fitting.

She was handsome, articulate, and strong-willed. Her smile was radiant. On seeing her from afar, his first reaction matched his usual perspective. On their introduction during her interview, to him her eyes lacked signs of compassion. Perhaps the drive to succeed caused her to steel herself against such feelings. He did not know. He did know he felt no attraction towards her then, Later, at the first retreat, he felt his first impressions were too kind. She was a woman – the only one in his life for whom he could find no warm feeling.

His administrative career was over. He was 43 years old and had had enough. Being Herself, She smiled that smile and never once said "I told you so." He wished She had, because he would not have minded – Her smile made everything better. All in all, his years of administration, when done, reminded him that the actual worst day of his life was the first day of a backpacking trip across Oregon with Rick. That trip started in his parent's living room while She, Rick, and the maintenance man sat talking.

LET US GET BACK TO PACKING

H E CELEBRATED HIS 36TH BIRTHDAY om sabbatical in Chicago at an elite university in Chicago, where he interacted with professors there. These interactions helped him understand his place in the academic world. He met LH. Their joint work led to a published article. He sat in on a course by RDB. Both men were scholars of the first order. He made a truth-filled self-appraisal: although he felt intellectually equal, he judged himself less prepared and disciplined – inadequate early study the cause, and lack of motivation an additional culprit. With diligent study in graduate school and on the job, he transformed himself into a scholar – just not of the first order. In a sense, he was an excellent engineer in a room of physicists. Anything they thought up, he used well. He made peace with this appraisal.

Every week day, he commuted to school from the home of his parents. He and She shared his parents' home with his brother Tom and Tom's girlfriend D. His parents' home was available because after they retired, they square danced their way across America, living in a tiny trailer they pulled after them. To get to school, he took an early train to the city, walked to another station, took a second train to the south side, and then did the reverse on the way home.

When he was in the city, She worked in a ceramics factory where She poured slip. She did not want an office job. She did not want to sit at home. They had no children. She enjoyed pouring, disliked the winter roads, and felt good earning money. His brother Tom, assistant manager and cook at a Poppin Fresh restaurant, brought pie home every other day. At first, he brought all sorts. Tom, She, and D tired of eating pie, no matter the type. Not the maintenance man. He loved pie, cherry pie best, and, eventually, that is all Tom brought home. The maintenance man kept eating cherry pie until he had a middle-aged, midsection -- more than 30 pounds overweight.

His brothers Herb and Rick would come by the house to visit and gab. Herb not so much, he kept busy providing for an expanding, expensive, family. Recently divorced Rick, with no children, spent his free time on motorcycles. One evening the maintenance man and all his brothers decided to go to Watkins Glen to see a Formula-1 Grand Prix. They went.

From the main highway into Watkins Glen, the four brothers and Herb's brother-in-law drove into chaos. Four-wheelers roared up and down a dirt road, harrumphing through mud. Drunks in beds of these monster trucks tossed firecrackers at people everywhere. The brothers carved out a space to park, put up a tent, sniffed cocaine to little effect, then switched to beer. Nearby, four men from Canada parked their huge box truck filled with firewood, bunks, and cases of Molson. To the maintenance man, it was clear

The race was a clarion call to a tribe to gather for a vast bacchanal –warriors in charge. Outnumbered women were pummeled by the chant, "Show us your tits!" "Show us your tits!" everywhere they went The maintenance man did not understand why a woman would be there, or lift a t-shirt to display. Everything was coarse, alcohol-fueled, exciting, disconcerting. The night before the F-1 race, the Canadians kept a huge fire roaring. The fire attracted the brothers, other nearby campers – about 15 men– and one young, drunk, woman. One of the Canadians started flattering her, putting an arm around her shoulder, and working her. He wanted her to fuck him, and all the other men, too. He kept asking her to pull a train. She neither agreed nor disagreed nor, perhaps, understood a thing he said. As he kept on, she changed the subject. The Canadian managed to coax her to get in the truck and lay down on a bunk, but she got back up and returned to the fire. In his mind, the maintenance man felt excited, wondered about fucking her, and ashamed of thinking so. It was his struggle between love of women in general, and a base response to this individual woman who lacked self-awareness. She stumbled near the fire. He went over, helped her to her feet, and said quietly,

"Maybe it's time to go to bed." She nodded and started to walk away. She wobbled. He took her arm and asked,

"Which way?" No one said a thing, or moved to interfere, so he just walked her in the direction she pointed. Every time she paused, he asked,

"Here?"

"No…. there" as she pointed further away. At last, she nodded. He stayed until he saw her go into a dark tent, laid down, and mumbled something. He left. He felt he had done a fine thing. Facing his animal spirits, wanting to have sex with her, he did not. He kept his re-affirmed oath to Her. On his return to the fire, Herb said he was a good man, but with a tumult of contradictory feelings, he doubted that was true. He was not so sure any of them were, yet he felt his actions placed him on the right side of loving women.

The next day he bought a red t-shirt with a gold emblem containing a black horse. It was a Ferrari shirt. Ferrari won the day. What he loved most about the Glen was the smell of nitro burning as the cars blasted down the straightaway, but all in all, one Glen was enough for him and he looked forward to get back to Her and dog Free. But when he walked into his parent's home to see them, She said

"Free died."

All he did was suck in a big breath of air. His first, best dog suffered from Valley fever for some time. The sickness debilitated him, and as the disease progressed, the maintenance man carried Free from place to place, as needed. Free struggled to be his old self, but kept declining. When he left for the Glen with his brothers, the maintenance man thought Free would be okay until he got back. He was wrong. She put his body in a plastic bag in a freezer so he could bury Free and say goodbye. He took the bag and a shovel to a spot by the river and buried his friend, but he did not say good-bye until 4 months later in Mt Jefferson Park in Oregon.

He ended up in the Mt Jefferson wilderness in Oregon because his brother Rick told them he wanted to hike the Pacific Crest Trail. She asked,

"Why don't you do it then?"

Rick answered "I'm waiting to do it with my friend Craig."

"Is he willing, does he know you want to do this?"

"Yes."

"Well...?"

"Well. he is on a contract on an oil rig in the North Sea. He will not be back for a year."

They talked back forth, and it seemed what Rick needed most was a partner on the trail. So, the maintenance man asked,

"Would you go, if I offered to go with you?"

"I guess so. Have you ever hiked or backpacked anywhere?"

"Nope. How hard can it be? There must be books to help get ready."

"Okay."

"Okay, let's do it?" or "Okay, I think I will wait for Craig."

"Okay, let's do it." So, the hike across Oregon began in a lower middle-class, living room of a house on a river, the house in which their peripatetic parents raised four sons, and having done so took off to square dance everywhere in the U.S. She was not about to set foot on a trail, but She was all in with saving, budgeting, and spending to make it happen. She wanted Rick to fulfill his wish. They bought a book, **The Complete Walker**, by Colin Fletcher that he read, some parts over and over, to make lists.

He possessed no backpacking equipment. Armed with lists, they shopped. Lists were perfect for him – as he loved to spend money but disliked perusing, comparing, and assessing options, as well as going from store to store in search of the best deal. Fletcher passed judgment on equipment and made lists. In a good way, Fletcher was a snob –in the wilderness you want to have the best equipment and minimize failures. For the most part,

The two brothers adhered to the lists, save one item. When the maintenance man bought a big, brand new, top of the line, Keltie backpack, Rick decided to stick by his midsize, not top of the line pack that had served him well. The maintenance man did not object. To get the best boots, in their only true search, they drove all over the city to find pairs in their sizes. Some items were available in a single store – tent, stove, utensils, Swiss army knife. Some items they bought turned out to be unnecessary – wool pants, big buck knives, an extra flashlight. One item caused consternation – food. What food do you carry on a 30-day hike across the parts of Oregon absent stores and restaurants?

You can try salami, homemade pemmican, and beef jerky. They did. These were the first items the novices gave to hungry trail walkers. One couple they met were trying to do the trail on brown rice and lentils. They cried with joy when the novices gifted them a five-pound salami. Others were happy to get two zip-lock bags of pemmican and five bags of jerky.

The novices settled on freeze dried meals as their principal source of food. Mountain View sold a variety of freeze-dried dinners. Count the days on the trail, subtract three (for planned stops for regular meals at three points on the trail, like Timberline Lodge), multiply by two and they had the number of meals to buy from Mountain View. They spread their purchases over five or six choices (Mmm good, Chili Mac) and were all set – for dinner. For breakfast, lunch, and snacks,

They improvised. For breakfast they chose instant cream of wheat or oatmeal with powdered milk, raisins or bacon, and tang. For lunch, they settled on dried soup and added freeze-dried peas and corn. Peanut butter or cheese with crackers, and Milky Way candy bars completed lunch. For snacks it was Milky Ways and freeze-dried ice cream. Foods like raisins, sugar, and powdered milk they manually repackaged into baggies.

Once assembled, everything, except salami, pemmican, and beef jerky, was sorted, sealed, and packaged into large, zip-lock bags, each containing a day's rations. They sorted the big bags according to trail segments. How many for the first segment before the first mail drop, how many in that mail drop to last to the next, and so on. The mail drops were boxed and addressed. She supported the hike by taking the packages to the post office, buying postage, and mailing them off. All this dividing, boxing, and mailing depended on a variable about which they had no clue: how fast did they walk on the trail, more accurately how many miles a day did they cover. To provide leeway, She mailed each package a couple of days earlier than their best estimate. Since the food was sealed in airtight plastic, it was no problem if a package sat in a post office a few extra days. The salami, pemmican and beef jerky were supplies for the first segment, and never went in the mail. They bought, sorted, packed, planned, and boxed in the evenings after he got back from the city. When he and She drove back to Arizona, everything but Rick's gear went with them.

Just before noon on July 3, he boarded a flight – Arizona-Utah-Idaho-Oregon. His luggage was an 85-pound Keltie packed with meals and all his gear. He got a coke each time he changed flights or modes of transportation. God only knew he was going without for weeks. A 65-cent bus took him to Portland. A $3.40 bus took him to Cascade Locks at the foot of the Pacific Crest Trail. Rick was waiting. They talked a bit, walked about a mile, and set up camp in a clear spot under some power lines near the start of the old access trail to Pacific Crest Trail. There were little gnat bugs everywhere so they zipped themselves into the tent and went to sleep. Judging by the difficulty of that one-mile walk,

He worried about the old trail they were taking up to the trail proper. His worry did not dispel his fatigue. He went right to sleep. After breakfast, they started out, went a mile in the wrong direction and backtracked, then started out again in the right direction. Switchback after switchback, all day long. comprised the access trail. Just before switching back, they could look down and see the Columbia River, recede a little more, then look up, and see another switchback. There was no end to the trees and no top of the trail. He grew tired, uncertain, and stumbled more, stopped to rest on each switchback, and had a vision of death by heart attack. On those switchbacks, resentment at Rick's choice to use his mid- sized pack – it carried significantly less gear – entered his mind and grew. The weight of his own pack dragged love of brother down a ravine of resentment. That they went through the water at a rapid rate made matters worse. He kept thinking he would die, and as the day wore on, he added thirst as another probable cause of death. He could not think of a worse day in his life. He asked himself, "Is this the last day of my life?" then added, "And you thought you would die laughing." Saying that to himself made him chuckle, and for a moment, feel better. But,

They had to keep climbing. About 7:00 that night they reached the top and knew this because the trail no longer went up. It went up and down. They drank the last of their water. The map showed Tea Kettle Spring was close. They only had to find it. They asked the map where they were, and where Tea Kettle Spring was, but the map remained silent. Near the beginning of the Pacific Crest Trail in Oregon was what his fatigue-befuddled brain supplied. They walked each way for a bit, sat down to rest, became thirstier, and decided to head south. They walked, stopped, questioned their choice to go south, decided to walk another 15 minutes, and did. Right at the 15-minute mark they saw a sign for the spring. Not one to mention God often, all he thought was "God bless us, we're not going die."

They filled their bottles, waited – the long wait – for the iodine to kill the cryptosporidium, giardia, and other malicious creatures that inhabit spring waters on the Trail. They drank their fill, then re-filled the bottles. He was not going to die of thirst…today. Tomorrow? Who knew? When tomorrow came, they waited in their bags until the sun lit and warmed the tent, got up, dressed, and had their first breakfast on the trail. What? Cream of wheat with dried fruit, tea, and tang. After breakfast, they filled water bottles, packed dishes, stove, sleeping bags, and tent. A trowel went in a side pocket of the Keltie, with a rolled-up ground cloth, and a sealed bag of garbage. By ten o'clock, they rolled out. Up and down, up and down, up and down. Hard on the ankles, hard on the knees, hard on the shoulders, they kept at it until one in the afternoon. Lunch. They had soup and big slices of the greasy salami. Tasty but not enjoyable – they resolved to offload it at the first opportunity. Back to up and down. At 6:30, they stopped, having made eight miles in 8 ½ hours. All the joints on both their bodies functioned, but complained, and exposed skin was covered in bug bites. They unpacked and set up camp, had dinner, cleaned up, relaxed for a while, and went to bed about ten, for a sleep not bothered by sounds of the forest. If they entertained the notion that things could not get worse,

They were wrong. Very wrong! The next morning was overcast and damp. No sun warmed the tent, instead left it dark. They slept until ten. After breakfast, clean-up, and packing, it was noon before they started. The day remained damp and overcast. Two rangers, checking the trail, heading in the opposite direction, told them to prepare for rain. They took out their rain gear, covered their packs and themselves, and kept walking. A mile later, it started to rain. The rain increased as the temperature dropped. They walked, slipped, and slid along the trail, looked for a place to stop, set up camp, and get out of the rain. They found nothing suitable. By 5:30, they decided to stop, and pitched the tent right on the trail. It was bad trail etiquette but they thought, correctly, no one would come along the rest of the day or that night. Everything was inside the tent, most of it wet, despite the rain gear. Cooking dinner was out of the question. They took off their wet clothes, ate some snacks, got into their dry ("God bless us, we will not die from hypothermia") sleeping bags, arranged the gear so they could stretch out to sleep. They did sleep well, and the following morning they stayed in their bags until the rain stopped just before noon. They ate more snacks, put on a set of dry clothes, and set out for Lost Lake at three in the afternoon. The trail passed above and to the left of Lost Lake. With a store and campground lakeside, they decided to stop, and, when the next day turned clear and sunny, dry all their gear. At their pace they were a day away from the junction with the Timberline Trail. The junction was about 13 miles from the Lodge. Two good days of hiking would bring them to civilization, not to mention their first mail drop. It took three. Late starts did not stop. Stops for foot care increased. Stops to eat became moments of leisure. If they counted the day of arrival in Cascade Locks it took seven days to reach the Lodge, about 46 miles. On the leg into the Lodge, two Canadians who had walked the whole Trail from Canada flew buy. A few words passed back and forth,

"How long have you been hiking?'

"Since May."

"It's kind of cold, are you warm enough in a t-shirt and shorts?

"No problem, the ice fields in Washington were a problem, but this chilly air is nothing."

The novices, in their long pants and wool shirts, just looked at each other and smiled, then threw a last word at the backs of the two men proceeding into the novices' future.

"See you."

"Not likely." They threw back. True. In a few minutes they went over a ridge line and not were seen again.

When the novices got to the top of the ridge line, there were some boulders where they sat, rested, and snacked. They took out some cheese and crackers and were joined by audacious black and white birds – about the size of a robin – who dared to sit on a shoulder, or a hand, held palm up with a little cheese and cracker. The maintenance man wore a red wool cap that attracted hummingbirds who neither tarried nor lit down, as there was nothing in it for them.

Accommodations were rough at the lodge so they got a ride into Government Camp, found a motel, and felt they were in heaven, with showers, laundromat, post office, and a fine French meal at the Swiss Chalet restaurant. At the post office, they collected the mail drop, and off-loaded weight. They put an extra stove, heavy knives (keeping only the Swiss), books, extra pants, belt, moccasins, and foot powder in a box they returned to Her. They spent the second night in Timberline Lodge waiting for morning to come to renew the hike – clean clothes, new food, less weight, feet in good shape thanks to the protection of moleskin. That is when they met John H. who did the 46 miles from Cascade Locks to Timberline in 2 days. He carried virtually nothing, a sleeping bag, water, and snacks. About 5' 6" tall, weighing maybe 130 pounds, like the Canadians, he traveled light and fast. He said he was waiting a day or two at the lodge to be resupplied by his dad who was at every spot where the trail crossed or neared a road or campground. This kept weight down, and permitted John to move fast. It was a wonderful system for speed hiking. By contrast, the novices chugged along at a leisurely pace each day, because, on the trail,

They got up when the tent was warm, ate a good breakfast, packed up, and took off between ten and noon. Two or three hours after the start, they unpacked for lunch, ate, packed up again, and hiked three or four hours, then stopped with plenty of daylight left to unpack, set up camp, make dinner, clean up, talk, then sleep. The routinely did nine or ten miles a day. Each new morning, they did it all over again. The maintenance man found he had to cinch up his pants because his waistline shrank noticeably – a carabiner through a couple belt loops fixed that. Two days out from the Lodge, after doing 12 miles the second day they were heading into Little Crater Lake in mid-afternoon. John H passed them going in. Twenty minutes later, just as they reached the spot, John H passed them going out, and said,

"It's too early to stop. I am going on to ...." Someplace, but he was already past, moving fast, and never seen again. The novices were happy to stop a little early, enjoy the clear blue water of Little Crater Lake – which must be a spring feed sinkhole or limestone subsidence because it is so small and the water so clear. Unpack, set up, dinner, bed. What a life. His body was satisfactorily tired. He usually wanted to eat, clean up, and go to bed. He did not think of Her. He did not think about women in general. He did not think about sex. He thought about water, walking, and waiting for the sun to warm the tent, and some nights what food to have the next day, a choice dependent on what Mountain View dinners remained. For all their fear of bears stealing food, despite discussion and thoughts about bears,

They never saw one. Once they surprised three elk watering in a pond near the trail. The elk took off and made loud crashing sounds as the disappeared through the undergrowth. They crossed paths with three men, two women, a few dogs, and four or five mules heading to Canada. The men had sidearms. The site of pistols caused some anxiety, so after pleasantries, the brothers moved on south, took a side trail off the Crest Trail to a point where they thought they would not encounter that party again. The following morning, still alive, while Rick slept, the maintenance man got up early and quietly left the tent.

He sat down to start the stove. On looking up, he saw a doe less than 20 feet away, that looked at him without fear. She sauntered off after a few minutes. After the morning rituals, the brothers moved on south.

The days of July ticked away. Unpack, eat, clean, sleep, pack again. Do it again. Occasionally, they met a hiker. Conversations were brief. All had destinations. Stopping to talk was not in their plan. As they talked with others, the novices felt their plan was distinct. They had all summer to walk but no specific destination – except Rick wanted to cross Oregon and make it into California. They never got up early – they preferred to wait for the sun to warm the tent – despite fellow hikers who extolled early starts that enabled them to complete a lot of miles before it got hot. Their concerns were limited to finding water – they never missed a chance to fill and treat their water bottles – to unpacking and packing every day, and to foot care. The wild life that drove them mad was

The mosquitoes that became more numerous and aggressive the further south they walked. Their worst encounter was at Top Lake, a ¼ mile off the Crest Trail, two hundred feet in elevation below the crest. Once visible, the lake looked like a wonderful spot for a swim, to fill bottles, and rest. With each step down to the lake, the humming of mosquitoes increased. They rubbed on Cutter's without effect. The humming was incessant. They talked about getting into the lake to get away from the blood suckers. Not more than a few steps later they were in full flight back to the crest, and then down the trail several hundred feet. A few predators pursued, but the Cutter's finally repelled them. On the dry, east side of the Cascades, mosquitoes swarmed at each water spot (lakes, ponds, slow sections of streams), that is, at each spot they had to stop for drinking water. For some reason, the bugs were mostly absent from the springs in Mt. Jefferson Park which gushed crystal clear water out of the earth. They thought the water was safe and drank deeply – delicious! Wrong. Diarrhea, explosive diarrhea, appeared two days later and stuck around until the end of the hike. At home, he took the cure for giardia, and later still he learned all water on the Trail must be treated.

The most remarkable thing about Mt Jefferson Park was that the maintenance man thought Free would have loved ranging all over the valley, and when he thought of Free all the tears he had sucked back into his body when She told him Free died came gushing out like the springs, clear but salty. He kept thinking about his friend Free all the way across the valley and as he was climbing out, he thought to say,

"Free I love and miss you. I will always remember you, but I want your spirit to stay here where you can be free all the time. Goodbye my good friend." With those words he let Free go, and headed up to the ridge line across to the hot, dry east side of the Cascades. They pushed their pace because the food packs were almost gone and the next mail drop was down the trail a good way. They made the drop before the packs ran out, but the pace strained their feet. He made a list of foot ailments: he had, numb big toes, blisters on his Achilles tendons, sore ankles, sore balls of his feet, and sore tendons.

Above the ankles everything was working well and feeling okay, but foot problems never left, and, with diarrhea a daily event, the maintenance man thought about home more and more. And

That two idiots who brought two stoves, four knives, and a useless salami should have brought two trowels.

A trowel interlude: hurry up!

A fact of their trek: eating the same food at the same time, and sharing genetic backgrounds, their body functions synchronized, not all to good effect, for example, in pooping. After eight or nine days on the trail, when one had to stop to poop, the other did too. Trail etiquette (go well off the trail, dig a hole, six or eight inches deep, poop, use a little toilet paper, make sure everything gets in the hole, cover it, and press the earth down), created a friendly duel to get the trowel first. The first would go off the trail in one direction, while

The other headed to the opposite side but stayed close to the trail. The first would dig his hole and shout,

"Ready?"

"Yes." The trowel would fly down to the trail. The second would scramble for it, go off the trail quickly, dig furiously, drop shorts and underwear, then move them out of the way of

The foul smelling, semi-solid, diarrhea that exploded from their butts. Thank God the need to poop occurred only about once a day – giardia considerate in that regard. Still, it was tiresome. Most of the time, they were on the dry side of the Cascades, thinking about and looking for the next water spot, happy to get to one, unhappy a horde of mosquitos waited to greet them. They met people heading north, but everyone was uncomfortable, so conversations were short: where are you going to (coming from); what about water; what hurts?

The maintenance man fixated on Crater Lake Park: could he stop there? Would his brother react well? They talked. Not much. Rick seemed okay with the idea. They agreed to wait until they arrived at the lake to make a final decision. Fate intervened as

The novices traversed a long hot, dry, desert-like pine forest on the approach to Crater Lake. On the long, slow, uphill slog, Rick's pack fell apart. He had to carry on with the remaining functional strap over his shoulder, both hands and arms keeping the rest of the pack together. They were offered and took a ride up to the top of the park. What a spectacular lake! So blue! So far down! They set up camp and discussed options. Rick's pack was useless. The maintenance man decided to go home. Rick decided to go on. They traded packs. The best gear went in the Keltie. Everything else went in Rick's pack to go to Arizona with the maintenance man. The next day, Rick went on. He got as far as Ashland, Oregon before the heat stopped him. From there, he hitchhiked to a friend's home in California.

The maintenance man caught a ride into Medford, a flight to San Francisco, and another to Phoenix. He was home that night. He was alive, still 36, and unpacked one last time. The first thing She said

"You are way too skinny." He was at his high school weight, all his pants were too loose, and he had about two weeks to get ready for fall classes. Happy at home, he binged on cokes, cheeseburgers, and fresh foods he had not eaten for a month. The Keltie and his gear eventually returned to Arizona. He lovingly packed all the gear into the Keltie and stored it away. It remains there to this day. Another leftover of the hike was his definition of backpacking: every day you have get back to packing.

HE CHOOSES RESEARCH AND
FINDS A FRIEND TO THE END

WHEN HE BECAME AN ADMINISTRATOR, he and Morris ended their collaboration: both wished to do research on topics other than subjective well-being. The maintenance man needed something closer to his graduate school training. Kevin was in preschool. She with a smile that made him smile increased Her handmade crafts –crochet, jewelry, and stained glass – and offered Her work at small craft shows. She tired of these shows when what she sold failed to justify the work of setting up and tearing down displays. She opened a store to sell her work and consign the work of others. The landlord played on Her desire and enticed Her to sign a lease with poor terms. At the end of the lease period, facing poor terms and sales, She closed the store, and began a home-based, appointment only, business in which She offered typing, word-processing, data entry, editing, and transcription services to small businesses and individuals. The business suited Her. After She met with a client and completed Her tasks, she was alone – in a solitary life She favored (Rot in hell Hop). Alone, she labored to convert depression into positive energy to face today and prepare for tomorrow. She declined drugs for depression. She chose to work through Her episodes alone. Yet, from him, She accepted hugs, being held, and encouraging words, but rejected analysis, directions, instructions, and problem-solving –too intrusive, too constraining. As best he could,

He respected that She addressed Her issue Her way. Thus, he accepted his share, and more, of efforts to raise Kevin. When Kevin was in preschool on campus, they ate lunch together, traveled to and from school together, and spent time at home together. The games that kid imagined, and the rules by which they played drove the maintenance man crazy. At a young age, his son lived in an irrational world, and the experience of raising him caused the maintenance man to respect all women who raised one or more children without going crazy or killing them.

Having earned tenure prior to arrival of his son, nearly all pressure at university was of his own making. Time spent in class engaged him – he had matured into an effective instructor. With a nonstop, classroom pacing style, he came out of class physically tired and mentally refreshed. However, out of class he needed tasks that engaged his mind. Even though he lacked a strategic career goal, he rejected the idea of spending the rest of his academic career sitting around like a pool of stagnant water. Like a day at dawn, a single notion illuminated his thoughts: he needed to collaborate: With whom? He knew, but

Ray had not spoken to him – aside from shared administrative tasks and during an attempt to transfer to psychology -- about research since the day, many years earlier, when Ray visited his office and asked what he thought of research, to which he had replied, "Not much." A poor answer, he now thought, when thereafter Ray did not speak to him. Ray seldom reversed judgments of persons holding contrary opinions on matters important to him. He put the likelihood of Ray's willingness to collaborate at one in four, or less. However, because Ray was the only professor in the college doing research that interested the maintenance man,

He went to Ray's office. In a cautious, somewhat formal manner, they reminisced about fights with the old dean, and commiserated with each other about the greedy, petty woman who was current dean. Ray waxed on about his sabbatical: in Italy, he sat in weak, flickering, lamp light late at night at a kitchen table in a cold house north of Rome trying to write letters home; he flew to Cairo to ride camels near the pyramids; and he explored the east coast of Australia. Everywhere he went, he made personal contacts that led to research opportunities for him, and, better, for his students. Ray lived the ethos of a research university: study, work, publish, take advantage of every opportunity, help graduate students advance. Yes, publish – everyone must publish,

publish everything! Beyond this, Ray possessed qualities seldom, if ever, seen in ordinary, self-righteous, passive-aggressive, pusillanimous professors. He was: a world class fabulist, devious, and charismatic with ambiguous morals – qualities that attracted, rather than put off, the maintenance man, who judged himself of questionable moral character from time to time, so he said,

"Ray, I'd like to work on research with you." Ray leaned back in his chair, lit a cigar, and looked at the maintenance man without speaking. As he did, evident to the maintenance man, a scale in his mind weighed negatives (he said he did not think much about research) against positives (he fought a dean with facts and reason, took over as chair becoming an ally in efforts to protect the department, and liked to smoke). In the end, Ray said,

"Let's give it a try" as he leaned forward and offered a Swisher Sweet. Thus, began, first a collaboration, then a friendship that lasted 17 years – until cancer ate the life out of Ray's body. Long before their collaboration, Ray had had a brilliant career. He had impressive, well-earned accolades earned by devotion to research, by unflagging efforts, by ignoring norms of behavior, and by a drive he felt for having lost time to less noble pursuits. Of these, he said not much. Rat revealed mere glimpses of his adolescence to the maintenance man: he drank heavily from youth on; he spent time in a youth correctional facility; and he married young because it was, then, the right thing to do. He talked of his grandfather with great respect (a Kentuckian who willed himself to die rather linger in a slow one) and from whom he learned, "Love many, trust few, always paddle your own canoe." He did. Experiences in his youth caused him to respect the military – particularly the navy. He never served, but his fabulist mind created L-SHIP, a vessel constructed to train graduate students to do research. L-SHIP was born, lived, and died in the period the maintenance man and Ray did not converse. Ray encouraged graduate students on L-SHIP not to interact with him. Some did anyway, e.g., Rick.

L-SHIP had Admiral Ray, line officers of various rank (graduate students), ordinary seamen (undergraduates who performed low-level tasks for extra credit), and adjunct officers (faculty collaborators). Line officers earned promotion by being responsible for and completing research tasks (creating materials, designing studies, supervising junior officers) –the more important the tasks the higher the rank. This navy produced notable levels of paper presentations and published research in its short existence. All who earned ranks earned Master's or Ph.D. degrees. Those who were unfit for duty were cashiered. That participants in L-SHIP accepted its fable is a measure of Ray's charisma. That they performed morally vague actions to keep the ship afloat indicated not only charisma but also an ability to convince others to do so. Ray called it "head rightening." Faculty were not immune, for example,

Adjunct officers Keith and Howard, both department chairs, looked away when L-SHIP crew used department copy machines after hours, appropriated reams of copy paper, disappeared boxes of large manilla envelops, and regularly entered locked spaces – all to keep L-SHIP afloat, steaming ahead. Ray's prowess as a fabulist started in his youth when he invented stories about why he was at the beach rather than school, why he was dizzy not drunk, and why he walked on a mountain road, not far from an unseen wrecked car he had driven off the road – all stories created to keep himself out of the hands of authority. His most lasting fable -- the National Organization of Instruction, Science and Education – he conjured from nothing, peddled to four graduate students (M, D, T, and O), and led all to perpetrate the fable through time, and across generations of students,

The National Organization of Instruction, Science and Education (NOISE)

With research a rationale, Ray created NOISE to enable the five founding members to afford to attend the established annual national research convention. NOISE met on the same dates and in same location as the annual meeting of the national organization. Absent an accepted paper at the national meeting, you "presented" at NOISE. "Presenting" helped secure travel money at research universities. Thus, the five were more likely to obtain travel funds which they pooled to rent a suite in which to stay. Ray wrote bylaws that vested decision-making in these five "founders." Members -everyone else- lacked authority. They approved founders' decisions by voice acclamation at NOISE business meetings. When founders became professors with reliable access to travel funds, they got their own rooms, and the suite became; a dormitory for graduate students, a place to sit, a bar serving drinks at near cost, and a spot for late night conversation. Like some fables, NOISE took on a life of its own. As the founders aged and basked in career accomplishments and praise, the origin of NOISE faded. Steps were taken to make NOISE respectable: real paper sessions were held in the suite; Mandatory dues (founders most, students least) funded the suite and bought alcohol; Bylaws were rewritten and brought democracy to members; A banquet was held each year; and, finally, someone completed legal work to make NOISE a non-profit organization. Before all this, Ray invited the maintenance man to NOISE the year after they began to work together. After Ray died, SCIENCE (sexually confused idiots emitting nonsense and crap endlessly) transformed NOISE from its original intent to mirror the perspective of modern universities. With the transformation complete,

NOISE kicked the maintenance man out, based on anonymous complaints by SCIENCE about things he may have said. With Ray dead, the maintenance man left, his parting comments only pointing out the lack of due process, yet he treasured memories of early times spent at NOISE.

He remembered arguing about signs with Gary, a clever fellow in a pudgy body. Gary worked with Don on signs, and with the goats on Don's farm. Gary was pushed from his university, even though he had tenure, by SCIENCE, or people worse, because he said the word "nigger" to demonstrate words have emotional power. Did he know what happened to him was a harbinger of a poorer future across the academic world? He was intelligent, so the maintenance man thought yes.

The maintenance man remembered being talked into a fishing trip on the open ocean, out past San Francisco Bay. He agreed to go, paid his share, and went to the hotel doctor for a prescription for a drug to combat seasickness. He offered some to Ray – who, a man proud of his heritage of living by the ocean, declined. The maintenance man said nothing, took his pill before the boat headed out. The Bay was calm. The fishing boat rocked him gently back and forth. "Not too bad" he thought. After the boat passed under the Golden Gate Bridge into open water, a twisting motion entwined itself in the gentle up and down, and, not long after, many "fisherpersons" were at the railing, chumming the water with their breakfast. And Ray? He turned green, went below, and sat down. He willed himself not to go to the rail. The maintenance man suppressed laughter that wanted to saturate the boat and surrounding sea. The former admiral had a difficult trip. What a day! What was the haul? One salmon.

He remembered meeting five women who possessed joy. He was interested. Their joy had nothing to do with academic accomplishment. He honored the limitation of his oath, felt proud he kept it, but tested the boundary that separated what his oath required and other behaviors. Talking with these five in different years was the essence of being human for him, and lacked the jousting that occurred with male colleagues. The men seemed like roosters – crowing, while the women seemed like canines, listening intently to understand, and, like humans, searching for what say next, given what they had heard. Had he other lives, he could have loved each of them.

He remembered traipsing all over different cities with various walking companions, looking for memorable places to eat. He remembered NOLA for the single best meal he ever had, four courses with matched wines. Thank you, Emeril. He remembered a café in Montreal where a counter woman smiled when he said, "Je suis désolé, mais je ne parle pas français." As she smiled, in English she said, "But you are" with a heavy French accent. A woman's warm smile always provoked his own. But because he and Ray played a game of who could out do the other in a fabulist's world, he remembered most clearly the year the suite held a costume party, and

Ray coaxed an admiral's uniform from a graduate student on leave from the U.S. Navy to get his Ph.D., but did not inform the maintenance man of the costume party until they arrived in New Orleans. He told the maintenance man about the party as he grinned a warm, avuncular smile tinged with a twist of "I got you" in his eyes, tacked on the end of his smile. That look sent the maintenance man on a hunt for materials to create something to match or exceed the admiral's uniform. He had no luck in costume stores. Costumes, or costume materials cost too much. Besides, paying defeated the game. The day of the party, coming into the hotel, the maintenance man noticed that the bellhops, doormen, and luggage carriers wore uniforms reminiscent of British India uniforms –red cloth, epaulets, brass bits everywhere. The doormen even had white helmets. His joy exploded at the possibility to outdo the Admiral. He even anticipated victory! To the hotel manager, he described his need and Ray's presumptive claim to costume supremacy. He promised to return the uniform in good condition. The manager smiled, called the doorman on duty, and instructed him to outfit the crazy man. He did. At the party, the British India army officer saluted the admiral, with a twist of "I got you too" in his eyes and tacked on the end of his smile. Such things complemented their friendship formed in joint research. These, and tobacco which

Ray never quit. He had persuaded the maintenance man to start smoking again during hours he tried to convince him to be chair. They smoked the rest of Ray's life. Cigars replaced cigarettes -- Swisher Sweets, Ray's first choice, and later, premium cigars for the maintenance man. As Ray was dying, his doctors and family tried to stop him from smoking, but he, still of sound mind and proud, asked the maintenance man to keep him supplied. He did. Perhaps being a smoker from his youth caused the cancers that killed him. Perhaps not. One thing is certain, by the time he asked to keep the cigars coming, smoking was a comfort, not a killer. Ray's death reminded the maintenance man of the death of Ray's grandfather as he had related it. His grandfather refused extraordinary efforts, lay down on his bed, declined food and drink, and died. This was how the maintenance man saw it, as he walked home, crying, from Ray's house hours before Ray died. Such memories gave form to their friendship.

Work is friendship

Across 17 years, the substance of their friendship developed during the hours they talked and argued in Ray's office. Although they talked a bit about university politics, most of their conversations were about research. The maintenance man comfortably discussed and argued with Ray as he came to understand the theories underlying the two focal topics of their research. For the first half of the 17 years, they concentrated on feedback in verbal learning, with an emphasis on a learner's confidence in recognition or recall of learned materials. The second half focused on dual coding theory, i.e., learning from images and text covering a topic to be learned. Their work had its own rhythm. First,

They would light up, then chat a bit. Depending on the state of studies in motion, graduate students came to the office and gave updates. With issues of analysis, the maintenance man took the lead. With issues about theory, Ray did – and the maintenance man chimed in from time to time. After attending to current work, they spent the rest of the time talking about the implications of their studies, as well as implications of research by others. If a conversation led to an idea for a study, a graduate student was summoned and assigned tasks to initiate a study. For this to work,

A cohort of hard-working graduate students was essential. These few, brave, persistent souls created materials for each study, produced the materials, collated packets of materials for subjects, organized and oversaw collection of data, and completed analyses of the data. Across the first ten years of their collaboration, there were four distinct cohorts of students. Efforts of these cohorts produced more than 20 peer-reviewed articles, and twice as many research presentations at national meetings.

The first and last cohorts were unnamed by the fabulists, but the second and third were called Zulu Dawn Noon Dusk (DND Zulu for short) and Cool Hand Luke, respectively. DND Zulu is a published author on an article in the ***Bulletin of the Psychonomic Society.*** As always, the name was an oblique reference to something real. DND

Zulu was active in a period of strife caused by a bad dean. Cool Hand Luke reflected the command structure the professors used. Ray was Boss Ray, the maintenance man Boss Willy, and, two male graduate students (K and M) were nameless inmates expected to work day and night. Two women (J and J) formed the last cohort, both older than average graduate students, both mothers of special needs children, both unbending under relentless pressures of caring for family, conducting research, and preparing for the master reading list seminar. One Cool Hand Luke inmate, a roly-poly little fellow, by dint of his hard work, and both women of the last cohort by dint of the load they carried with energy and perseverance, were favorites of the Bosses. One J evoked those other feelings in the maintenance man. Each student who finished the master reading list seminar completed a Ph.D. Some students started the master reading list seminar but did not finish. They changed programs and worked with other professors. The master reading list seminar was difficult for everyone, including the Bosses, because

The seminar, a fabulist concoction of Ray and the maintenance man, covered a list of research articles, essays, book chapters and books –5000 pages – about learning, cognition, spatial and verbal memory, language, and instruction. The seminar, "voluntary" for both students and faculty, met three hours every Thursday night for 20 weeks. Each week, students were expected to "master" about 250 pages. "Master" meant read, understand, and respond to any question asked about the readings for the week. Notes were forbidden. A tough slog for all, but they became the navy seals and army rangers of academia. The Bosses were proud of those who completed the seminar.

The teapot incident

One night, the maintenance man aggressively questioned the J who provoked feelings in him. Her face turned red and there was a bit of glare as she returned his gaze. He should have been more sensitive. He saw he had pushed her to simmering – not his intent – trying to stimulate an assertive, articulate, give no ground answer. He did not relent and pushed a bit more. Her head started moving back and forth, and up and down, like a knob on an old-fashioned teapot. He was about to push just a little bit more when Ray said,

"I think it is time for a break. We will start up again in 10 minutes." And

He and the maintenance man went to the office and smoked a cigar, where Ray said

"Boss Willy, ease up, will you?" It was an earnest request, so he nodded, and when the seminar resumed, he asked

"J, would you give us your best response to the question I asked before the break?" She did.

The women relaxed a bit. The bosses relaxed a bit. From then on, the maintenance man asked questions a bit more gently, and remaining seminar nights passed more collegially -- but the expectation to master the information never left. Boss Ray was First Boss.

Good and bad cops

Boss Ray liked students to view him as a good cop or uncle. He cast the maintenance man as a bad cop, and happily described him so. Boss Ray would say, sure, he had to maintain discipline but Boss Willy was responsible for all the difficulties the program heaped on students. Did not Ray have an easy-going style in and out of class? Did not the maintenance man run his classes as constant stream of questions asked of every student, randomly distributed across students? If a student did not know the answer, did he not keep asking the student more and more basic questions until the student gave a correct response? Yes, it was all true, and when a student brought an issue to Ray and asked for relief, he said,

"I would love to give you an option, but Boss Willy just won't allow it. You know how he is. You can go ask him if you like." Nearly always, the student would leave, nodding agreement, but not to find his/her way to the office of the maintenance man. Once.

Mick, the roly-poly little fellow, came with a question on how to complete a statistical analysis. The maintenance man knew a careful reading of program documentation would lead to the answer, so he said,

"Mick, I could give you the answer, but to do that, I would have to read the manual. So, instead, you should go back to your office and read the manual until you find the answer. Do not be afraid to try a few different things. If one thing does not work, try another. You cannot break the computer by making mistakes." On hearing that, Mick, head rocking like the knob of a teapot, left, read the manual, and eventually solved the problem. But all these shenanigans did not completely hide the fact that

The maintenance man had a hard shell covering a soft heart. He gave chance after chance to those who performed poorly, or failed to execute as expected. Ray gave chances to a point, until he decided a student was irretrievably deficient. While Ray gave the maintenance man a second chance (after 11 years of silence), students were not as fortunate. Being Uncle Ray, without exception, he gently counseled the deficient few out, forever.

What a choice! Who was the bad cop? Even now, the maintenance man cannot decide.

After the cohorts

After J and J received Ph.Ds., there were no more cohorts, no more research requiring graduate students. The maintenance man was 52 years old when the Bosses chose to create two scales, the first measuring attention deficit hyperactivity disorder (ADHD), the second measuring attitudes and behavior toward money. To shield this work from rapacious, intellectual property policies of the university, they worked at home and created Lumir Research Institute, a legal S-corporation. They identified Lumir as owner of the scales. Neither scale generated sales. Lumir continued to exist, and through it, the Bosses pursued personal financial gain. Mick, the roly-poly little fellow, gained an interest in Lumir, in exchange for venture capital provided by himself, his parents, and his aunt Lou.

ALL THE TIME HE AND RAY
CONDUCTED RESEARCH

Boss Willie came to campus early. On Wednesdays, he ate lunch with JH. Over time, others joined them, so that often five or six persons ate, and argued issues of the day. One exuberant fellow, Jack, not an academic, inhaled internet news and consumed conspiracy theories. As a complete conservative, he animated discussions. Boss Willie, vaguely libertarian, often sided with Jack as he confronted the rest – all longtime liberals. When Jack died, dynamics of the group changed. Argument diminished, and many in the group were content to simply discuss their medical and personal issues.

Jack had been the spark that ignited firefights of lively discussion. Death extinguished his spark. For Boss Willie, two significant outcomes had their origins in the lunch group.

First, at a lunch, JH said that he wanted to retire early, but probably would not because of objections by his wife. Early retirement interested the maintenance man, who earnestly investigated early retirement and found that an agreement might include: permission to keep statistical analysis software bought for him by the university; eligibility for his son to attend university at faculty rates; a retirement income based on his average salary over his best three of his last five years (the university assured him of a 12-month, rather than 9-month, salary for his final three years – artificially creating his three highest years); and, importantly, credit for each year of service raised from 2% to 2.2%. At 2.2%, his retirement income was only a little lower than his current academic year salary. That a life-plus- survivor option (She received the same income were he to die first) was all he needed to convince Her. When he described these facts to Her, She sighed with relief and consented. Lifetime guaranteed income eliminated Her financial concerns, She felt free to act on Her belief he would be happier out of the university. He was uncertain he would be happier, but he wanted to try. He was 51 years old when he signed the three-year agreement. Ironically, the bad dean left before him, and after his retirement, the budget line never snapped back to his original college, rather it returned to the hands of university administration –assigned where they thought best. Such is the nature of agreements in universities.

Second, after Jack died, with the lunch bunch focused on personal health and other uninspiring topics, the maintenance man tried to convince the group to do something different, something bizarre or absurd, something to bring joy to people, absent political or social consequences. The bunch scoffed. As a chorus, they asked,

"Like what?" He had nothing specific in mind, so he had to pause for a moment to conjure up an absurd behavior a group of old men was capable of undertaking, When he did, he said,

"Like riding bicycles across the country and inviting people to find us and toss water balloons at us." His friends regarded him as if he suffered dementia ("Oh dear! Another one round the bend."). So, he continued,

"No, no, seriously… think about it. Say we start in Seattle. We can probably get to Idaho without much notice. By the time we reach Minnesota, we might get local interest. It might drift to the Internet, go viral, and by the time we get to Chicago the ride might be a noticeable event. If so, just imagine what Cleveland, Philadelphia and New York City would be like. So many people lined up to lob a water balloon." His friends continued to consider him crazy – none agreed to do it – while in his mind's eye he foresaw a joyous, fun-filled time. They ended the discussion with a question, dismissively delivered,

"How would people find us?"

"We'd have a blog to report progress, and give clues to our whereabouts." From then on, every one of his comfortable liberal friends declined to discuss or entertain the notion, but

Three years later, on a tour he called the Tour of Water Balloons, the maintenance man bicycled alone from Canada to New Orleans, with his 92-year-old father driving a van stuffed with bike parts and supplies, only to find that NFL football spoiled his arrival in Jackson Square – because the Square was barricaded for a Super Bowl Experience, a commercial celebration accompanying the spectacle of men bashing each other, prancing around like gladiators, and being loud and obnoxious.

When last checked, one or two videos of the Tour remained on YouTube. He never went back to tell the lunch bunch what they missed, nor smile with a twist of "I got you," He was 65 years old and more mature when he finished the Tour.

How did the Tour go? Like this.

PREPARING FOR THE TOUR
OF WATER BALLOONS

EIGHTEEN MONTHS BEFORE HE STARTED the Tour, he began to train. For 2-3 months before that, he rode a stationary bike nine minutes a day. He was 64 years old, 65 pounds overweight. The stationary bike bored him, so he gave it away, bought a Trek 1.2, and cycled city streets. He rode with caution because She expressed concern for his safety, but managed to encourage him. He had concerns too – he felt the 65 pounds each time he walked or pedaled, so he began with five-mile rides – and planned to increase to 40 miles a day over time, He figured

The more he rode 40, the more likely he could do 50 or 60 a day during the days of the Tour – and thus, be able to finish the 1440-mile Canada to New Orleans route in less than a month. He made lists and plans (more than for the Pacific Crest Trail) that covered equipment – van, bike, spare parts (tires, gears, pedals, derailleur), shoes, tools, oils, and patch kits – personnel – his father and Sam, his father's Shiba Inu – and promotion – t-shirts and videos. He saved money. Despite encouraging him, She refused to allocate family income to the Tour. She said Lumir provided enough income for him to self- fund. He did.

Beyond plans musings filled his mind. He imagined a many-purposed blog: to report day-to-day progress; to challenge people to find him and toss a water balloon; to build a following so advertising revenue defrayed costs; and, to have a record of the Tour. He wrote a blog and it became his record of the Tour, but when no more than twelve people found and followed the blog, there was no advertising income. He imagined a paved path 18-36 inches wide going from Canada to New Orleans located just beside the streets and highways he pedaled. He saw himself cycling that path from end to end. He imagined people in cars coming up, passing him, reading his t-shirt, and wondering about the Tour of Water Balloons. He imagined some might find the blog, or find his YouTube videos, and learn he invited people to find him and toss a water balloon. By the 12th of July in the year of the Tour,

He had lost 32 pounds and cycled 20 miles a day. As the day of departure neared, Arizona days were at their hottest, so he got up in the dark and rode as the sun came up. Vanessa at Landis Cyclery helped him choose wheel sets, tires, tubes, tools, extra spokes, flashers, shoes, clips, and two pairs of padded shorts, while Jori and Jim taught him to maintain his bike. Brand-X Custom T-Shirts delivered his t-shirts. After he spent $2500 on all that, he still lacked a laptop. Finally, he picked bought a laptop, a Verizon broadband card, and a Flip video camera -- all to document the Tour. He was amazed he also saved enough money for gear, travel, and living costs on the road. He was close to ready three weeks early, which prompted him to think long complex experiences are comprised of many simple events – each easily accomplished with perseverance. All his simple preparatory tasks were done.

After reaching 20 miles a day, he kept postponing an increase to 40, or even 30, miles a day. He might have claimed the heat stopped him. In truth, it was inertia. Once he achieved a milestone, say going from a 5 to a 10-mile a day ride, he reveled in reaching that milestone and enjoyed the reveling. He enjoyed telling others about each milestone. Yet once achieved, that milestone failed to motivate him to work toward the next one. To work toward a new milestone required an exercise of will. Inertia was an implacable foe in the struggle to prepare. Case in point, one Friday after six consecutive days riding 20 miles, he woke at six – sun up – thought about his 7:30 breakfast with Frank and Mike, a business lunch with employees of Lumir, and heat. He skipped the ride. When he stopped his routine, he had to overcome the inertia again.

For him, the antidote came from others. After he told friends about the Tour, they asked questions. Initial questions included: are you exercising (not yet, but soon); what type of bicycle do you have (I don't yet; but I will get one soon); what is your route (I cannot tell you; but I am riding across the country); are you going this summer (not this one; but next summer}; is someone biking with you (No, no one; Do you want to ride along?). As he answered initial questions, others arose. With each new question and answer he took a small step closer to the Tour. He could not stand to fake answers, so his progress was inexorable.

At first, he talked of a Seattle to New York ride with his lunch companions. After they declined, he thought it would be too easy to pinpoint his location and pummel him with water balloons every day. He did not like the idea of crossing the Cascade and Rocky Mountain ranges either. He got all the going up and down he ever wanted on the Pacific Crest Trail. To avoid these issues, he chose to start at an undisclosed location, report his progress in a general way with clues as to his exact location – a tactic that required his blog to "go viral." He chose to cycle from Canada across the "flat" middle of the country to New Orleans. He wore a Tour t-shirt of his design every day. He did not want to hide.

On August 6th, he left Arizona for Wisconsin to meet his Dad. His father's company made him happy. His Dad was mellow, a skilled tool man—handy to have around given the maintenance man lacked skills with all hand tools.

As departure drew near, he obsessively checked and re-checked to-do items, and kept thinking it would be nice to be on the ride when he either had everything or did without. The first video he posted on YouTube was "**The Tour: Kent St Prologue**." He had talked with the colonel in charge of the Air Force installation where Lumir provided services. The colonel, who encouraged him to show people how to throw water balloons in a safe way, permitted him to record the video between two Air Force buildings. The video began with instructions, viz: (1) stand still; (2) toss underhand; and (3) use clean tap water. In the video, he suggested these steps to preserve his well-being and minimize a crash-related injury that might end the Tour. Following these instructions, separate video segments showed the wrong way to throw balloons first, then the correct way.

He loved the Flip camcorder for its single operating button, simple way to transfer videos to a computer, and cost – 129 dollars. As always, news and talk show pundits pontificated about the state of the country. He judged these assessments to be self-serving, elitist, and dyspeptic. He wanted to see for himself. He was anxious to go. His sense of well-being was high. He had mastered critical elements of documenting the Tour; built his exercise capacity, learned to power the pedals on up and down strokes; done essential bike maintenance; created and uploaded a blog; and created and uploaded a video file. He had fun saying good-bye. He wandered around the Air Force installation, and talked to people he liked. He sent a package of Tour t-shirts to his Dad, which prompted his father to call and ask,

"What are all these yellow shirts for?"

"Did you read the back?"

"Wait a minute" and put the phone down. Soon he was back on the line and said, "Oh."

"Yeah, they're for you to wear on the Tour."

"Okay." The maintenance man realized he needed to ask,

"Dad, do you have a current passport?" and his Dad said

"Wait a minute" and he was gone again. The maintenance man waited three to five minutes – smiled and laughed to himself -- and then heard,

"Yeah, why?"

"You may need it to get back in the country from Canada."

"Okay, I'll take care of it."

"No, it will be taken care of when we leave with the van."

"Okay." At 92 he took his time, stayed mellow. The maintenance man looked forward to traveling with him – it might be the last time they talked. And he was certain he would hear many of his Dad's stories more than once – life's costs and benefits rolled together. He worked his list, for example,

Item 5 was making motel arrangements for the first three nights. Completing the Tour was uncertain, so he did not plan any further in advance – the van, laptop, cell phones, and a relaxed cycling regimen supported being flexible. As he searched the web for motels along his route, he heard Her in the kitchen making a familiar sound

"Mmm." The music of that sound evoked memories of many delicious foods he had eaten to its accompaniment. From his desk, he shouted over his shoulder,

"What are you eating?" and had those savory memories smashed by two words,

"Brussels sprouts, want some?" as the memory of the taste of brussels sprouts drove out (like bad money driving out good) memories of tangy nectarines, amazing flans, and mouth-watering roasted and grilled meats.

"Uh, no thanks..." He felt a need to ride to rid the taste of brussels sprouts from his mind, which was when he thought: a lot happens in my mind that does not happen anywhere else. The next day

He got up at five and, ten minutes later, was on the road. There was a very light, misting rain and a cool, gentle breeze as he rode. He pedaled a mile and a half west, turned north, and as sunlight streaked the sky, he saw dark clouds on the western horizon. The light mist changed to typical Arizona rain – big drops, far apart. A mile later, the rain was steady and thorough – smaller drops, plenty of them. A half a mile further he was drenched, his back a black streak from wet grit thrown up from the street. He started to get chilled, and thought about hypothermia, as his chilled state reminded him of being on the Pacific Crest Trail. He finished one loop, and did not do a second one. It was the first rain he had ridden in, and the revelation that he could do ten miles in the rain without rain gear was enough learning for one day. He checked his rain gear.

Four days before leaving for Wisconsin he pedaled 40 miles for the first time – with energy and daylight to spare. He believed he could do 40 to 60 miles per day on the Tour. He felt satisfied he had overcome inertia and reached that important milestone. At the same time, he understood his 64-year- old body had to be respected for what it could and could not do. With that ride done, he believed he could make it across the country on a bicycle. He hoped God bestowed those who passed him on the highway awareness of the limitations of bicycles, as well as the wisdom to act accordingly. The very next day,

He suffered severe back pain all day. He skipped riding and wallowed in fear about the threat to the Tour. Was that the way it was going to be the whole Tour? He took some aspirin, rubbed on Icy Hot, and trusted that his back would improve. He soldiered on but the following day it was "Ow!" Ditto the day after that too. He took the bicycle in for its final tune-up. It returned in perfect condition. He added Icy Hot and aspirin to his packed items. He also put in some Gum disposable soft picks for teeth – the best thing ever for getting food particles out from between teeth. He tested the laptop. It performed well sending and receiving e-mail and uploading blog posts. He finished packing by 6:00 p.m. He wanted some time to sit around and think if he had taken care of everything. In prayers that night, more wishes than dialogs with God, he hoped for cool, windless days, and flat, well-paved roads with clearly marked bike paths – all the way from Canada to New Orleans.

He said goodbye to Her and his son. None of them were fond of long or emotional good-byes, so off he went. He spent three days in the car, traveling interstate highways, smoking cigars to ensure he stayed alert and did not drift into drowsiness. On the way he stopped for a night to visit his cousins Jim and Carol. The following day he traveled across the plains to Ames, stopped for a night to visit with friends Phil and Rose. The next morning, he traveled across Iowa and Wisconsin to Rick's house.

The first thing he did after arriving, was visit his brother Herb, who suffered from both a stroke and kidney failure, in a nursing home. It was an unhappy visit. Herb neither ate any of the special food treats that he liked so much when the maintenance man had visited him the previous May, nor talked (except to say yes or no), nor even smiled when teased about things that had previously cracked him up. All in all, Herb seemed very beat down and that first visit ended when he vomited, and became cold and clammy. The attendants took charge, took him off, put him to bed, where he laid, his face ashen and drawn. The next day, after he had finished dialysis and had had a nap, he felt and acted better but still neither said nor did much. His unwillingness to talk provoked feelings of despair and helplessness in the maintenance man, who reminded Herb of the Tour, said Dad would be back in four to six weeks, and hugged him good bye. The rest of that day, the cyclist and his father drove to the Canadian start point about 250 miles north of Rick's home. It rained hard the whole way and there were a lot of little hills. At home, he only thought about flat roads and sunny days. Hills he was confident he could tackle, but rain was uncomfortable and dangerous. As they drove, he thought about Herb. He told himself to make sure he said the most important things he had to say to friends and family…you never know. At the motel that was their staging point, they unpacked. Next, they drove to the border, then back to the motel.

They scouted and set up points to rendezvous along the way.

PEDALING THE TOUR OF WATER BALLOONS

THE FIRST DAY OF THE Tour, they ate a continental breakfast and got to border just before 0900. In his musings, skies were sunny and roads were flat, but that day, skies were overcast, sliced by chill breezes off Lake Superior, and 100 meters inside the border was a hill higher than anything he had ever pedaled up. On the way up he slowed to walking speed but did not dismount. On the way down he went so fast he feared he would crash, yet reached the bottom unscathed. The road had wonderful, wide shoulders. They planned to rendezvous after six miles because of the hills and because his back still hurt, although so much as the week before. He was happy he had made no commitment to anyone to finish this ride, just to try, but knew he would be depressed if he did not finish. He finished day one.

Following an excellent French dinner, they discussed weather and road conditions, walked Sam the Shiba Ihnu, and went to bed. As he drifted into sleep, he thought: if you act behave as if something is real, one day it might be. He was on the Tour.

They were at it again at nine the next morning. Four hours and twenty minutes later he arrived at his destination. A brisk, cold wind chilled his face the entire day. After setting out the spots he wanted his Dad to stop, his Dad stopped where he wanted. Energy foods served him well, as did the warm van when he could find it. His back felt fine as he rode, and the chorus of the U-boat sailors in the film **Das Boot** echoed in his mind: "It's a long way to Tipperary…, It's a long way to go. "

Some rules dealt with adversity. They agreed to drive around cities. Driving through cities would have introduced trouble identifying and meeting at rendezvous points, and he declined to cycle in traffic in unfamiliar cities. They agreed to keep going south. If conditions turned extreme, they would drive south 40 miles and search for a place to stay. The third day he missed a paved bike path and pedaled an extra five and a half miles– thankfully the shoulders were still three to five feet wide – but the wind, right off Lake Superior, blew steadily at 25-35 mph and ambient temperature did not reach 70 degrees the entire day. He was discouraged when the wind required that he pedal downhill. At day's end, they checked into Whispering Pines, then went to scout the road ahead. When they returned to the room, Sam asked, "Where's my bed?" At 1930, they retraced 44 miles back up the coast. A call to the motel of the previous night had confirmed the bed was there. Oh, that Sheba! She knew where she wanted to sleep.

Before starting the next day, they got a call from Brian, Herb's son, and learned that Herb had been moved from his nursing home to a hospital. Details were limited, but his doctor speculated Herb had had a heart attack. The Tour team was depressed but chose to keep on going – neither one father wanted to sit at the bedside of an unconscious loved one. The cold (60 degrees or less) and steady, strong, wind only increased their malaise. There was a bright moment when he rode by a doe and fawn standing stock still not more than 20 feet away on top of a small bluff the bike path went around. On uphill portions of the ride, he was down to walking speed by the time he reached the crests. He found that he had to use all the gears – a possibility he had told folks at Landis he never imagined doing. The next day,

They moved away from Lake Superior and a heavy rain fell all day. They drove along the length of the Willard Munger Trail waiting for a time when the rain might stop. It did not, so they headed away from the trail and toward the next starting point. After a few miles it stopped raining, and they found a county road that he thought would make a good segment for the day. He put on his gear, got on the bike, and took off on a deserted road with his Dad following behind and clocking him. Somehow, he made it onto Loon Lake Road and made a big circle back toward the point where he started. That was enough for him, so they packed up the bike, scouted the run for the following day, and found a motel right at the end of the run – right on a lake. No bad news on a call to Illinois was good.

The next day was cloudy, temperatures from start to finish ranged between 67 and 74 degrees, light breezes blew from the east, and the roads were flat. The day was as he dreamed the Tour would be. He was calm, so his mind let him remember the day before –flustered by riding in a big circle. They met Cliff, who had made two cross-country rides, and was now on a trip from Williston, North Dakota to New York City on a reclined bicycle. Cliff was looking for a shortcut to Hayward, but they could not help. That day a glitch occurred when Dad forgot to check his watch as he went up the road. At one point the maintenance man was certain that he had gone well past his usual stopping distance, so he called his father and after an unproductive conversation, said,

"I'll call you back in a couple of minutes." He pedaled around a big bend looking for a landmark for his father to find, and right there, maybe 300 yards ahead, was the van, the dog, and his father, not all that far from where he had called. That evening, they met a couple doing a huge load of laundry. He told them about the Tour, the water balloons, and the blog. They said they would check it out when they returned to Iowa. The maintenance man asked if they voted for Obama, and the man cracked the maintenance man up when he said,

"The first time."

The following morning a thick fog replaced predicted thundershowers. He did not want to be on the road in the fog, so he skipped the initial part of the ride on a county road with narrow shoulders, and went straight to the Old Abe Trail – a straight shot to the Falls on an abandoned railroad bed paved with asphalt and quite level. Not more than two miles along the trail a deer crossed his path. Right after, he got a business call that startled him. He might have jumped; except he was clipped to the pedals. If he had been riding on a highway, he would not have heard the ring -- the silence of the woods was broken only by bird calls, insects buzzing, and that damn business call. Determining stopping points was a snap because there were two places his father could intercept the ride and he made both.

There were two aspects of the Tour he appreciated most keenly as he rode. First, his age and physical condition (pretty good, but not tiptop) led him to carefully select on what roads to ride, what weather to ride in, and how much fatigue to endure. Second, traveling with a hard-of-hearing, 92-year- old man (who refused aids) revealed the little ways aging affected his father. He adjusted to his father's poor hearing, but kept being surprised by unexpected moments of forgetfulness. Though not part of his plans or lists, the Tour turned out to be more about he and his father than about water balloons.

He could not see it, but he imagined a sky hook attached to the back of his bicycle that somehow hooked the jet stream and pulled it south as he pedaled that direction. For two days he began in cold, wet conditions and reached warmer, sunnier, conditions by the evening. He posited the jet stream was pulled south by an inexplicable force. Since he was the center of his universe, he reached the conclusion he was that inexplicable force. Despite a backache – his imagination also fueled a sense of bemusement with life. After seeing many persons in many different job and life situations, and after talking to them, he thought it ludicrous that politicians presumed to tell the multitudes how to run their lives. What gall! In the end he just said to himself, "Forgive me, I am only human" and kept pedaling.

The next morning, he woke with severe and immobilizing back pain and thought, with feelings of regret, guilt, and shame, that he might have to give up. He got up, peed, and dressed – pain. He loaded the car -- pain. They went for breakfast -- pain. They drove to the start point – severe pain. He geared up and did a short test ride around a parking lot. A miracle occurred! When he got off the bike – the pain was gone. Altogether gone! He wasted no time, remounted, moved out of the parking lot, looked up to see a hawk take off from a nearby tree, and fly just over his head. When he turned onto the road, the hawk turned in the same direction. The hawk drifted ahead, beat to a higher elevation, his shadow moving along just ahead of the maintenance man, getting smaller and smaller until it was gone. Thoughts of pain went off with the shadow, and he pedaled on until

A mile or so ahead, he saw what he believed to be a branch or pipe on the road and part of the right shoulder. He shifted hands to veer enough to the left that he not run over it. Just before he passed it, the stick bent in the middle, one end reared up and bent back, and the whole thing glided into the grass – the first, and biggest, garter snake he had seen in 40 years. Many miles down the road, he entered a small valley, populated by uncountable yellow and white butterflies. The road and shoulders were littered with bodies of those that had met the machines of men. A live one flew just off his right shoulder for two or three pedals, another flew right in front of him, got caught in a swirl of wind above his heart, and stayed there for one or two heartbeats – each sharing moments with him before flying off. He shed tears when he thought the life of a butterfly is short, sweet, and simple. What do we have that is so much better?

Much later, he thought that the hawk, the snake, and the butterflies all took a bit of his pain off with them because the pain in his back left for good. It was neither medicine nor science, just bits of the road.

On August 23rd, after driving through a garish oasis of a town named after the Wisconsin Dells, just south of there, they entered an endless string of hills. The road that runs through these hills rises and falls sharply – a road built on steep inclined planes of ascent and descent to master the minor elevation changes quickly. He spent the day trudging up each plane and racing down the other side – ten, twenty, thirty miles of it. There were two hills he walked most of the way up. For the first hill, his body said stop pedaling and he did. For the second – the longest hill of the day – he slowed to less than walking speed and his muscles ached with pain. Flies buzzed around and landed on his face. When he swatted them, his bike wobbled. He had a vision of being swatted by a truck zipping along at 65 mph, and finished that hill walking.

Rest stops went smoothly. During the next-to-last stop, they talked about the last stop. The maintenance man said

"OK, we will stop when highway 23 reaches highway 12. Find a place to park on one of the corners, and I will find you."

"OK, I will stop at 12 and park" his father answered and off he went. Forty minutes later, the maintenance man reached the target intersection, but found no dad. He rode a block further, still no dad. He fumed, and said to himself,

"I've lost my dad; She is going to kill me" as he thought of Her reaction to the news and pulled out the cell phone to call his father. It went to voicemail; he hung up and called again. They devised this two-call process because his father could not get his cell out of his pocket (where he felt it vibrate [as his ears did not hear rings]) before a call went to voice mail, but still had it in his hand when the phone rang again.

"Yeah?" his father's friendly voice

"Where are you?"

"Oh, I'm lost someplace, where are you?" he replied.

"I'm at the Kwik Trip across from MacDonalds in Dodgeville."

"OK I will be there in a bit. Bye." The maintenance man waited and waited. Soon he needed to pee – urgently! Another two-call – his father was a way away, so he went to the toilet. A short time after he came out, his dad showed up. Phew! His dad went to bed early because while the maintenance man did forty-two miles on the bike, his father did more than 100 on the road – and never saw the highway 12 signs, and the maintenance man had forgot to tell him the name of the town. As the maintenance man drifted off to sleep, a last thought wafted through his mind: clear simple messages create simple days. Good advice that did not stick because the next day,

They started in Mineral Point on Highway 23, a nice road with adequate shoulders, rode to Highway 11, packed the bicycle, and drove east to Monroe where they unpacked the bicycle and he took Highway 69 to the border where it became Illinois highway 26. It was there he discovered they missed another rendezvous for two reasons. First, neither saw the state border sign, if it existed at all, and second, a town, Oneco, was on the map but not on earth. There was no cell phone service, so he ended up going all the way to Freeport, where they met by simple good fortune, and both thought it would be good to stop for the night.

The day after was a disaster! Illinois roads! Phooey! They found no road with a semblance of paved shoulders. All were narrow – he decided to avoid such roads. A goal of the Tour was to have fun, create fun for others – not die on inadequate roads. Depressed, they went shopping, got their room, showered, and went to dinner. That night he went online and signed up with Rails and Trails, and found a 60-mile trail along the big river. He told himself, "Tomorrow I will be somewhere between Clinton and the Quad cities." Then he thought he would cross the river to Iowa and check out the roads there. As he went to sleep, he thought: some days you just get on with it.

The next day he rode the 60-mile Great River Trail from Savanna IL to the outskirts of the Quad Cities – a flat paved way comprised mostly of bike trails and some county roads. From their stopping point, they drove around the Quad Cities to the Iowa side of the river, hoping that Iowa had roads with adequate shoulders. Nope. They did find a combination of roads he was willing to take to Burlington. Doing so, two phenomena struck his fancy. First, he rode along the top of a levee, perhaps two miles long, higher than the surrounding terrain comprised of swamps, the river, or rivers, with short cropped grass on both sides of the levee. His eyes were focused some yards on the path ahead, to avoid pitfalls, and caught sight of some graffiti painted on the path. He looked down, just in time to read "Ain't life grand?" and had to smile – it was the only graffiti he had seen to date and it perfectly fit his mood. The second phenomenon of note was the Thomson prairie. Grasses and plants of the plains, three to four feet tall, extended in all directions. How did settlers get across such expanses? Thinking that reminded him of the Pacific Crest Trail odyssey filled with packing and unpacking experiences. On the bicycle Tour, he found there were also morning and evening packing experiences – about an hour and a half all told – plus, something he did not do on the well-marked Pacific Crest Trail – he had to find a path to pedal that he deemed safe. Trucks rushing by at 70 mph were quite distressing, so he tried to minimize their likelihood.

Doing laundry was not covered by pre-trip planning. At home, he wore seven shirts, seven pairs of socks and seven pairs of underpants, plus a pair of pants, each week. His laundry chore was one-load, once-a-week. However, because he sweated through 7 or 8 shirts a day (leaving 7 in reserve) and other clothes needed cleaning, doing laundry became an every-other-day affair, requiring them to find a motel with washers and dryers.

He spent the next morning on a nice ride on country roads between Muscatine and Burlington. Deer, yellow-bodied, black-wing, and cardinal birds, a donkey, an immaculate brick church, the Apostolic Christian Church, and the Iowa River -- highlighted the ride through sparsely populated southeast Iowa. From Burlington they found no decent routes south. They crossed back into Illinois, stopped each time they spotted a motel, and were frustrated repeatedly by a series of motels did not allow pets. One family-owned motel welcomed them. They went out, scouted roads, did laundry, ate, and prepared for the next day.

He rode 45 of the 50.4 miles south on county roads to Taylorville (skipping a gravel patch and two sideways sections). Aside from the rained-out day four, he had ridden and scouted roads every day, and they had not taken a break. He felt karma at work, because a balloon festival was underway near Taylorville, and that evening many balloons were being inflated and tested for liftoff the next morning. His father loved hot air balloons. The sight of them always lifted the maintenance man's mood. He asked his father if he wanted to stay over for a day of rest and see some of the festival, and was surprised when his father said no. The maintenance man sensed,

His father wanted to get home as soon as possible. Like Her, his father worried when he rode alone on country roads. Starting, stopping, and searching for route and town signs disoriented him, and they found that the best way to avoid disorientation was to have his father drive down the road for 6 minutes and pull over in a safe spot where he had time to walk the dog and read a little. The ride into Taylorville was against a steady breeze on rough roads. Finding a motel and scouting took 10 minutes (It was a straight shot on Nokomis Rd to Mulberry Grove). As they had some free time, his father said it was time for new tires. He had seen an old friend -- a Walmart Supercenter – and had to visit. Tires were as good excuse as any.

On the road from Taylorville to Mulberry Grove, big hills, a head wind, heat, humidity, and a head cold reduced him to exhaustion, so he stopped after doing 39 miles in three and a half hours. They hunted for a suitable road south, ended up in Waterloo where they decided he would try Route 3 down to Cairo. Given his current level of performance, it was at least a two-day trip. When he could, he looked for signs of anger or malaise among folks he met on the Tour, but found none anywhere on the path he cycled. He saw farmers, truckers, waiters and waitresses, many closed businesses. If people were angry, they did not share it with him.

The road out of Waterloo was perfect and a seven A.M. start meant two hours of riding in cool temperatures. Thirty miles out of Waterloo the shoulder deteriorated and disappeared altogether. They picked up the bike and drove until, on a new section of highway, the shoulder was good. They stopped, unpacked the bike, and he started riding again. Soon after, the shoulder disappeared. He had reservations, and his dad was completely against continuing. It was his father being serious, so he recorded it as a 40-mile day. About 40 miles from Cairo, good shoulders returned and he decided they would get a motel in Cairo and return to do that stretch.

From the look of things, no funds from Obama's stimulus package made it to Cairo – they could not find a single habitable motel. Grand old buildings crumbled. Nothing seemed new. They crossed the bridge and headed west into Missouri, where they found a route that looked good and ended at a ferry to carry them back across the big river to Kentucky. The night before,

As he waited for the local news to give the forecast, he realized that the three to five hours of riding each day was the calm part of his day. Mornings they packed the car, took Sam for a walk, and went for breakfast. After a ride, they found a motel, unpacked, and took showers. They shopped daily for drinks, ice, snacks, gas, as well as occasional items like toothpaste and gum. Alternate days they did laundry. He walked Sam twice – the last a long walk – so Sam would sleep through the night. Writing the blog, editing the videos, and uploading them took about an hour. While these details filled his day, he was pleased he spent so much time with his father. Despite a hearing loss, lapses in memory, and a bit of confusion on the roads, the maintenance man loved to listen to stories of earlier times. One evening, his dad told his side of the separation from Isabelle. As she told it,

Isabelle was the heroine of her story. She did not identify the cause of the separation. Both stories agreed that Aunt Marge drove to Chicago from Long Island, picked up his mom, himself, and his brother, turned around and drove back to New York. He saw his father crying when he said goodbye – at his mother's behest – but in telling his side, his father neither mentioned the cause of the separation nor admitted his tears, and his mother did not answer, nor ever mention, the tears. In two and a half years in New York, a man named Lou entered and left his mother's life. Neither parent ever mentioned Lou after the reconciliation. Their stories diverged on events of the reconciliation. She said she called his father, agreed to reconcile, and they all went back to Illinois when he came to get them. Thereafter he and Isabelle had two more sons, and both parents seemed at ease with each other. When the maintenance man was in college, Isabelle told him that she loved his father more than ever.

Her life's dream was to have four sons. She did, and only ever expressed love for all four, except when driven to anger or exasperation by one, at which time her typical response was to launch something through the air toward the offender – most often Herb – who was adept at setting her off with a few choice words. The single worst incident happened just after a family dinner. Herb had made a smart-ass remark as she filled a Tupperware container with creamed spinach. Not bothering to fasten the lid, or choose another object, she sent it flying at his head. He ducked under the table as the lid came off the rotating container and creamed spinach created a green blood splatter across the ceiling and down a wall of the kitchen. She stomped away as her husband and boys howled with laughter. Herb tried to clean it up, but mostly smudged green into the ceiling and wall.

His father's version of reconciliation added two details Isabelle never mentioned. First, his father told him that he, on his own initiative, drove to New York to try to work out their differences. When he got to Sarah's house, he knocked on the front door, Isabelle opened it, and, on seeing him, said, "What are you doing here?" then slammed the door in his face, whereupon his father returned to his car and drove back to Chicago. His father never reported what he thought, but said he responded "It will be a cold day in hell before you see me again" which must have covered a much more hostile thought. Who knows?

Second, his father said that later Sarah told him that after he drove off, she, Sarah, told Isabelle to sit down. Then she said, "Dear, you are going to have to choose. Either you make up with that man and get on with your life, or you go get a job so you can get your own house, and get on with a new life, but, by God, you will not be living in my house much longer."

No participant in the tale, not his father, not his mother, not his grandmother ever said who said what after that -- maybe it is better that way – but his father made a second trip to New York, and a reconstructed family left together for Illinois. Over his own life and marriage, the maintenance man gained respect for his father and mother, for their commitment to marriage, for whatever let them reconcile and live out their lives until her death, delayed some 50 years, from heart defects caused by rheumatic fever in childhood. Her death was swift. As his parents prepared to go to a square dance -- a retirement passion – she bent over to tie her shoelaces, then kept on going head first into the floor. Paramedics said it was likely she died in that moment, as she was dead on arrival at the hospital.

His father's recollections initiated a period of reflection and introspection as the maintenance man pedaled alone on the bicycle. One thing was certain, he had none of his usual reactions to women encountered on the Tour. This absence of curiosity and interest did not occur to him until later, when he attributed his absence of interest to a complete engagement with mundane tasks of the Tour, with talks with his father, and with moments of introspection sparked by those talks.

A night later, they found a Quality Motel at the intersection of an Interstate and a local road. The latter looked good for biking and turned out to be part of the Mississippi River Trail that went on down to New Orleans. They decided to make the rest of the Tour on that Trail – but lacked maps and directions. Road conditions, still caused them to skip down the road. Where Minnesota and Wisconsin had roads that supported continuous riding, those in Illinois and elsewhere had not. The maintenance man estimated that when he reached New Orleans, he had cycled more than 800 miles on the bike, and driven more than 3000 miles in the car, to complete a journey Google says is 1440 miles long.

As he pedaled the next day, he thought about their good fortune. After 16 days, they had been rained out once. Further, as they continued south, cool weather followed along. Although some days were in the mid 80's, only 3 or 4 days were truly hot. That day was overcast and windy, and he became chilled while riding, a peculiar sensation because when he stopped, he got hot immediately. His sweat soaked at least one t-shirt every 10-12 miles – changing helped him focus and remain calm. At their last rendezvous before stopping, they talked with a man named Mike B who rode up in his pick-up. All three talked about cycling. Mike gave them helpful information about the Mississippi River Trail, told them about the Tour of Corn, as well as the ferry. He started to leave when he slammed on the brakes and said "Oh, oh! I don't think the ferry runs on Monday and Tuesday." Their jaws dropped, but Mike whipped out his cell phone and called the ferry. All was quiet as he listened, and then said,

"You are in luck. The ferry runs 7 days a week now."

Not long after, as they waited at the dock, he thought, for him, the third-best thing of the day was meeting Mike. The second-best thing was being sole passengers on the ferry which came across just for them after they pressed a button on a pole. But the best thing was hearing his father say,

"I am glad we came this way. Ever since you mentioned ferry, I wanted to cross the river" which caused the maintenance to smile because he thought, "Sometimes you do what you want – for yourself and for no particular reason -- and you end up in harmony with the whole world around you." Putting a period to his feeling, after the crossing, they had one of the best hamburgers of their lives in a café called MeMaw's in Hickman TN.

The last day of August they completed 42 miles of the Mississippi River Trail between Dyersburg and Munford TN. A 16 and a half mile, flat stretch ran along the top of a levee. The remainder was up and down little hills – but the heat and humidity climbed up without respite. He also found that Beaver Road from a church outside of town down into Munford was the shortest stretch of road with the most dogs running free, willing to chase him, and force him to pedal faster and faster. Jack Williams terriers being the most persistent buggers. By the end of the day, exhausted, he contemplated a rest day. That afternoon they discussed plans for the remaining days and decided to wrap up the Tour in New Orleans in 5 or 6 days. As they unpacked the van, they discovered the laundry bag was missing, along with two pairs of socks, some underwear, two Tour t-shirts, and a cribbage board stored in the bag. Oh well! That clinched it. The next day, they did chores and shopped. They went to the bank, ate breakfast, bought cigars, drinks, a cribbage board, ice, gasoline, washed the car, and drove to Greenville, Mississippi to scout the next leg south.

They stayed at a Days Inn in Greenville for two nights. Greenville, a town mostly situated along route 82/278 and Mississippi 1, burdened by an old downtown struggling to survive, caused him to feel sad – so many fine old brick buildings empty and deteriorating. A smaller version of Cairo. The first night they drove around looking for a place to eat, with little luck. They used Magellan to find restaurants. A list of types appeared, among them Italian. He asked his father,

"Would you like Italian?"

"You bet, I love Italian," came the answer. A single tap displayed Fermo's Italian Restaurant – the only Italian restaurant listed. What the heck, he tapped again, and they were directed to an old building with a sign stating Keppler's, not Fermo's, Italian. It was Italian, so they went in. The place turned out to be a gem, because there, in Greenville, Keppler's prepared solidly good food. They ate dinner there both nights.

The next morning, they drove to Rosedale and he biked back to Greenville. Near Lake Bolivar he met a man named Steve coming out of a field of cotton. The maintenance man asked Steve about short cotton plants he had seen earlier along highway 61.

"Different varieties" Steve answered, as he offered a bottle of water that the maintenance man declined,

"No thanks, my father is around here somewhere with a cooler stuffed with cold drinks. Can you tell me about Lake Bolivar?" which the maintenance man had thought was the Mississippi until Steve referred to it by name.

"It used to be the main channel of the Mississippi, but it was completely cut off when the river cut a new channel. That happens a lot along the river."

On the following day he had a great ride and traveled his longest distance. Just after he made a last video clip, and his father had driven off into the future, he pedaled into Issaquena County – where Mississippi 1 turned hostile to biking.

The fourth of September began in a disappointing way. They left Vicksburg to look for a route toward Prentiss where the maintenance man wanted to take the Long Leaf Trace the next day, but they did not find a road with a discernible shoulder. They chose to switch the search to "county roads," which had no shoulders but very little traffic. They specifically looked for 478, but never found it and ended up driving to Prentiss. They arrived at 10:30. As it was early, he decided to do the Long Leaf Trace immediately. With a little trepidation he sent his father off to Hattiesburg 43 miles south via two roads he clearly marked on the map. Off his Dad went. Later, he learned his father got lost and made a side trip to Columbia – 30 miles to the west of Hattiesburg. Fortunately, he set himself straight and only had minor problems finding the trail end in Hattiesburg. With the diversion, he only had to wait an hour for the maintenance man to appear at the trailhead. The Trace turned out to be a Mississippi gem – 43 paved miles with light bicycle traffic, essentially all downhill from Prentiss to Hattiesburg. He exuberantly shouted "Whoopee!" a couple of times coasting on down the Trace.

Getting close to the finish he mapped a route for each of the next two days – one from Lumberton to Nicholson, the other from just west of Pearlington into New Orleans. By his calculation, he would exceed 800 pedaled miles on the way into Jackson Square, New Orleans. Unfortunately, route 11 from Lumberton to Nicholson, which looked like a perfect 41-mile ride when he was planning it sitting in Hattiesburg, turned out to have a tiny ribbed shoulder to warn people when they ran off the road. They spent the rest of the day finding and setting up the final ride into New Orleans. He formed an analogy based on a military truism – no long ride by a 64-year-old man survives intact when it encounters roads built just for cars. The next day,

They took old route 90 out of Mississippi and across Louisiana to Bayou Sauvage National Wildlife Reserve. From there, only a 12-mile journey into New Orleans remained. He rode all the way in to Jackson Square where he wanted to do a couple of "victory" laps. Didn't happen. The greedy, garish, commercial NFL Experience gobbled up the entire square. Ordinary citizens had to pay to enter. The Tour was over. The only water balloons ever thrown were those he solicited for **The Kent Street Prologue**. When he could not enter Jackson Square, he pedaled out to the spot where he left his father. He knew his father was ready to leave New Orleans and had no desire to stick around for an outstanding meal in any of the innumerable places that served such food. He felt strongly that when your father is tired, you had to get him to bed. When he is ready to go home, you had to take him. As for himself, he felt relief and a sense of accomplishment at the end of a ride he had conceived in jest, started, and finished. So,

They left New Orleans 30 minutes after the last stage and returned to Wisconsin after two days of hard driving. He visited his brother in the nursing home each of the following two days. Herb was declining and the maintenance man came away discouraged. He said his goodbyes and headed home. On the way, he stopped to visit friends Phil and Rose in Ames. He and Phil made a deal for some of his excess bike gear, including two extra wheel sets that bedeviled him the whole Tour, as he never needed them, but had to keep packing and unpacking them into and out of the van. On the remainder of the drive home,

He pondered how, if in any way, the Tour had changed him. He started with the thought that he finished in the same place he started – in his own skin, asking: did I learn anything? Have I changed? What's next? All his answers seemed to start with "That depends." How so? In truth, he told himself: I gained no new first principles, had one mystical moment pedaling through a valley of butterflies, and found little evidence the country was ill. He learned his father was satisfied with his life for traditional reasons: he said he was fortunate to have two different women to love and be loved by, to have had and raised four sons to be productive adults of whom he was proud, and to have had a career doing work he loved. The maintenance man learned new details of his father's life: his best friends were life-long friends from high school; He managed a bookstore; and He had no desire to document his life for others. For the maintenance man, it was illuminating to see how, at 92, his father coped with limitations age visited upon him; to observe that they were able to travel from Canada to Louisiana and spend 26 days and nights together in close quarters; and to see that his father was still a vital human being who affected people in his own life in a positive way. These made the Tour valuable. "Is that it?"

No, there was more. For the preceding ten years, he had made his views public in articles written for a local Arizona newspaper, and in conversations with anyone who would talk with him. His beliefs – against big, central, government, for lower taxes, for less social intervention, for individual responsibility – were embedded in a pessimistic outlook for the near future. On the Tour, he saw that most folks focused on their own lives, and that they seemed to manage well – he took this as a positive (in a great flywheel of society sort of way). On a personal level, he learned he could pedal a bicycle 40 miles a day, day in and day out, and found that reassuring, as it gave hope for a future like that of his father. He accepted that he was still himself, a person who liked to smoke hand-rolled cigars, go to casinos to gamble, eat well, and wanted to visit skeptics (former lunch companions and friends) who lacked faith or interest in such a trip. He thought of singing "Na, Na, Na-Na-Na-NA," and asking, "Who's crazy now?" Then he thought there is no rational basis for faith – you either believe or do not, and, being or becoming enlightened is self-evidence. As it always is.

PANDEMIC, VACCINES, BULLOUS PEMPHIGOID, AND THEIR CHOICE

WHEN THEY MET, SHE WORE a girdle. He regularly asked or urged Her to stop wearing it. She did, and they became physically and emotionally entangled. - He suggested many actions She might or might not do. If She did not, it was for him to adjust. They closer they became, the more She disclosed of her abuse by Hop. Her telling made the maintenance man ashamed to be a man —that men could do such things. For Her, he tried to alleviate Her alienation, never forced a thing on Her, rather tried to provide time and space for Her to choose. He offered comfort. She fought depression by gaining and retaining control of Her mind, Her body, and Her choices. Her way precluded choices he wished to make on Her behalf, but he had to let it go. As for his attitude toward women, after

He shared his views with Her, and after his affair with J B, after he foreswore sexual intercourse with women, they found a compromise: he never brought his views or behaviors towards other women into Her life; She never asked. They had conflicts. How to nurture Kevin raised difficult conversations. Kevin was central to their lives at home, and they dealt with problems that plagued him as he grew up, a process that lasted until Kevin was in his early thirties. By the time the pandemic arrived, Kevin lived in his own home and did not present daily concerns. Her faith in vaccines -- she got annual flu shots -- translated directly to getting the COVID vaccines as soon as possible. He had a different view. A positive take on his view would be that fighting off illnesses, rather than using vaccines, strengthens the species. He did not trust reports on the effects of COVID vaccines, because long-term studies of adverse effects did not exist, and because COVID was only slightly more fatal than influenza. Unlike flu shots, she asked him to get the COVID vaccines. For her, he did. After their second shot, problems appeared that brought him face to face with his dilemma. The problems started when

Her skin began to itch. And itch. And itch. Over-the-counter remedies failed and She could not refrain from scratching. The itching persisted. She thought they might have an infestation of bedbugs or mites, or some other parasite. They tore the bedroom and other, oft-used, areas of the house apart.

There was no evidence of biting creatures. She saw a dermatologist who asked about detergents they used, identified an ingredient to look out for, and suggested alternatives. He also prescribed a steroid- based skin cream. Because they had detergents with a proscribed ingredient, they discarded them. She reviewed information on steroids and decided not to use the cream, or receive pills or injections of steroid-based compounds. The itching persisted, and

Her breathing got more difficult. Having stopped smoking five years earlier, and having observed improvements in Her breathing, this difficulty disheartened Her. Her energy for ordinary, daily activities diminished. These conditions persisted from April through June, and then

In addition to itching, blisters appeared -- first on Her legs. The blisters would fill with liquid and break. Her scratching broke others. The liquid made her clothes damp and uncomfortable. She changed frequently. Her fatigue limited her usual activities, so he started doing Her laundry and other chores to reduce Her need to move around. She returned to the dermatologist. Before the visit, the maintenance man investigated the condition. Doing so, he concluded she suffered a rare, auto-immune disorder called bullous pemphigoid. She took its description to the dermatologist who confirmed the diagnosis. Bullous pemphigoid exposes the flaws of modern medical practice, because

The cause of the disorder is unknown. No cure exists. Doctors prescribe a palliative treatment – steroids. Without a cure, the dermatologist sent her home with a prescription for a steroid-based skin cream –again. She did not fill that prescription. AS for his dilemma, What should he do on Her behalf? Were Her wishes to be disregarded? Unlike any number of issues for which he had an opinion, nothing he knew or felt helped answer these questions. It was not as if this were a new problem, because

Since they first met, they held many opposing views. On some issues, he or She might not be interested, and the interested party prevailed. He liked to spend, She preferred to save. When She discovered he kited checks, she stopped that behavior. Despite keeping an accurate checking account, he had no interest in budgeting or saving for future needs. Her interest was strong, thus, when he suggested She keep the financial accounts, She accepted at once. Conflicts were more intense when they both had strong, opposite, views on an issue. How to deal with the bullous pemphigoid was such a case. He wanted to act, including using steroids, to combat the disorder. Although described as rarely fatal, in Her case, the disorder got worse, and he worried She might die. Nevertheless, She retained control of what was done, and never relented, leaving for him only behaviors that eased Her difficulties with daily living.

The itching and blistering spread to the arms, later to the midriff and back, and finally to the scalp. Upon breaking, a blister became a sore on the surface of Her skin. Over time, some areas cleared up, skin sores started to heal, but scratching prevented complete healing. As the disorder encompassed more of her skin, her fatigue increased and he observed a noticeable decline in Her resilience. She slept a lot. The blisters continued to soak Her clothes and the bedclothes, all of which required a regular change, wash, and dry. In early August, She slept alone in their queen-size bed and he changed, washed, and dried the sheets every day. One night, She woke up, called his name, and told him

"I am scared."

"What's happening?"

"I cannot breathe."

"Stay calm, breathe in slow and deep, then breathe out." Moments later,

"It is not working. I still cannot breathe. What can we do?"

"I don't know anything I can do to help you breathe. Perhaps we should go to the hospital." To this, She said nothing. He knew She did not want to go to the hospital. Then she said

"I am scared. What should I do?"

"You must think about a doctor or the hospital. You must tell me what you want to do, because if it is up to me, I would take you to the emergency room right now. Do you want me to take you to the hospital?"

"I don't want to go, but I have to. Yeah, take me." On hearing this he said

"Hold on. We will go as quick as possible." Then he jumped up and Gathered some of Her clothes and personal items, found her a robe and slippers, dressed Her, put Her in an office chair, wheeled Her to the car, transferred Her to the front seat, locked up the house, drove to the hospital, ran for a wheelchair, helped Her sit, and wheeled Her into the emergency room. The moment he told admitting staff She could not breathe; they wheeled Her off. Thirty minutes later, they called him, and took him to Her treatment room. She breathed through an oxygen mask, talked as if she were disoriented, and asked when she could go home. He had no answer. They waited. A doctor came into the room and started right in, addressing them both, but talking to Her

"I believe you are okay for now. The oxygen will make it easier for you to breathe."

"Can I go home now?"

"In my opinion, you should stay here, let us conduct some tests, and see what's happening." The maintenance man asked,

"What about Her skin?"

"We will have a wound nurse examine her tomorrow and find a course of action." She asked

"When can I go home?"

"Let's see what the tests show, okay." She remained silent, so the doctor asked him,

"Do you have medical power of attorney?"

"Yes, but She understands what you are asking. It Is for her to decide." He faced her and asked,

"Are you willing to stay in hospital so they can conduct these tests?"

"What are these tests?" The doctor responded

"Oh, some blood tests, and heart and lung examinations...."

"And after that, can I go home?"

"We will see, but most likely you will be able to go home."

"Okay, I'll stay." The doctor nodded, stood up, and as he was leaving said,

"Someone from admitting will be with you soon. They will have some forms for you to sign."

He left. They waited. A person from admitting came. She signed permission and consent forms. A staff person came, picked up her bag of items, disconnected the oxygen, and wheeled her off. It was late, past visiting hours. He was told to go home and return during visiting hours the next day.

While at home, a night nurse called and said She was being difficult. He asked the maintenance man to talk to her. She wanted to come home. He said She had to stay the night because there was nothing that he could do for her problem breathing. She agreed to stay. The next day

He returned early and found Her in better condition. The first thing she asked

"When can I go home?"

"I don't know. I'll ask the doctor when I see him" which was a difficult promise to keep because doctors made and completed rounds before visiting hours— an instance of medical practice designed for medical practitioners, not patients or family. It did not help that She had a cardiologist, a pulmonologist, and a phlebotomist attending her: each practiced his/her specialty. Consequently, her heart was examined and given treatment, her lungs were examined and given treatment, and her blood was drawn regularly, tested, and results examined. Another doctor, the hospitalist in charge of her case, was like a general contractor in charge of a construction site. No doctor addressed the bullous pemphigoid, except to put her on a steroid, which the maintenance man had to demand that they quit administering – per Her wish. For her skin sores they called in a wound nurse who dressed some of the worst wounds and left. He managed to meet with the hospitalist who said that she could leave in two days, as no purpose was served by keeping her in the hospital. Two days later,

He took Her home in time for a subdued 55th wedding anniversary, a quiet dinner, a hug, and a kiss. The next night an oxygenator with a 50-foot tube was delivered to help her get enough oxygen. The relentless nature of the bullous pemphigoid continued: some sores healed, new blisters formed and leaked, new sores followed, She suffered extreme fatigue. As part of Her treatment, for six weeks, a physical therapist came and worked on mobility and breathing with Her. The physical therapist told him She was her fifth client of hers who had taken the vaccines and then exhibited bullous pemphigoid. As a scientist, he believed double-blind experiments most effectively revealed cause and effect relations, but what the therapist told them stunned him. A rare disorder,

Bullous pemphigoid in five patients of one physical therapist, all occurring after receiving the COVID vaccines, was an improbable coincidence. Her doctors had treated her breathing, but did nothing for the bullous pemphigoid. Once she rejected the steroid palliative, they threw in the towel. With respect to recovery from the disorder, She was on Her own.

She was afraid of falling from the queen-size bed, so he cleared the dining room and put a twin bed against the wall, followed by a sofa which he put against the twin bed. The wall and the back of the sofa provided guards that prevented a fall. He slept on the sofa every night so he could hear Her if She needed help. From September 2, when She returned home, his days were all the same. Each morning,

He got up first. When She woke, she went to the bathroom. Depending on Her choice, either before or after breakfast, he helped Her put on clean, dry, bedclothes. She went into Her office to sit down. He made breakfast and brought it to Her. While She ate, he pulled out the couch, stripped the bedding from the twin bed and put it in the washing machine, after which he made up Her bed with clean, dry, sheets, a dry, absorbent pad, and blanket. When he finished the bed, he moved a load from the washer to the dryer and started a wash load with Her clothes and the pads dampened during the night. On trips to the bathroom or back to bed, sometimes She walked and sometimes he wheeled Her in Her office chair. On all trips, he had to keep the oxygenator tube free and clear of obstructions. Her fatigue caused Her to sleep many more hours than normal. Between one and three times a day, but always before She went to bed for the night, they treated the worst of Her sores with MediHoney and nonstick bandages. However, the bandages aggravated Her, and during the night, as She slept,

She pulled them off. Most days, three times a night She woke because a damp nightgown or bedding made Her feel cold. When She called him, he woke, moved the couch away from the bed, and helped her change. If the pad, sheet, or quilt were also damp he changed these while she went to the toilet. After he changed them, he washed and dried them right away -- there were only two quilts and three sheet sets for the twin bed. Two appointments a week for six weeks with the physical therapist helped her breathing. She achieved an oxygen uptake score sufficient to make use of the oxygenator optional. After the sessions with the therapist ended, they kept the machine and She continued to use it, especially at night. From the end of October, all of November, and until the end of December, Her extreme fatigue continued. She spent many hours a day sleeping, and had less of an appetite for the breakfasts and dinners he fixed. His routine remained the same, but his level of concern increased, and when he suggested using the steroid cream for the itching, she refused, so both frustration and concern occupied his mind. At the end of December,

She had another episode of very difficult breathing and they returned to the hospital. She did not recover any resilience during the first two days after admission. The nurses expressed a great deal of concern. She slept most of the time when he or Kevin visited. On January 2nd she woke up while he and Kevin visited and she said to him

"Bill, am I dead?" and he answered

"No, you are just very sick" to which she said

217

"No, Bill, I am dead." And then fell back asleep. He left the room to go and cry. Later they came back. He let Kevin talk to Her alone. Then he went to be alone with Her and whispered in Her ear,

"Sherry, I love you. I may not have loved you the way you wanted me to love you, but I have always loved you. I still love you." She simply slept. The nurse said she would probably sleep for several hours, so he went home to do some chores. A nurse called and said that her breathing difficulty had increased, and the doctors asked for permission to intubate. He asked

"Does that mean She would be unable to talk?"

"Yes."

"In that case, I do not give permission. She did not want extraordinary measures taken to extend Her life."

"Okay." Two hours later, a nurse called and told him

"I am sorry to have to tell you that Sherry passed away this afternoon." He was two days past his 77th birthday, She was 3 days short of Her 77th birthday. They lived together during four years of university and 55 years, four months of marriage. They had chosen cremation. Neptune Society came and took her body away, and returned Her ashes to him two weeks later.

THOSE WHO LEFT BEFORE HER

HER DEATH WAS THE SIXTH in his close family. He felt like the engine of a train; loved ones like cars he pulled; each car filled with shared life. Death decoupled a car – easing the pull, but painting the car with sadness. Although he might add cars, that meant new, unknown, loads. Isabelle, who carried him to life and loved him all of hers, was the first. In early November, six weeks before his 49th birthday, his father called from New Mexico, and said,

"Mom died today." Tears engulfed him. He started to sink to the floor. She had to put Her arms around his pulsing chest to help him stay standing. Later, he recalled nothing else of the call. He drove to New Mexico. Sarah, her nephew Smitty, his brothers Herb, Rick and Tom, and his Dad greeted him with hugs, smiles, and tears. He heard his parents had been preparing to go square dancing, that his mom wore a big, swooshy, square dance dress, that she bent over to tie shoes, and that she kept going down – most likely dead when she hit the floor. Before the memorial, locals stopped by the house and talked about her. At the memorial,

A minister, who knew her not, gave a heartfelt blessing, and began a eulogy. Listening to a stranger talk about his Mom struck the maintenance man amiss. That feeling moved him out of his seat, toward the podium, where he took the minister aside, and whispered

"Father, I appreciate that you came today, but you did not know my Mom. I do not want to offend you, but I believe it would be better for her friends and relatives to have a chance to say publicly what is on their minds. Would you please be brief, and then invite them to do that?" In a kind voice, the minister answered

"Sure." He did. They did.

After the service, those who spoke expressed their gratitude for being able to do so. He kissed his Mom goodbye. Sarah kissed her daughter goodbye. The body was taken for cremation. Days later, his father had her ashes interned in Fort Bayard National Cemetery – in a spot next to the spot waiting for him. Then like a cloud of ashes in a swirling wind, the gathered departed. Sarah flew to Orlando, where she lived and cared for herself in her own house well into her 90's, until

An ankle broke in a fall and reduced her mobility. Unable to leave the house or care for her yard – her remaining passion – her resilience declined. Smitty moved her to a nursing home in Largo, where he visited daily. She was 97 (the maintenance man 55) when her body stopped working and forced her strong will and Irish moods to stop. On her death, individual memories of her were cemented like bricks in the wall of his mind. He recalled a morning, at nine or ten years, when he observed her as she put on a brassiere after a bath. She put her arms through the straps, bent forward to fit the cups to her breasts, stood up, and fastened the clasp in the back – a fluid, continuous, act done with the grace of a woman secure in her body. His mother had been shy about her nudity, his grandmother had not. She called herself a practical nurse, and one time,

She took him to a big house where she cared for the children. Before they went in, she said, "You are going to meet Tom, a colored man, who is my friend. Be nice."

Then she took him to the kitchen sat him down with Tom, who spoke to him in a soft, clear, husky voice – like a father. For that, and because he was his grandmother's friend, the maintenance man liked Tom. A second encounter with a colored person occurred with his aunt, when she drove him and his cousin Lorraine into New York city for a show at Radio City Music Hall. A car crossed their path and narrowly missed them. In a loud, bitter, angry tone, his aunt shouted, "Learn to drive nigger!" The tone of her voice frightened him. He had never heard the word "nigger" before. He was curious about its meaning, but felt no emotion. Fourteen years later, he met, talked, and lived with another colored man – no longer colored, but black – his roommate.

For some years they were friends, but life style differences led them to drift apart.

His Mom, aunt, and nephew liked to tell a story about Sarah. When you walked down Brook Ave, turned left on Park Avenue, and then down Park Ave toward town, on the right, there was a fire station where his grandfather Herbert and buddies volunteered. They drank Ballantine Ale at the hotel bar next to the firehouse, ostensibly, prepared for an alarm. Mostly they loved the ale and the crack. It was safer to drink at the hotel than in Sarah's kitchen, where once upon a time they drank, got drunk and brawled, and where Sarah, at five-foot three, stepped up on a stool, waved a carving knife under his grandfather's nose – about six feet off the ground – and said, "Now Shorty, you'll be drinking somewhere else." And, knowing her as he did, he and his buddies went off to the hotel.

Three moments were crystal clear in his memory. The first occurred when his mother, brother and he lived with Sarah. Occasionally, at times he was alone with her, she moved in close to him, as if a conspirator in some devious scheme. Then she would say

"Billy, they are going to send me to China." He would hear these words with naïve belief, fill up with fear of the loss of her, and utter,

"No! Grandma, don't let them do that." He did not know who they were or why they were going to send her to China, but with his whole soul he wanted her to stay.

"You won't let them take grandma away, will you?"

"No!" He knew he would resist any attempt to seize her and take her away. He had no clue what he would do. He just knew it would not happen. And, as his mind swirled in a current of fear, apprehension, and anger, she suddenly smiled, gave him a big hug, and said,

"It's okay, I know you will."

Later, in his early adolescence, she changed China to "a home for old people." By then, he knew it was a game they played, perhaps a way for her to express, in a public manner, an underlying fear. She remained independent into her 90's, then permitted Smitty to move her into "a home for old people" after she could no longer walk unaided. But the maintenance man was stung by the irony: she ended up in a home for old people, and despite all his protestations as a child, as an adult he did nothing to stop it.

The second moment occurred when his mother and grandmother (God bless them.) took him aside for a private chat one afternoon, a day or two before his wedding. "What is this about?" he asked himself. Isabelle spoke

"Sit down there on the bed, son." She pointed to a spot opposite where they sat. He did.

"We want to talk about you getting married."

"Okay. Everything is fine." Thinking they needed a word of encouragement about their part in the proceedings.

"That's good, but this is about you." And Sarah added her emphasis.

"That's right. You, precious."

"We want to know if you know what you need to do." On hearing these words, he thought – "Oh! Oh. This is about sex. Please do not ask how or what sex we have. I do not want to tell my mother or grandmother anything about the sex I have," but he only managed to mumble,

"I think I am okay there."

"Do you know what's important?" Mom. "Yes, do you?" Grandma.

"I think so."

"Let me tell you just one thing then."

"Okay."

"You have to be sure you satisfy her."

On hearing these words, the thought, "What does that mean?" filled in his brain. Clearly, a secret had been kept from him. The woman he was marrying never mentioned satisfaction.

"Son, do you understand what I am telling you? Mom again. "It's important you understand." Grandma again.

"Okay." His soft muttering.

"Do you?"

"Sure." But he did not understand. Later, after they died, to his regret, he knew he should have said "No, tell me what you mean." If he needed more explanation, he should have asked for details. He did not. Instead, he spent years trying to ensure She was satisfied with everything, everywhere – when likely they just wanted him to understand orgasm is important in the sexual life of a woman. They both died before he even thought he should ask them what they meant. It was also later that he realized they had taken him aside, risking embarrassment, perhaps fearing ridicule, out of love for him, by giving him their view about making a woman happy. They also asked

"Do you love Her?" Mom.

"Yes. I do."

"Are you sure?" Grandma.

"Yes. I am." He was. And they both said

"Good!"

Off they went. As they left the room, his smart-ass mind said to itself. "I hope they're satisfied." Then smiled, and went off to do something himself, forgetting for the moment the idea of satisfying a woman.

The third moment happened after his mother's death, which devastated his grandmother – both her daughters preceded her in death. She had watched her daughter Marge waste away from cancer, but had had time to say goodbye. His Mom, her older daughter, who nagged Sarah to stop smoking cigarettes before they killed her, died suddenly. There was no goodbye. The maintenance man and Sarah were sitting alone, when she said, with a steady flow of tears down her cheek., "The worst thing in my life has been living to see both of my children die. It should not be so. I am ready for the Lord to take me." In that simple moment of loss and pain, he lacked words of comfort, had no smart-ass comment to make her laugh, only a hug.

What did the maintenance man realize about these three women in his life? This. Isabelle urged him to be himself – choose and be. Yes. That Sarah and Isabelle set boundaries to guide him to a productive life. No question. That those two, and She, supported his choices throughout his life, despite occasional misgivings. Always. That their hearts and minds worked for his best interest, his happiness. Of course. He loved all three, in ways distinct and unique to each. That they provided experiences that formed the basis of his concept of woman.

Yes. That in their human frailty and imperfection, they sparked some misguided behaviors. True, but still he loved them. And he realized a long time later, that after his LSD trip, when he returned feeling love for all women, that that feeling was simply an idealized distillation of his experiences with three real women.

His father mourned the loss of his wife for a short period, hung out with and traveled to various parts of New Mexico with pals, passed time with women friends of his mother, and after a year or two, stopped seeing them. He said they all wanted to marry him, but he was not interested. He deflected their interest. He met a woman on his own, grew to love her, and married her. He sold his house and moved into her double-wide trailer. The trailer sat on a lot that he immediately improved by planting fruit trees, installing outside lights, building a workroom in a permanent garage, and creating a system to water the trees and a garden. With his hands busy, he was content. They lived two happy years before rapid-onset Alzheimer's disease destroyed her mind. She became paranoid, began to repeatedly call the police to report he was stealing her money or trying to kill her. In the end, his father called her son who brought her to his home in El Paso. Then the son helped her divorce the maintenance man's father, who packed his tools, clothes, and dog into his van and drove to Wisconsin to live with his son Rick. Sadness visited the maintenance man's family again, when

After his divorce, his brother Herb rented a shabby apartment and scrambled for money to comply with the settlement. Prior to the divorce, Herb got a full dose of heartache when his beautiful daughter committed suicide in her early 20's. After the divorce, only one of his remaining five children visited him on a regular basis. He developed kidney disease that required dialysis two or three times a week. Unable to work full-time, he worked part-time at Home Depot. The maintenance man started sending him $600 a month, an arrangement that lasted more than a year, until Brian, the eldest son of Herb, found him unconscious on the floor of his bathroom – a victim of a stroke. Herb ended up confined to a nursing home, on dialysis, with greatly impaired speech, and, miraculously, the same brilliant smile that he wore

– all through his life -- when poking fun, making smart-ass remarks, sassing Isabelle, and just enjoying life. In the nursing home, when the maintenance man visited him for the first time, Herb conveyed that he had fallen in love with one of his caregivers. He and the maintenance man were a lot alike. The maintenance man made several visits before he and his father left on the Tour of Water Balloons, and more after the Tour. In the latter visits Herb's pallor was unhealthy, he did not eat treats brought for him, and he was less responsive. His smile was nearly impossible to provoke. After each visit, the sadness of the maintenance man grew. In a matter of a few months his nephew called with the news,

"Uncle Bill, dad died."

"I'll be there as soon as soon as I can get a flight."

"Okay. See you then."

"Yeah."

As with his mother, he was not able to say goodbye, nor was he able to kiss his brother's forehead. Cremation. He delivered a short eulogy for Herb. Through sobs and tears, he said,

"My brother was a good, hard-working man who provided for his children." To his brother's children, each addressed by name, he said,

"Never doubt that your father loved you. He did." To both his children, and his brother's ex-wife, the maintenance man revealed,

"I am happy to say that at the end of his life, despite all his difficulties, he found a new person to love." And to himself, the maintenance man thought

"I hope his last thoughts were of his children and his new love."

Herb's death diminished, but did not extinguish, his father's liveliness. His father got up each morning, walked Sam the Sheba Innu, had breakfast at the Little Red Schoolhouse restaurant, and worked in the yard and garden. He missed Herb, said so, but it was his way to move on with life. He continued to work with his hands on stained glass and other craft projects. He did not wallow in grief. He helped Rick, with whom he lived, by doing chores around the property, and by buying food and sundries for daily life. He made friends with a down and out woman across the street, and helped her as much as he could. It was not a love interest. One day, while taking Sam for a walk, he slipped and fell, and

His end began. He was taken to the hospital with bruises, cuts, and exposure, not hypothermia. All things considered, after the hospital transferred him to a nursing and recovery center, his prognosis was good for a 94-year-old man. His condition did not improve. It was as if, once his body stopped moving, his mind discovered he had had a full life, and decided it was time to go. In the time between admission to the recovery center and his death, the maintenance man flew to Wisconsin and was with his dad. He had a motel room a ½ mile from the center and visited afternoons and evenings. On his father's last day, a caretaker fed him a full meal. His father died at 10:30 p.m. He was called back to the center. Before Neptune Society representatives took his body to cremate, the maintenance man kissed his forehead and said,

"Goodbye, Dad." No tears, simply sadness.

The maintenance man arranged his father's memorial and reception, resolved his finances and estate, disposed of his personal effects, and ensured his ashes were interred next to those of his wife. His father lived simply. Over his life, he acquired insurance policies, financial benefits from military and union participation. He did not discard, consolidate, or simplify any of them. He preferred cremation to burial, and only arranged for the small plot in Ft Bayard National Military Cemetery where the ashes of Isabelle had been interred. Three years before, in Wisconsin to rendezvous with his father for the Tour of Water Balloons – as executor of his father's trust –the maintenance man spent days with his dad in banks and credit union getting himself listed as a transfer-on-death recipient. He also had a copy of his father's trust papers and a list of his credit card accounts. Consequently, before the Tour, he felt prepared to settle his father's affairs, but feeling prepared did not actually make him prepared. He discovered,

Death created a myriad of opportunities to experience frustration. For a transfer-on-death, Bank of America required his father's death certificate and his own personal identification. These funds he placed into a trust at Great Lakes Credit Union – requiring another death certificate and personal identification. For IBEW (a 60-year member) benefits, a death certificate and union documentation. The process was similar for two John Hancock insurance policies, a Liberty Mutual policy, a Metropolitan Life policy, and a Manulife policy – all required a death certificate, personal identification, and relevant company documents. Some entities accepted scanned and emailed documents; others required a physical copy. Upon request, the Defense Finance and Accounting Service determined he had veteran benefits due. There were credit cards to pay and close. There was a car he decided should go to Rick, and did, after receiving an okay from Tom, his second living brother. The maintenance man had to dispose of his father's interest in a family trust, created in the 1800's by a Chase family member, his father's great-great-grandfather, that dispensed earnings from trust holdings to living descendants. He divided his father's trust interest among three surviving brothers and five surviving children of Herb – all properly recorded with the executor of the trust. As to

The final details required to settle the estate, doing final taxes for his father and for the trust of required the most attention. Finding and gathering the required documents and details, contacting his father's CPA, and arranging delivery of documents to the CPA was time-consuming and comprised of tasks the maintenance man detested. Proceeds of the estate were dispensed. Neptune Society shipped his father's ashes to Arizona. The maintenance man drove them to Fort Bayard National Military Cemetery and had them interred. And that was that, except departures kept coming. A year later,

Tom, his youngest brother, was diagnosed with lung cancer. He went to University of Chicago Medical Center for treatment, changed his diet, and made other life-affirming changes. He seemed to improve and took his wife to Las Vegas to celebrate an apparent victory. The maintenance man drove from Arizona to Las Vegas to see them. Tom was full of optimism and hope. To no avail, he died a little over two years after his father. Tom's death provoked less emotion than those of his wife, Sarah, Isabelle, Herb, and his father. Despite living with Tom during the year of his sabbatical at the University of Chicago,

The maintenance man knew Tom least well. He left for college when Tom was three. During summers home, he worked and visited

Her. During the year at the University of Chicago, when they might have learned more about each other, the maintenance man was at school all day, and Tom worked nights. Most days, they passed each other on their way to separate lives. After his marriage, Tom spent more time with his own, growing, family and the large extended family of his wife, choices the maintenance man accepted. He also respected Tom for pursuing an interest in the guitar, for being a positive and productive businessman, for working on behalf of his children, and for committing to a life-long relation. Viewed from his distant point, the maintenance man thought it a life lived well.

How did the maintenance man feel about these three men in his life? Just this: that each one optimistically chose a path in life, and did not settle for one forced by circumstance, tradition, or family. That each chose a path that required skill, perseverance, tolerance, and, sometimes a little audacity.

The four brothers owed their existence to the audacity of their father. While he was being trained for Signal Corps duty for the Pacific campaign, on a leave from training at a base in New Jersey, he decided to spend some time at Coney Island. He had ten cents and a return train ticket in his pocket. As he walked along the Boardwalk, his heart went pit-a-pat, his mind went blank, and his penis twitched when he saw Isabelle standing with a girlfriend at a railing. He did not hesitate. He knew what he wanted. He went up to her, and – as recounted by both parents later – the conversation went something like this

"I like you."

"So?"

"So... I would like to get to know you better."

"I'll bet you would." She had a smart-ass mouth, too.

"What do you say? Would you like a coke or something to eat?" At which point the story gets murky, except all agreed, the last thing they remember him saying was,

"But I only have ten cents, so you will have to buy this time." And

That was how their courtship started, how trips to Merrick entered his father's life, how they married, how they moved to California, how he laid telephone lines behind MacArthur while that egotist kicked

Japanese ass across islands of the Pacific, how they had two kids, separated, reconciled, had two more, and then lived until death parted them. It was their love story. The maintenance man could not think of a better one.

After Her death

―――――――――――――――

THE MAINTENANCE MAN THOUGHT ABOUT how to be responsible with money, the maintenance man realized his behavior toward money stemmed from three notions – having "enough," being able to "spend freely," and avoiding "slogging" -- notions imperfectly linked to financial and life principles like saving, earning or paying interest, investing, the money-value of time, and planning. For him,

Having "enough" emerged from specific decisions (like Hers to be debt-free and frugal). He recalled Lao Tzu wrote, "He who knows he has enough is rich." He and She chose to eat well, live in comfort, and enjoy life. Money earned satisfied these choices, hence they viewed work as a fair trade. When money was tight, they eliminated choices, and when it was ample, they added them. In a mind experiment, he compared his quality of life with those of ancient kings and rich persons of the 19th century, and doing so, believed that he was not then nor ever poor. They did eat well, lived in a warm home with hot and cold running water, flush toilets, owned reliable cars and mobile phones. When he and She talked about money, one or the other would say, "Even in tough times we have not been poor." For Her, financial security was a thing apart – She achieved freedom from debt, covered bills well ahead of due dates, and saved – always. Doing so made Her happy, so he let Her; he did not share that concern, and

Once basic needs and joint choices were satisfied, he saw remaining money as disposable -- to spend at their discretion – but She saw it as a hedge against future needs and unknown emergencies. A different notion possessed him: spend freely, without thought or care. This animal spirit collided with Her indomitable wall of frugality.

Their financial conflicts began and ended with what to do with such money, or whether they even had any. A compromise came to pass: his principal salary (with social security income added after retirement) became the family fund She managed. From the family fund he had an allowance for lunches, gas, and spending money, which he could spend freely. The consequences were his. His allowance, which never exceeded 40 dollars a week, barely kept his animal spirit alive. From time to time, She surprised him with money for an impulse. Hence, while he worked at a university, his desire to spend became a well of pent-up impulses. After leaving the university,

With a consulting business established, he gave Her the money to bring the family fund to its pre- retirement level. That done, She did not oppose him spending the rest. He loved spending. He bought state-of-the-art Pella windows for the entire house. He bought new cars for Her, Kevin, and himself. He paid most of the cost of a townhouse for Kevin. He gambled. Over 27 years, he gambled and lost more than a half a million dollars at Indian casinos. Bemusedly, he referred to these losses as "reparations."

As he continued to spend and gamble, feelings of reward diminished, although the habits lived on. Unlike ensuring "enough" – a source of pride and achievement –feeling good after spending or gambling faded fast. Habit kept him working, but a sense of "slogging" increased.

Slogging described what he felt when he worked with little or no purpose. He imagined a meadow covered with deep mud. Each step across being a separate task – difficult, filled with the danger of losing this shoe or that. If the goal –the other side of the meadow – diminished in value, the trip became more difficult. It was a slog. His work was the same, but the reward was not. Although he imagined or thought up "uses" for money – which worked the moment he fulfilled an impulse, even these imagined uses lost purpose. With gambling, he realized that he won money using money, and, over time, always lost more than he won. A vicious circle. Slogging. Each negative aspect of work increased the "slog." He recalled that soon after they married,

He chose to be responsible for earning money, and She chose to keep finances in order – choices that fit them well. In graduate school, despite meager earnings, they were comfortable. Their health was good, both were in school, and campus entertainment cheap – the sense of slogging never entered his mind. They made do with a used car and a small apartment. Only the last few days of each month – his stipend exhausted – did they feel a bite, mostly at dinner when they routinely ate tuna casserole, or spaghetti with a can of plain tomato sauce, or eggs and toast. They had each other. It was enough. In the year he became a professor at the university by the great shallow lake,

With a salary seven times greater than the assistantship stipend, they did not slog at all. She paid off his school loans and saved money. They ate at Irv's delicatessen or other local restaurants whenever they wished. They went to concerts and movies. They had health insurance, but neither children, new car, nor a house. In the two years after he resigned, between academic jobs –

Working to get by was trying, but not a slog. He drifted through jobs. She clerked for an insurance company to sustain their life style. Living so did not deter them from buying a school bus and traveling around the country with their friends Doug and Dottie. The bus trip ended in Tampa, money exhausted, and, for the first time, they faced real need. Dog Free added expenses, and after they moved to a kitchen- less, apartment, they both had to work. They did without health insurance, concerts, and movies but ate regularly at Alvarez, a good restaurant in Ybor City. Months later,

After he walked on campus without prospects and obtained two, consecutive, one-year, temporary, positions, the act of getting up to speed for those jobs distracted him from university issues. He did not consider or criticize university policy or politics. His faith in the ideals of a university remained intact, but began to fade after he obtained a permanent position and continued working. Chicanery masqueraded as a pursuit of noble goals in hiring practices. Colleagues, otherwise quite honorable. put aside academic principles in exchange for social and political milestones: he despised the creation of university positions for an un- or less-qualified spouse to insure the hire of a desired spouse. Such practices diminished his support for affirmative action.

His salary dispute taught him how naïve he had been about faculty salaries. He believed salary was linked to performance, particularly published research. When he was ignored in a salary adjustment scheme, he was angry, given: (1) his research productivity was among the highest in his college; and, (2) less productive, faculty received so-called market adjustments. Such legerdemain reduced his support for affirmative action from tepid to nonexistent. He concluded that a noble goal had been corrupted.

For nine years after the bad dean left, he walked across campus to work with Ray. There was not a whit or whiff of slogging to their collaboration. They talked, smoked, did research, and trained graduate students – he left university petty politics and corruption to others.

As the maintenance man approached 51 years, a friend, JH, expressed an interest in early retirement, and the maintenance man became interested because of their talks. He found that the age plus years of service criterion of 80 meant he could retire when he reached 54 years old. He discussed the matter with Her and She said,

"You should do it if you want, but I have one concern."

"What's that?"

"Will our income go down?"

He had done the calculations and explained that their retirement income would be about 80 percent of his pre-retirement academic salary. As any reduction in income disturbed Her. He also told her that the retirement income would continue unchanged even if he died. This fact helped her relax, but not entirely – so he said

"I will make up the difference somehow."

"How?" she wanted to know.

"I will start a consulting business. I am sure an applied statistician can find work in the real world."

"Okay then." She said in a flat, final, trusting voice. So, he decided to do it and went to talk with Ray, who asked about details, particularly about the time course of a potential deal.

"It's a three-year agreement." He told Ray.

"That works. We will be done with our last cohort by then. What do you plan on doing?"

"Right away I am starting statistical consulting to meet family financial needs."

"You should do it. There is nothing to come back to here. The department's gone. Everything is about teacher education now. There is no place here for what we do."

The maintenance man concluded Ray was looking toward his own exit, and felt he could proceed because they would have three years to work out a plan to keep working together. So,

He negotiated, then signed a three-year, early retirement agreement. During those three years, he methodically built a consulting practice. A few clients were graduate students and faculty who feared or failed to understand statistics, others were administrators of school districts facing imposed, state test and performance reporting requirements. Doing these limited, mundane projects, he earned three to four thousand dollars a month for 30-35 hours of effort, and receiving these funds eased Her concerns about finances. He maintained a four-day a week, on-campus, presence. On a day set aside for consulting, sitting in his office at home, he received a phone call. A woman introduced herself as Pamela, and asked,

"Is this statistical consulting services?"

"It is."

"I am inquiring about the possibility of working in the firm." She talked with a peculiar accent he could not place.

"Well, I am the entire firm and right now I work one day a week."

"Oh." Projecting a sense of 'well, that's that.' As an afterthought, he said,

"But I am willing to meet for coffee and discuss possibilities."

"I could do that."

They met at the student union on campus. She was a slender, attractive American woman – visibly pregnant – who talked, he concluded, in a peculiar quasi-British way, whose husband was an engineer recruited by the College of Engineering. She described her background in statistical education and her work for the National Health Service. As she described her skills and interests, he saw what she preferred matched what he did not – close to a perfect fit – and his mind turned to how they might work together. When she said she wanted to work part-time, he decided they had to work together, and they agreed to do so. Their approach to work developed quickly, in that

They met clients together; both expressed their ideas for completing tasks – although she would defer to him on issues involving advanced analyses. After a meeting, they discussed who would do what: he communicated with clients to work out data access; She took charge of "backroom" operations most of which she handled at home. A combination of personal computers, the internet, and SPSS software made it possible to operate a business, S and D Statistical Consulting Services, from two homes 35 miles apart, without ever having a formal office. From time to time, they encountered a client whose personal attributes or analytic task was too much of a slog for him. Because Pamela willingly took on these jobs, they never turned away a client. On such occasions, he felt vindicated and satisfied in his first impression that they matched so well. For him, being able to work and talk with her without effort was a source of joy, even though she was a flaming liberal infected with the blight of British socialism. Accepting this, his view ended up in the category "You cannot have everything."

An education colleague, Jay, recommended him to Bernice, a vice president of marketing for a San Diego firm that had embedded the entire K-8 curriculum in English, mathematics, and social studies inro PC-based, animated, instructional narratives. Over four and a half years, he conducted evaluations of these programs in multiple states. Free to conduct these evaluations according to his best judgment, he found the programs had a positive effect on student achievement. For four consecutive years ending in 2001, he completed meta-analytic syntheses of all the evaluation studies conducted: their products were effective, and the San Diego firm used this evidence to be become a publicly traded corporation. In the years the firm contracted his services, he earned enough to meet his, financial obligation, expand Her emergency fund, gamble regularly, give his brother Herb a monthly check, and spend in a way that fulfilled his pent-up impulses. He did not save. Other clients provided additional income which he and Pamela shared equally. He spent his share of that as well. In the final two years of the retirement agreement, as he engaged in both consulting and full-time work at the university, he and Ray graduated their last students, then turned their attention to new ventures.

They purposely decided to turn away from purely academic interests toward the notion of using their academic skills to make a boatload of money. To deny the university a claim to proceeds from their efforts, they transferred meeting, discussion, and activity from the bunker on campus to Ray's home, then went to work. With an ironic chuckle, one would say

"Fame and fortune are just around the corner" to which the other would respond,

"I can feel the breeze." Then both would light a cigar and attend to the task. They chose to follow two paths to success. The first path involved development of two paper-and-pencil tests, with the first measuring attention deficit hyperactivity disorder (ADHD) and the second measuring knowledge, behavior, and attitudes toward money.

The ADHD scale transformed attention deficit and hyperactivity symptoms listed in the fourth edition of the **Diagnostic and Statistical Manual of Mental Disorders** into straightforward statements that test takers judged did or did not describe themselves. The money scale contained 100+ items. For 80-plus items, respondents judged if an item described themselves, and for 20 knowledge items answered true or false. The initial norms for the ADHD test were developed using student samples, while the norms for the money scale were developed using general population samples. An effective, micro-computer delivery and report-generation system was created for the ADHD scale. Following a modest marketing effort, several copies of the entire computer-based package were sold. At that point, they encountered, for the first time during their collaboration, the need to invest significant amounts of money – rather than thought, discussion, and effort – for these two enterprises to proceed, which, to their surprise, neither of them had an interest in doing. Searching for and selling their ideas to potential investors threatened to be a long, uninteresting slog. Neither had the ambition to make that journey. With interest and efforts in the scales stalled,

They shifted focus to a second path to fame and fortune – forming a behavioral science consulting firm. Between them, they had contacts with Navy and Air Force persons who had provided one or the other of them small contracts to assist, measure, and evaluate training effectiveness. So, their plan was to expand such contracts. With his retirement agreement completed, and with Ray still at the university, the maintenance man won a small contract with L-3, a defense firm, to provide statistical consulting to the Air Force Human Research Laboratory. To fulfill the contract, he spent a morning a week at the lab visiting and talking with government scientists and contractors who worked for Boeing, Lockheed-Martin, or L-3. He advised and assisted on several analytic tasks -- interactions that opened the door to their second path to fame and fortune. He did not know then how taxing the slog toward future fortune would be. But,

The most important research at the lab required obtaining a top-secret security clearance. That was a slog! The slog began the moment he started to complete form SF-86—the single most intrusive tool in government procedures to ensure secrets are kept– 29 sections and 130 pages of questions delving into every aspect of a person's life – all required detailed, accurate, answers. Imagine trying to remember or recover exact addresses of every place you ever lived and names, addresses, and supervisors of every place you ever worked. Imagine having to know full names, addresses, and occupations of every friend and relative. Imagine 10 pages of questions about physical and emotional health, seven pages about experiences with police, five pages about illegal drug use, four pages about alcohol use, seven pages about finances, and five pages about personal associations. Imagine a host of other sections equally intrusive. All requiring full, truthful answers. Imagine having to swear an oath to affirm the accuracy of the responses. Then,

Imagine two FBI agents entering his home and reviewing his SF-86 responses under oath. Finally, imagine them contacting neighbors, employers, close friends, and other sources to inquire about his character. No question, for him, it was an endless slog through his whole life, past and present. To access sensitive, compartmentalized, information, like intelligence gathering methods, meant more inquiries, interviews, and training. More than six months after starting the process, he was cleared and received a badge that permitted access to classified top secret, but not compartmentalized, information (he had no need to know). To enter secured areas was a slog. Entry required that he sign in and leave all electronic devices with a guard. Exit required him to sign out and collect the devices from the guard. He had to leave any notes he took inside the secure area. Once cleared,

He consulted with government and contract personnel on classified projects. He met a young scientist, Brian, working as a contractor – an employee of Lockheed-Martin – and helped him with analyses of data he had collected in graduate school. They eventually discussed and collaborated on several projects as the maintenance man became more familiar with work at the lab. They became friends. Unlike research conducted with Ray,

Research at the lab did not excite him. There were many surveys, lots of input from subject matter experts, and a near total absence of true experiments. Further, Air Force line officers influenced studies proposed by government scientists because they provided the money that funded the research. The maintenance man observed that these officers seldom understood the intricacies of research methods – including the benefits of randomization, sampling, eliminating confounding conditions, and forming and testing hypotheses. Consequently, in the time he spent at the lab, only one project ever stirred his interest – a microcomputer-based pilot performance measurement, evaluation, and feedback system that collected data from the lab's integrated system of four state-of-the-art, airship simulators. Brian was the architect of this system, but its creation was the work of a few computer scientists. The maintenance man added nothing to its development. He kept slogging. He continued to meet with Ray to discuss general, nonsecure aspects of lab work. By 2004, their subchapter S corporation, Lumir, had been in existence for 5 years. They decided to put aside all efforts on the scales and concentrate on behavioral measurement research, specifically by focusing on obtaining Air Force contracts. Ray made one trip to the lab to re-establish contacts with scientists he knew there, but day-to-day efforts fell to the maintenance man who worked on site regularly. By the time of this decision,

The maintenance man had observed, learned, and decided that Brian, the young Lockheed scientist was the most dynamic research person at the lab. Further, Brian had a strong working relation with the most dynamic government scientist, and those two were responsible for Lockheed obtaining significant amounts of contract money. In private conversations, Brian expressed disappointment that Lockheed did not reward him at a level commensurate with the amount of contract money he secured. The maintenance man sensed opportunity, suggested to Ray that they offer Brian an interest and position in Lumir, in exchange for Brian's efforts to secure contracts. Ray agreed and they did so. Brian, a measured risk-taker, asked for time to decide. They honored his request. Beyond the intrigue of poaching talent from a big defense firm, the slog of defense work continued apace for the maintenance man. In mid- 2004,

Brian was a lead member of the team L-3 assembled for the competition for renewal of a 5-year contract to remain prime contractor. When L-3 won the contract renewal, Brian joined Lumir as CEO, and significant contract income was assigned to Lumir. They hired the lead software engineer who wrote the critical coding elements of the pilot performance measurement and evaluation system. As these events transpired, in late 2004, Ray received a diagnosis of cancer, withdrew from Lumir to face his end, and died in March, 2005. From 2005 until 2015, Lumir grew from three to 15 employees with a gross income of two million dollars per year. Fortune loomed, but sadness at the loss of his friend dampened its allure. He preferred his friend's companionship to wealth. Absent the joy of working with Ray, and not yet a close friend with Brian, slogging became permanent. He was 60 years old. For relief, he gambled. By 2010, he limited his activity at the lab to necessary policy and contract meetings, Lumir staff meetings, and focused on administration of company payrolls, contracts, and meeting federal security requirements. Just a slog through deeper mud.

The pilot performance measurement and evaluation system attracted wider attention within the Air Force and from competing companies. By 2015, Lumir staff were traveling across the country and world-wide, thereby attracting even more attention. In late 2015, a competitor offered to buy Lumir, and

Both the maintenance man and Brian were ready to sell. A deal was negotiated and closed in May, 2016. Proceeds from the sale rolled in for three years. The maintenance man supplemented family funds, spent freely, and gambled, but slogging for money ceased.

EVEN A SLOG HAS HIGH POINTS

His high points came near the end of active participation at the lab. Both were unrelated to contract work; the first occurred during an annual fund raiser, and the second occurred when the maintenance man imagined and made real the Tour of Water Balloons.

The fundraiser took the form of an auction in which various humorous, half-humiliating, humbling acts were proposed for personnel present at the fundraiser. An act was proposed for an unsuspecting victim. The remaining attendees bid to see it happen. Most bids ended at 10–15-dollars. Attitudes of Air Force personnel toward contractors led to somewhat more humiliating acts proposed for them. To the maintenance man it all seemed harmless. Then the base commander asked for bids to see the maintenance man swim the length of the base pool (some 200 feet) in his clothes. Caught by surprise, the maintenance man shifted from a quiet, composed, professional demeanor – adopted for the sake of his company – to a close approximation of his former smart-ass self. The commander himself started the bidding, and said,

"I'd pay 15 dollars to see that happen." To which the maintenance man asked

"Is that with or without shoes?"

"Without. We are not interested in seeing you drown." To which the maintenance man asked

"With or without my sports jacket?"

"Without. We are not interested in ruining a good – it is a good sportscoat – isn't it?" In which the maintenance man detected a little more than a gentle barb. So, the maintenance man said,

"To be clear, the base commander would like to see a scum-of-the-earth contractor swim this pool in his socks, pants, dress shirt and underwear? To which the commander said,

"Yup." Hook set, but mindful of the good cause, the maintenance man responded,

"Well, the scum-of-the-earth contractor will bid 25 dollars to see it not happen." The commander took the bait.

"30 dollars."

"35 dollars."

Alternately, 40 and 45, 50 and 55, 60 and 65, 70 and 75 dollars were bid, and the commander paused. So, the maintenance man said,

"I guess wages in the private sector beat those in the Air Force." There was more than a bit of laughter among the attendees, so the commander said,

"100 dollars." And the maintenance man relented, took off his shoes and coat and jumped in the pool. Before swimming, he asked for someone to swim alongside. After the shock of the water, he did not know if he could make the distance. A couple of grunts, prepared for this eventuality, jumped into the pool, and shadowed him to the other end. Exhausted, he climbed out to a round of applause, picked up his shoes and coat, went to his car, drove to Walmart, bought jeans, a shirt, and some underwear, returned to work and finished the day happy.

The second high point was the maintenance man's attempt to generate some viral publicity for his fancifully labeled 2010 Tour of Water Balloons. He filled 200 balloons with water and took them to the lab, solicited lab personnel to throw these balloons at him as he rode past on Kent Street. He conceived this event as an instructional exercise as well, one pass to demonstrate inappropriate methods and one pass demonstrating acceptable methods tossing a water-filled balloon at a person on a bicycle. The exercise was a rowdy, rousing success, although the video never went viral. At last check, several Tour-related videos are still available on You-Tube.

BECAUSE OF HER, HE TOURED THE BEAUTIFUL WORLD OF SPANISH

AFTER THEIR TRIP TO D.F., the sprawling, noisy, capitol of Mexico, where shyness kept Her from speaking Spanish, She led him through what he should say, and one brief, halting sentence at a time, they proceeded through a week of sights, sounds, and dining.

He remembered devoted pilgrims trekking to the Basilica of Our Lady of Guadalupe—most walking, some crawling, some on their knees, and a solitary man on his stomach. What faith! From the window of his hotel, he watched people living on roofs of buildings opposite. As he and She walked the streets or rode the metro, hands attached to despairing eyes sought money, dented their budget, and stirred feelings of responsibility. Why so many? He had no idea.

He acquired an abiding interest in Spanish, and pursued it by taking university courses. Regarding fluency, he judged himself mediocre, yet took comfort in warm responses of native speakers when he conversed with them. Most of his time at home and work, he lived in an English world, had no thoughts of immersion in a Spanish world, yet, – surprise – after Arpanet became Bitnet, a Spanish woman and a Spanish-speaking Basque woman used that medium to contact him, and

Life-long friendships flourished. The Spanish woman, Juana, requested his articles, and any others he might have, on meta-analysis. He copied, boxed up, and sent everything -- to her stunned surprise. Via Bitnet, he described his work on subjective well-being, and further e-mails led to a joint study of subjective well-being among Spanish elders. He traveled to Barcelona and stayed with her and her family.

After the visit, they traveled to Madrid and presented the results at an international conference. In time, they published the findings. In Spain, he fell in love with España. It was the first of many visits.

The Basque, Nekane, contacted him the same way. They collaborated on articles (two with Juana) on meta-analysis, Euskera-Castellano bilingual education, and psychometric qualities of Lumir's ADHD scale. On a trip to España, he first met Nekane in a train station in Donostia, and then she, a devil-may- care, demented, driver, chauffeured him to Ordizia – her pueblo. They presented a paper in Lisbon. His animal spirits were enchanted – on a path to being aroused – by her exuberant femininity, but after telling him of her love for her future husband Victor, he, always, simply treated her as a friend. Later, she came to the United States to present a paper at a convention of an educational research association. Nekane stayed in their home with them, then she traveled with him to the meeting.

For the maintenance man, trips to Spain formed a collage of images and memories. He could not separate one trip from another. Every trip, he visited Juana in Barcelona and Nekane in Ordizia. The two were distinctly different. Juana, mature, reserved, and analytic, was a thorough scholar. Nekane was enthusiastic, excitable: she pursued scholarship colored by politics of the Basque country. Through their own communications, Juana and Nekane became friends and collaborators. Each became a catedrática – an academic achievement of the highest order. Each, and her family, provided stable moorings for his trips, so that his memories of España entwined with memories of the families who opened their homes to him.

Pedro, husband of Juana, spoke no English, loved to take the maintenance man on trips around Barcelona. On the first visit, Pedro took him on an evening tour of the area around the Universitat Autònoma de Barcelona – just a set of academic buildings to the maintenance man. Instead of driving on El Diagonal, he drove along a parallel frontage road very slowly. The maintenance man sat next to him.

Juana sat in the back seat. Pedro reached over and touched his arm, then pointed to shadows along the sidewalk as he slowed the car.

244

A woman emerged from the shadows and approached the car. As she did, she opened her blouse to present a full view of her bare breasts. Pedro asked,

"¿Qué piensas?" The maintenance man replied

"No he visto algo como eso en los Estados Unidos."

Pedro laughed, then he and Juana had a brief, rapid conversation that the maintenance man failed to understand, while Pedro continued driving as before and pointed out one or two more women who did the same thing. Pedro started a conversation, interspersed with the question,

"¿Me entiendes? To which the maintenance man inevitably replied

"Un poquito"

As they drove out of the area, the maintenance man wondered, then asked

¿A esas mujeres les molesta la policía?

"No."

"¿Porqué no?"

"Porque no son mujeres."

"¿Qué?"

"Ellos son hombres."

Men! Publicly displaying breasts! Soliciting sex. From men? That he had never seen in the States, and hoped he would not.

A second night, the three visited the magic fountains of Montjuïc, a display of myriad colors and innumerable fountains gushing water, synchronized to music, first seen at the Great Universal Exhibition of 1929. Other tours explored the Gothic quarter, Barceloneta and its beach, the abbey of Santa Maria de Montserrat, home of a black Madonna, and buildings designed by the architect Antoni Gaudi.

Each time in Barcelona, he visited la Sagrada Familía – a vision of Gaudi – whose construction began in 1882, and neared completion 140 years later. Simply magnificent, La Sagrada Familia is the one man-made structure that strengthens the maintenance man's belief in the importance of faith.

In España, in Madrid, he was on his own. He strolled El Parque Retiro. He visited the Prado to view the paintings of Goya and

Velasquez, then went to examine the painting *Guernica* by Picasso. That huge canvas depicts effects of a carpet-bombing campaign, in which planes of the Luftwaffe's Condor Legion and Italian Aviazione Legionaria, both of which comprised Franco's nominal Spanish air force, bombed the Basque pueblo of Guernica during the Spanish civil war. After Franco prevailed and became dictator, he initiated carpet-bombing campaigns against the languages of Cataluña and the Basque country. With his death and adoption of the 1978 accords of autonomy, Catalan, language of Cataluña, recovered, but Euskera, language of the Basques, continued to have an uncertain future.

He traveled with one small bag that contained a pair of pants, three or four shirts, a jacket, three or four sets of underwear and socks, nicotine gum, and toiletries. On trips of 15-20 days, he needed to wash clothes. His first time in Madrid, this need led him to wander the streets to find a lavandería. He set off from his hotel with a plastic bag containing all his dirty clothes. He wanted a coin-operated, self-service, laundromat. To achieve his goal, he used a frank approach. He advanced toward a friendly face and asked,

"Disculpe, ¿sabe dónde hay una lavandería donde puedo lavar la ropa? "

Some said no. Some gave him directions which invariably led to a tintoría. In every tintoría, he discovered helpful people that would wash and iron (or fold) his clothes, but under no circumstances would they let him wash his own clothes. After several such encounters, he headed back to the hotel. On his way, another Spanish lady came into his life. She was

Dressed in scruffy jeans, beautiful, young, with blonde hair and a slender build. To his surprise, she had a wooden baton hanging from a leather thong wrapped around her wrist. She stepped into his path, and he asked himself, "What's this?" She spoke rapidly. All he understood were words for hotel and room. He assumed she wanted to return to his room with him, nevertheless, again he asked

"Disculpe, ¿sabe dónde hay una lavandería donde puedo lavar la ropa?" She stopped talking. He asked again. "¿Sabe dónde hay una lavandería donde puedo lavar la ropa?"

She shook her head no. More disconcerting, she gripped her baton, and stepped back from him with a puzzled, miffed expression. He thought she might hit him with the baton. She did not. Then he thought she might think he was asking her to wash his clothes. She said no more. She turned away. So, he said

"Adios señorita" and turned and walked toward the hotel again, and

As he neared the entrance, an idea lit him up – a ray of hope – which led him to a taxi stand in front of the hotel, where he asked the first driver, muy amable,

"Disculpe, ¿sabe dónde hay una lavandería donde puedo lavar la ropa?"

"No hay." There was no laundromat where he could wash his own clothes. He asked "En todo la ciudad, no hay?"

"Sí. Y no hay en todo España."

Amazing!

More amazing was the hospitality Sara and Iñaki, parents of Nekane, and Victor, her husband. Beyond opening their homes to him, as proud Basques, they took him to Txindoki, a mountain with a spiritual aura, located in the province of Gipuzkoa. They walked a road at its base, stopped in an inn for wine, while Iñaki described how he hiked Txindoki in search of mushrooms. In Ordizia, Iñaki led him on el rondo through the bars of Ordizia. On el rondo

The two of them would enter a bar, order a small glass of wine, and talk with friends and neighbors of Iñaki, finish their wine, and head to the next bar to repeat the ritual. On el rondo, he heard stories of the civil war from old men who experienced it as children. Hearing about the loss of parents, aunts and uncles, or other family members made sad listening. One old man sang Basque folk songs for him. The emotion of the old man's singing drew tears to the eyes of the maintenance man. On another visit, Sara and Iñaki drove him to Guernica where they had tapas and visited the Tree of Guernica, an oak tree, and a symbol of the independence of Euskadi.

After several trips, he sought a way to return the favor of hospitality that the two families extended to him. Giving physical gifts embarrassed him, so, for some time, he could not decide what to do. When Jordi, the son of Juana, came to the States, he drove to LAX to pick he and a friend up, then drove them back to the Arizona desert. As they drove along the Salton Sea, they were flanked by the Sea on the right and a great, long, freight train on the left. The Spaniards were astonished by its length. The maintenance man provided accommodations and took them to see the Grand Canyon. Yet, this individual act of hospitality failed to fulfill his desire to do something for the entire families. One day,

Reading the Wall Street Journal, he encountered a story about Rekondo, a restaurant in Donostia. The story told of two New York city wine lovers interested in drinking an obscenely expensive wine ($8000 or more per bottle in New York) with dinner. Via the internet, they learned Rekondo had a world-class wine cellar and a bottle of the wine they sought – at much lower price. They traveled to Donostia for dinner and the wine. Although the Journal article focused on economics – the cost of their flights, accommodations, dinner, and wine in Spain was less than the cost of the wine in New York city – the maintenance man's mind was aroused by descriptions of the restaurant, its wine cellar, and experiences of the New Yorkers. In a self-evident moment, he knew he would treat his Basque family to dinner at Rekondo, then repeat the gesture in Barcelona with Juana's family.

Rekondo, on the east slope of Mount Igueldo, overlooked the old city of Donostia-San Sebastian and La Concha, a scimitar-shaped beach that is the shore of the city's half-circle bay. The restaurant's terrace, dining rooms, and wine cellar exuded casual elegance in a simple, classical, manner that the maintenance man thought," perfect for dinner." He sat at one end of the table, between Iñaki and Luis Mari, father of Victor, while Nekane sat at the other end with Sara and Belén, mother of Victor. Amaia, Nekane's daughter, sat in the middle of the table. A waiter, holding the 100-page wine list, came and stood before the men. The fathers deferred and the waiter handed the list to the maintenance man, who started to review the list, then stopped because his ignorance of wines made making a choice just a random act. Consequently, he turned to the waited and said,

"Quiero lo mejor vino que cuesta unos dos cientos euros…" but could not voice a request for a recommendation because Luis Mari interjected

"Disculpe Guillermo!"

In the same moment, Iñaki took the list from his hand, indicated to the waiter to come back later, and began talking with Luis as they reviewed the list. The maintenance man tried to protest, to exclaim his desire for a wine to match the occasion, to use two hundred of the four hundred euros set aside for wine. They simply ignored him, continued to review the list, and agreed on a wine. They summoned the waiter and indicated their choice. Everyone ordered. The meal was good. The wine was good. The conversation was as good as the maintenance man could muster. The dinner was purpose-perfect.

In Barcelona, Juana, Pedro and two of their three children were his guests at a small restaurant – Pedro's choice. He also ordered. As in Donostia-San Sebastian, the food was excellent, but it was the spectacle associated with one dish that made an indelible impression on the maintenance man. The waiter brought a dish – about a foot long and two-inches deep – to the table with twenty or twenty-five small fish spread across the bottom. He displayed the plate of fish to the diners poured a little olive oil into the dish, displayed the dish again, and poured a second, unknown, liquid into the dish. The maintenance man anticipated eating raw, oily, fish, but the waiter stopped, looked at each diner with a quizzical expression on his face. He asked.

"Algo falta. ¿Qué podría ser?" No one responded. The waiter continued

"Creo que necesita sal." And proceeded to put an ample measure of salt into the dish, to swish it gently, and examine the contents. It was obvious that the mixture was still liquid, and as the waiter examined it, the same quizzical look spread across his face. He spoke

"Creo que todavía falta algo. ¿Qué podría ser?" A second time no one responded, although a sense of play passed among them. The waiter went on

"Es obvio que necesita mas sal, ¿no? And proceeded to pour another ample measure of salt into the dish, swish it carefully, and examine the result – still quite liquid. His quizzical expression returned. He asked

"Otra vez, creo que todavía falta algo. ¿Qué podría ser?" Now the diners understood the game the waiter played, so Pedro said

"Mas sal." And the waiter smiled and replied

"Si." He poured in a third measure of salt, at which the maintenance man started imagining what it would be like to eat small, oily, fish with that much salt. He reflexively took a sip of water. Meanwhile, after he swished the mixture again, the waiter appeared truly perplexed, faced the diners, and uttered

"Lo siento, pero, creo que todavía falta algo. ¿Qué podría ser?" To which all the diners responded "Mas sal." And the waiter smiled and replied

"Si." He poured in a fourth measure of salt, swished the mixture which had firmed up considerably, became perplexed again, and asked

"Señores, ¿creen ustedes que necesita un poco de sal? Laughing, they all gave their affirmation "Si!" "Por supuesto!" "Es obvio!" Of course, the waiter complied, turned the dish over onto a flat plate and with purposeful attention extracted the fish, one-by-one, from the salt and placed them on a clean platter, from which he served two or three to each of the diners, leaving the remaining fish to be selected by those who wanted more. The maintenance man, his anticipation intact, took a first careful bite on a small fish that had been placed on his plate. How could this be?!

The fish was delicious. Of course, there was a light fish taste. There followed a pleasant hint of olive oil, and finally, only the tiniest of hints of salt. How could this be?! He did not know. He did not care, finished those on his plate, and reached for the platter for more.

Other times he ate sheep's brains – no thanks; squid in its own ink with rice -yes; tapas – many ways to say "Yummy;" drank zumo de naranja natural – more please; and hot chocolate served with churros – outstanding. He saw aqueducts, churches, buildings with long histories, and universities. He used metros, trains, planes, and buses to travel. He met Angel, a professor who loved MacDonald's quarter-pound cheeseburgers. Asi, he spent time in España, but most of all he remembered his two friends, strong women, la Sagrada Familia, a tribute to faith, and a young woman of the street who wanted something, but not to help him find a place to wash his own clothes.

A LITTLE PENIS REACHES A LONG WAY

IN ENCOUNTERS WITH WOMEN, HE felt neither wise nor worldly, rather waifish. He and She made love thousands of times – acts inseparably tied to Her. With each of three other women he had sex once, with a fourth he made love twice. There were no others. Two incidents of a sexual nature set his moral compass right. On occasions he deliberately dominated encounters, he felt powerful which fused with his doubt about sexual prowess and with curiosity into an ambiguous blend that caused him to ask: on which side of the line between the light and dark am I? He asked himself,

"Am I corrupt? Is my soul intact?" He had no certain answer. For him,

Everything sexual began on Long Island while he, Herb, and Isabelle lived in Merrick with Sarah – as his parents sorted their lives. His aunt lived with her husband and daughter in nearby Valley Stream, and the sisters, with children in tow, visited frequently. After one sleepover, the children rose before the aunts, played, undressed, and examined each other. The body of his cousin fascinated him. Her vulva (the first and last he saw for years) was where he had a penis. In turn, the brothers' pre-pubescent penises intrigued her.

Instinctively, impulsively, immune to condemnation, his brother tucked his penis and testicles back toward his anus, put his thighs together, and announced,

"Look at me. I am a girl!" The maintenance man imitated, and asserted,

"I am a girl too!" And the three marched around the house naked, proclaiming,

"I am a girl. I am a girl. I am a girl." until they stood in front of the aunts, newly awake, wide-eyed, visibly restraining laughter. The words his mother uttered reverberate still.

"Boys, where are your little wee wees?" She used diminutives like "wee wee," "peanut," or "little thing," to refer to penises – his or any other -- and never used "dick," "penis," or "cock." Cheeky Herb answered at once.

"Right here, Mom!" as he spread his legs, restored his genitals to their proper place, and beamed with pride – this act mimicked by the maintenance man. Briefly stone still and speechless, the aunts' mirth burst, like sunshine, and illuminated the room. Their laughter laced their sputtered statements about how little boys and girls should play together -- as they hustled the children into clothes.

That morning set a permanent emotional tone to his relations with women: curiosity, mirth, a bit of "It's not proper," but not "You shouldn't do that!"

In thrall one day on seeing the full, naked, breasts of his grandmother Sarah as she dressed after a bath, she saw him and smiled. Without shame, she kept dressing, as if to say "It's just life." and added another nuance to that emotional tone.

When his parents' separation took him from a Chicago school with a half-year calendar to a Long Island school with a full-year calendar, and as the school staff judged him capable, he was advanced a half-year, missed introduction to multiplication, and, struggled with it at first. One day, as he oozed exasperation, a classmate came next to him, stood there, put her arm around his upper arm, rested her opposite hand on his back. She tried to explain. Hairs on his arms and neck tingled as they rose with goosebumps. He shivered as pleasant sensations sloshed in his mind. More nuance. Years later, at fourteen years old,

The maintenance man woke one morning –after only recently having stopped bedwetting – and found his underpants moistened by a viscous fluid where the tip of his erect penis brushed them. Had he wet the bed? No. Something else. He changed shorts, told no one, and asked: Had he come? Had he had a wet dream? Maybe. He recalled no dream. From then, sex in dreams meant wet dreams. Those dreams, as well as his fantastical, wide-awake musings about girls, differed from those about his grandmother or mother. He learned masturbation, with or without musings, caused ejaculation while awake, and unlike dreams, added physical nuances to the emotional tone of his attitude toward girls and women. The same year,

Two incidents added somber nuances to that tone. The first happened a day he was home alone. A three-year old girl, dressed in underpants and t-shirt, wandered there from her nearby home. He had her come in. She explored the house, touched this and that, and ended in a bedroom with him nearby. She acted tired so he had her lay on his bed, and patted her back. What to do? He wanted to move his hand over and down her body. Curiosity encouraged a desire to proceed, but like a visitor to a foreign border, he hesitated, wondered, and looked at her. She looked at him with wide, sleep-softened, eyes and made a small, apprehensive, not quite whimpering, sound that unleashed a sequence of memories: a cry of a baby bird he had crushed; his mother's sadness and disappointment; the words she spoke; the sense of guilt he felt on seeing her face and hearing her words; and, the experience of forgiveness at her hug. Instinctively, he knew it was wrong to yield to his curiosity about the little girl. The gossamer strand of those memories, like the thread of a spider's web, stopped him from touching her. He got her up, took her home, came back home, relieved somehow. Did he do right? He thought so – but still felt guilty– he had come so close! If she had not made that sound? If he had not told his mother about crushing the baby bird? What might have happened?

Later that summer, a second incident involved the maintenance man, his friend K, and the Y brothers – all from the same subdivision – as they traipsed through a forest along the banks of the river that flowed along the western edge of the subdivision. They sought adventure. They threw stones at large, sluggish, carp loitering in shallow pools. They picked up dead limbs, smashed them against trees, played at pirates, dodged each other's blows, and ducked in and out among the trees. This noisy crew rambled on until they reached a meadow of tall grass dotted with patches of red- and blackberries – bushes heavy with ripe fruit protected by nasty thorns. As they crossed the meadow toward the largest patch, K spotted a neighbor girl, 11 or 12 years old, who must have followed them after they passed her yard. K said as much. The boys dispersed to collect berries, and regrouped to eat them. Sitting there, K said,

"She's closer."

"So?"

"So, let's call her over."

"Why?"

"Let's see what happens." K had something in mind, but said nothing more. Rather, he called and invited the girl over. She came closer and stood nearby. K made his intent clear when he said

"Come here and take off your clothes for us." Neither the Y brothers nor maintenance man spoke. Silent, frozen observers, they waited. The girl shook her head no and moved a bit away. K continued to encourage her to take off her clothes. She kept stepping back. K stood up. She turned, walked away at a quick pace. K followed her, and said in a voice loud enough for both she and his friends to hear,

"Let's get her!" The others stayed dumb. The girl ran through the last bit of the meadow and into the forest. K followed 30 or 40 yards behind. The others followed K. As he ran, the maintenance man thought of the three-year old girl. Was this not the same circumstance? He ran a few more steps, then stopped. The Y brothers stopped. The moral circumstances of this episode differed little from the first. Why was it wrong? Why had he stayed silent? Did curiosity stop him from speaking out against K's request to the girl or his command to them? In that moment, he did not know. Minutes later, K returned, smiling, and said,

"She got home." The three said little, shuffled around, and looked for a distraction, then headed home. It took the maintenance man many years to understand that knowing an action is wrong is not sufficient to prevent being drawn into it. He had to choose and act correctly. On these two occasions he nearly committed sexual abuse. Twice, the same single thread of thought and emotion prevented it. He realized curiosity did not justify immoral acts. Restraint by him and consent by the other person became guidelines of his future behavior, but he could not articulate these guides until later. In mid- and late life, two social movements begun and promoted by women ("No means no." and "Me too.") clarified and confirmed his own conclusion. He accepted the premises of those movements, but not all the tactics of the latter. He felt satisfied with his perspective, but remained uncertain why he had not spoken against K's command. Ultimately,

The tone of his feelings towards women was nurtured by the care they displayed toward him, and by their actions toward him. He believed his concept of love rested on that tone. From fifth grade through senior year of high school, specific girls elicited hair-raising, tickling goosebumps and pleasant, sloshing, sensations, as well as the urge to do more – but he did not, because

He did not know how. Doubt and anxiety mitigated the pleasant sensations evoked by girls in his thoughts, dreams, and presence, and roiled the enjoyable emotional waters rippling in his adolescent brain. Some of his anxiety came from shame, rather from attempts by Isabelle to shame him -- she did not understand why he wet the bed. She tried many tactics to prevent it. Hours before bedtime she limited his liquids. That did not work. Sometimes, she woke him after hours of sleep and took him to the toilet to pee. That failed. She threatened actions meant to shame him. She threatened to put him in diapers – but did not— and to hang his urine-stained sheets in public – but did not. In the end, she washed his sheets, protected the mattress with a rubber sheet, and regularly expressed frustration. For the maintenance man, in all honesty, the surprise ("How could this be?") felt on waking in wet shorts on a wet sheet outweighed any shame. One day, bedwetting just stopped. A residue of anxiety about a possible relapse replaced whatever shame he had had.

As a member of the faculty of the university by the dry river bed, the maintenance man spoke of bedwetting with his friend Keith, an expert on enuresis who used behavior modification techniques to build devices to treat the condition. Keith's soft-spoken, rational views diminished his anxiety. Perhaps, he did not let go entirely of the feeling with which he had lived so long, because his mind found a place for the residue -- it accompanied him to classes, and to academic conversations.

Anxiety held him back a bit, but never silenced him – he loved to argue too much – about just about anything – and other aspects of his personality pushed him past doubt and anxiety. With girls,

It was different. For women and men alike, he saw them involved with more than seeing life in a rational way. He preferred being analytic, and looked for rational solutions to problems between himself and others. It helped if they held the same belief. In his view, girls, women, mothers, and grandmothers had more on their mind than rationality, whereas, boys, men, fathers, and grandfathers seldom did. For him, women (not all) looked for signs of the disposition of others towards them. He believed they did this to insure their physical, emotional, and psychological safety, whereas men (not all) watched actions and listened to others to decide what they had to do then and there – not to think ahead. Doubt did not help him understand this difference. Regarding doubt, he had his fair share. He was intensely curious about the girls he knew and saw. Puberty increased his motivation to do something, but

The facts that his post-puberty, flaccid, penis was small, that his erect penis did not ever exceed five inches in length (nor average girth), and that his culture deified BIG (tits and dicks), amplified his doubt. He had no direct evidence on which to gauge his ability to be good at sex, rather, only the information from his immediate environment of friends, family, reading, movies, and television – not one completely reliable. He spoke brusquely– even as a child. Doubt and brusque speech accompanied his intelligence, his confidence in his thoughts, and his tendency to be indolent. Overall, he felt curious, tentative, and unique, and wondered where his body and mind would take him? First,

During high school and first year of college, his qualities led to relations with girls that were both exciting (girls showed interest) and disappointing (he pulled back). He remained a virgin. Among his male friends, sexual intercourse with a girl was a holy grail. He thought so too. Setting aside a love of arguing, he was no different from his friends. As they did, so too he exaggerated his activities with girls, but never lied about his virginity. At the start of his second year of college, 18 years old, when he first saw Her Mona Lisa countenance and beautiful eyes,

He felt (knew, hoped) everything would be different. After a college picnic that started each school year, he asked her out. She smiled and said yes. In her eyes he saw both a bright, promising, future, and a lurking sadness. Her gaze radiated hope, sadness, and resignation simultaneously. She seemed like an elegant sloop dragging a sea anchor. He felt happy and full of anticipation. Their life together began. At first,

They dated —not exclusively. She dated both him and his roommate early in the semester. He had a few dates with others, but his thoughts relentlessly returned to Her. Curiosity confounded him. He wanted to touch every part of Her. After She set his roommate aside, they moved toward exclusivity. In their community of 400 students, being, or being perceived as, exclusive ensnared them in ritual. Couples were a topic of general interest. All knew who was with whom, talked or speculated about outcomes and prospects, and, on a need-to-know basis, raised questions. If he went out with another woman, first she asked

"Aren't you with Her?" followed by questions about his intentions toward herself. He responded

"Yes, but not exclusively." Eventually, he focused on Her, and on knowing Her in all ways. They became a data point in Mr. VB's record of couples who met at college and, in time, married.

Another ritual, with variations for good and bad weather, evolved from being at that small college in a small town in farm country, where students were not permitted to have cars. On evenings with clement weather, couples strolled to secluded, off-campus spots nearby, spread blankets, did what they wanted, assured others would respect the convention and not bother them. The woods and high grass around the campus served many. On evenings with inclement weather, after dinner, couples (save eight seniors who shared four rooms in the gym) hurried to secure a classroom in a classroom building, draped an article of clothing on the outside doorknob, went inside, and "studied." Occasionally, benign hooligans ran through the classroom buildings, knocked on doors, sometimes opened them, and said,

"Oops! Sorry," then laughed and ran on.

As He and She moved from less to more intimacy, they embraced the rituals. Sensations in his penis, and a mind full of curiosity, impelled him. She chose caution, but was also interested and curious. Because Her primary focus was academic success, before they "studied," She insisted they study. For him, that meant math and chemistry. They did, and often surprised the devilish hooligans with the firm assertion, voiced in unison,

"We are studying! Shut the door!" as they wryly smiled at each other. Even after they started a "study" sessions, sexual intercourse did not follow right away, or always. Mundane obstacles littered the path to intercourse. Before he accessed Her breasts, She had to teach him how her brassiere hooked and unhooked. And She found it quite amusing on the occasions when he fumbled for hooks on a back- clasping bra, and needed to be told the clasps were in the front. For him, for an interminable time, She wore a girdle. Doing so thwarted exploring Her genitals. He nagged her to stop wearing it. Her conflict between wanting the appearance of a firm fanny and becoming more physically intimate ended in favor of intimacy. Hooray! With the girdle gone, he kissed her mouth, neck. and shoulders, caressed her breasts, explored her vulva with his hand, fingered her labia and vagina. Naïve, he knew not the function of her clitoris. She had to guide him, and correct his behavior toward it. She kissed him, caressed his chest and back, and explored his testicles and penis, usually erect. They came to this state of intimacy in winter, when classrooms provided the only privacy for them, and entertainment for unattached, devilishly benign, hooligans who hoped to catch couples in an act of sex. They hesitated to go all the way, until

One evening they bagged the trustees' board room – carpeted, with a large table that blocked a view of the floor from the door. Imagine soft carpet instead of hardwood floors! Imagine the allure of concealment from hooligans! Imagine making love in a room set aside for hoity-toity college trustees and administrators! Imagine two adolescents hot for each other! It was perfect! They made love, and after,

Doubt impelled him to ask, "Okay?"

She replied, as a Mona Lisa smile lit her face, "Yes, okay. Relax."

From then on, they made love when they could. He did not lose interest or curiosity in other women, however, given his affection for Her, and his doubt, he put aside impulses to act. Their first winter as a couple, the maintenance man's family traveled to Tucson for a family reunion. On the three- day journey there, they ate in a variety of places, some of dubious quality. They ate Mexican food for the first time in Lordsburg. He had hot Mexican chili! Weeks after his return to school, well into the spring semester, he started to feel bad, peed bright orange urine, and ached all over. He went looking for Her at a basketball game. On his way and in the gym, students kept asking,

"Why are you so yellow?" "Why are your eyes yellow?" "Do you feel alright?"

"No, as a matter of fact, I don't."

"You should see the nurse." And so, the next day he did. In minutes he was in hospital, flat on his back, hardly able to move – feeling he did not want to live. Still very sick, happiness filled him the first time she was permitted to visit. Nurses came and went at all hours. They fed him mush, Jello, and pudding. They took blood to measure bilirubin to track the progress of his recovery. He missed classes for two weeks. After she was permitted to see him, every day she brought assignments, and left with what needed to go back to his classes. At the end of that semester, he achieved his highest grade-point average. He lost his ability to handle alcohol, and for the next 15 years did not drank, nor miss it, because She filled the hollows into which he had previously poured vodka.

The bond between them grew. He knew She did not like his sharp-tongued style of speaking to others. He tried to be less so. They shared a conviction that there was a strong bond between them. Jealous when other men showed interest in Her, he believed Her when She said he should not worry. He relaxed when She showed or said She liked his penis. She stopped wearing makeup when he said he did not care for it. They had no money, and made do with what parents sent. She tolerated and supported his gambling (pitch, a farmers' game, and poker) –by sharing money from Her father– because he won more often than he lost. When he won, they had treats and danced at the student union.

When he lost, they watched TV, went for walks, or studied. After sex, depression sometimes overwhelmed Her. She took a long time to speak about the source of Her depression – childhood abuse by Her step-father – but right from the first, She accepted his embraces, womaned up, and tried to live in the present. His efforts were palliatives. She spent years in thought and reflection, made inexorable progress, and became Her own person. He believed it was a miracle! Her struggle was a fixture of their life, but

Their first summer apart, there were immediate concerns. How were they going to see each other living 50 miles apart without cars? His dad helped in two ways. First, his dad's good friend Willard gave the maintenance man a janitor's job in a high-rise building on Addison Ave and Lake Shore Blvd, more than halfway to her home. To get to the job, he took the North Shore Line, then the El to Addison Ave, then walked to the building. After work on Friday, he took the El, transferred to a bus, got off at Canal St and walked to Phyllis's apartment. He often stayed over. If Phyllis worked Saturday, they made love after she left. Second, some Fridays he went home. On Saturday, his father would lend him the car to drive to the city with the stipulation that he return the same day. They did not have an opportunity to make love, and passed the time going for pizza, hot dogs, or Italian beef sandwiches, made visits to Maxwell Street, and drove to parks and dark places to make out.

His last two years at college, they were together most of the time. They studied diligently (She) or lackadaisically (he), did their work (She the laundry and kitchen, he as janitor or as a counterperson in the student union), ate together, participated in intramural sports, went to church, and enjoyed what diversions exist in a small, Illinois, farm town. Twice, for Christmas break, they rode the G M & O to Chicago. In the spring of his last year, after he had been accepted to graduate school, conversation turned to what they should do. He wanted Her to go with him to the university in corn country. His anxiety increased when he thought of going without Her. At first, she wanted to stay. She had made two very good friends (Fay and Judy) and wanted to stay close. Their finances made clear they had to live together to get by at the larger school. A tentative speculation followed,

"Maybe we should get married." Far from enthusiastically, she said

"I don't know." They left it there for a few days. One day, after courage swept away his doubt and anxiety, he said,

"I love you. Will you please marry me?" That was all he could manage. She looked at him, her eyes focused directly on him, a shy gentle smile on her face, and said in a soft voice

"Yes. I will." In that moment, there were no other words. After a bit, one or the other said "We have to tell our parents." And the other answered,

"Yes. We do." Thus, began a slog (for them) through wedding plans, choices, and the ceremony itself – their last moments of childhood, of meeting mothers' expectations and purported obligations. Dutiful, they met each expectation and obligation. Three days after the wedding, they found themselves alone in a brand-new, married-students, apartment on the campus of the university in corn country.

They were 21 years old, with money (not much, but more than ever before), and a reliable used car. They spent a lot of time on studies, but still traveled the state, spent time with friends playing cards and board games, and smoked marijuana (from the second year on). Along the way, She taught him to be gentler when they made love. She continued to make positive steps in Her struggle against abuse-induced depression. Toward the end of four years at university, She encouraged him to persevere and finish his dissertation, rather than quit and move to Canada. He heard Her and did. They seldom argued. When they did,

The most recurrent topic was money. He wanted to spend, She wanted to save. Assistantship wages supported neither well – rent and food consumed it all, leaving each with a pent-up desire to fulfill their money dream. In their last year, a friend, Richard, of Dr. WB provided the maintenance man with a point of contact at a university by the shallow Great Lake. When Richard left that university for another, the maintenance man slipped right into the friend's old job. Wages grew seven or eightfold. They felt rich! There were discussions about what to do, but the sheer quantity of money supported some of the desires of each. He balanced the checking account and wrote the checks until the day She saw red-ink in the balance column of the ledger. An argument followed. The result of this argument was that She became CFO, assumed possession of the checkbook, and kept it for the rest of their lives. His impulses to spend became "wants" in Her budget. Some got funded, some did not. He accepted the arrangement because She paid the bills, hid extra savings, and told him when he could fulfill a "want." He learned some restraint. At the end of the academic year, She gave him a receipt -- his school loan promissory notes paid in full. Save a mortgage, they remained debt free all their lives.

In the year he worked at the university by the shallow Great Lake, they smoked marijuana regularly, and used mescaline and peyote. After each had a miserable LSD acid trip, they did not use it again.

They lived up the hill from the university in the Coventry neighborhood – center of a counterculture comprised of old Jews, hippies, and habitual, hard drug addicts. Sporting dark shoulder-length hair and a full beard, he felt good when old Jewish ladies called him rabbi. They insisted he looked like a rabbi. Had use of hallucinogens transformed him into a spiritual being? Not really. In high school and college, he read about mystical experiences (e.g., *Zen Bones*, *Tao Te Ching*, and books by Watts and Castenada) and was drawn to message therein. Yet among choices life presented and by the decisions he made, none led that way. Instead, use of drugs freed him from inhibitions, boosted his moral relativity (e.g., "if you're not with the one you love, love the one you're with."), and led back to Her. On that path, the maintenance man enjoyed the company of women – he did not avoid opportunities for encounters of a sexual nature – yet throughout his life, he spent most of his waking hours with Her, or working with colleagues, or raising his son, and, content with that life, never deliberately altered it. Indeed,

He was no saint. The litany of evidence against such a claim was long and convincing. During his second year of graduate school, after the acid trip that produced the revelation that he loved women, he, Clive, and John created a rag called ABANARAPPOR for absurdity, anarchy, apathy, and pornography, handed it out on central campus, and argued with persons provoked by its content. One day,

He met an attractive undergraduate, chatted her up, and eventually they wandered to a secluded spot where they embraced and kissed passionately. After some minutes, they paused, moved apart, and she said,

"I have a boyfriend." He said he was married and asked

"What should we do?"

"Nothing. We should leave it at this."

"Okay." That was it. Right then, he felt aroused, disappointed, and relieved. They took different paths away. He never saw her again. On a trip to present a research paper at a regional conference in a nearby city,

He visited the former girlfriend of a fifth-year graduate student who dumped her. Devastated by the breakup, with a face etched by emotional pain into a mask of despair, she talked of her love for him, of her inability to understand why he left her, and of her despair going forward. When she began to cry, he moved next to her, put his arm around her shoulder. She rested her head on his shoulder, looked up at him, smiled sadly, and continued to speak of her pain. His hand cupped her face. He encouraged her to put her former lover behind and think about her future. As they talked,

Words and acts of comfort changed to caressing. She responded. They were on the well-worn path countless men and women journey – that ends with sexual intercourse. When he left to return home, he hoped she felt better about herself and life, but that did not ease a feeling of guilt nor prevent the questions he put to himself: why did he do that? Was he a predator? Was his soul intact? Why had an initial act of compassion ended in passion? And on and on...

A year later, living in Coventry, the woman called, told him she worked as a flight attendant, was doing well, was in town, and asked if they could meet. He asked, she affirmed, that she had recovered emotional strength and resilience. When she asked a second time about meeting, he said he could not. After a few more minutes, they said good bye. She never called again. Nor he she.

During the first of the two years they lived in Coventry, a small group of graduate students invited he and She to a party. He attended, She did not. He, and four graduate-students (a man and three women) smoked marijuana in the apartment of a fifth graduate student – an attractive woman. They played truth or dare. When the game ended, partially clothed people sat around and talked and gossiped. At the end of the evening, he and the woman living there found themselves alone, felt and expressed mutual interest, and had sexual intercourse. One afternoon days later, he smoked marijuana with another student from the department, and had sex with her. Throughout the remainder of the year, he and both women remained cordial, but chose not to be alone again.

Four years later at the university by the dry river bed, in his first year there, he fell in love with JB. the wife of a graduate student in his class. Possessing a wide handsome face, broad shoulders, normal breasts and hips, and beautiful, bright, gray eyes, he was instantly attracted to her! And she to him. They arranged to meet privately as often as possible – over the course of several weeks – usually in his office, frequently after an evening class – to kiss, embrace, and caress. On a day her husband was out of town, she invited him to her home. He went. Without pause, they kissed, embraced, caressed, then made love. Surprised that he felt for JB as he did for Her, apprehension clouded his feeling of love. Nevertheless,

He continued to meet with her. One day they visited a tiny orchard populated by hippies he knew. He lied to Her about needing to work at school, to spend the time with JB. They passed part of that day naked, in a sauna, and that evening made love for a second time. His love for both was unchanged, but both apprehension and a sense of guilt grew. The lie was the linchpin that unleashed his guilt. He had to do something.

When he exposed these feelings to JB, they talked, but neither saw a clear path forward. The more they discussed possibilities, the more certain he became – he had to tell Her. In the end, they both told their spouses about their feelings and actions. When JB told her husband, he divorced her. When the maintenance man told Her, She was visibly hurt, cried, refused to be hugged, held, or hear more, and said to leave her alone. He did. Days passed in silence. In that time, he thought about but did not see a path forward. He anticipated sadness and pain on all possible paths forward. Why was love so hard? Like so many times past, he needed to talk to Her. He waited until She came to him, and

First, She described how he had betrayed Her trust. The betrayal had devastated Her. Next, She expressed how She saw their near future unfolding. She did not know when she would feel like making love with him again. He answered, "I understand." She dismissed this with,

"Right now, I am not certain that's true." Then,

She expressed Her anger. Her Mona Lisa eyes turned hard, stared straight at him without warmth. His She was gone, and right then he only felt a fear of the loss of Her. He stood speechless. Just as well, for She had more to say. She went on,

"I still love you, but I do not feel any love for you right now. I feel hurt, and I do not know when that will change." He nodded. Finally, She said,

"You will have to choose what you want to do." And She left to be by herself—leaving him alone – whereupon he sat down to think. He knew

On one hand, he loved Her. Across ten years of companionship, She was his confidant, friend, lover, advocate for other ways to solve problems and treat people. She supported his choices when he made them. They were, but never called each other, soulmates. They had endured a lot together. On the other hand, he and JB were in the grip of passion. He called his feelings for her "love." No other word fit. He still felt intense, romantic love for her. He wanted both women, but She insisted he choose, and, unlike previous choices, She offered no guidance, or comfort, about the choice between passionate, romantic, new love or enduring, steady, committed love He might have chosen passionate love but for the fear of loss of Her. His emotions with respect to each woman balanced, like persons of equal weight on a teeter-totter – both suspended in air. In the end he remembered,

He had made a solemn oath during their marriage. His exact words were:

> I William Albert take thee Sharon Kay to my wedded
> Wife, to have and to hold from this day forward, for
> better or worse, for richer for poorer, in sickness and
> in health, to love and to cherish, till death do us part,
> according to God's holy ordinance, and thereto I plight
> thee my troth.

She gave an identical oath. He decided "till death do us part" was binding and inescapable. No amount of linguistic legerdemain altered the meaning. To choose JB, he had to break his oath. Once he understood this, he chose Her. He told Her. He said he would never have sexual intercourse (make love, fuck) with another woman. He never did. A long recovery of their marriage began. When he saw JB on campus or elsewhere, they talked. They still loved each other, but after his choice, their paths diverged. He was sad it had to be that way. He still loved them both, still was not a saint, because

Life continued to present possibilities when he was away (conferences, training sessions, parties – none of which interested Her), and he continued to be interested and curious about woman. At a party, an unknown graduate student came up to him and proposed they have sex. Stunned by her frankness, he asked,

"What?" and, right away, she said

"Do you want to go to my place and fuck?" He managed to say,

"I don't know if that's a good idea." And added, "I want to do right by my wife." She said,

"It's a 'sport fuck'." He had never heard the term, and asked,

"A what?"

"Recreational sex, no commitment." It sounded too good to be true. Disoriented by the request, uncertain about consequences, trying to do right after having foresworn intercourse, hesitantly he said,

"Thanks for asking, but I am going to say no." They said goodbye. She left, and he never saw her again, but she planted the seed of 'sport fuck' in his head. Over time he reconstructed "sport fuck" into 'sexual play (not fucking)," which involved kissing, embracing, laying naked, caressing, and oral sex, but never intercourse. At parties, he flirted and engaged in petting with different women.

He met a German woman at a conference on multivariate statistics. They kissed and caressed for hours before she left. At a Bayesian statistics training session; he met a Russian woman and they did the same. At a conference of NOISE in New Orleans he repeated this behavior with an English professor. For several consecutive years, at the annual meeting of NOISE, he met and played with one dynamic woman. Besides kissing and caressing, he tactilely stimulated her to multiple orgasms. She volunteered to perform oral sex. He accepted and enjoyed it. In three, other, consecutive years at the same meeting, he met S, with whom he felt he might fall in love. That first year they talked. The next year they kissed and caressed. She wanted to make love, but he said he could not. The third year, they kissed and caressed. He began to explore her body with his hands, but when his hands moved from her neck and breasts toward her genitals, she told him she had her period and asked him to stop. He did. They laid together for a short time, then returned to the conference. At home, an email exchange went on for a time, then faded. He never saw her again. Posted on her Facebook page, photos showed her happy. He sent her an email noting his impression. She did not answer and he did not contact her again. Also at home,

He had an encounter with a graduate student. Her apartment was a short walk from his office and he went there once. There was virtually no physical contact. They talked about sex. She described an ongoing relation with a professor, and expressed a willingness to engage in a variety of sexual play with him. Without any thought at all, he asked,

"Would you masturbate for me?"

"Right now? Right here?"

"Yes, and would you do it until you have an orgasm?"

"Really?"

"Yes." She reclined on the coach where she was sitting, unzipped her jeans, put her hand down her panties, and began to masturbate. He experienced a sense of power as she did, and did not know if it was the sense of power or the watching her have an orgasm that thrilled him, but the thrill differed from sensations of active participation. Different, not better. Thereafter, she came to his office about once a week when he worked at night. He would caress her breasts while she masturbated to orgasm. The first visit, after her orgasm, he asked her to perform oral sex. She did. They continued so for perhaps a dozen times over several months. By mutual agreement, they stopped. They recognized the absence of a real relation, and the absence of personal growth – only the pleasure of sexual release. She left to take an academic job in the Midwest. They talked a few times by phone, but never met again. Yet, watching a woman have orgasms, perform oral sex, and experience feelings of power excited and motivated him.

From his late 50's into his 60's, having erections became less certain. He and She made love less often due to his doubt about being able to perform. At the same time, he became a restless sleeper, his tossing in bed disturbed Her sleep, so She asked him to sleep in a separate bed. They rearranged the bedroom, brought in a twin bed, and he used it thereafter. In talks about making love, he described his doubt. She tried to reassure him. He told her how oral sex rather reliably led to erections and release, but She had little interest in oral sex, and by the time she became ill, they were not making love at all. In pursuit of sexual release,

The maintenance man set aside restraint, made arrangements of dubious value with women willing to engage in sexual play for money or other considerations. The first incident occurred by chance. After years of going to the casino alone, losing his stake or winning enough to declare victory, and going home alone, on leaving the casino one night, he encountered two women – sisters – sitting on a bench. They appeared distressed. He asked how they had done. They had lost, were stranded, unable to pay for a taxi. He offered to drive them. They accepted. At their house, the taller of the two offered to perform oral sex. He said yes. Her sister went into another room while she knelt in front of him, undid his pants, and sucked his penis until he ejaculated.

As always, he liked the release. As always, he was not free of guilt. And, as always, he kept this incident to himself. After which,

The idea that a casino was not just for gambling but also for meeting women, grew from nothing to a significant aspect of going. From then on, he gambled and observed women around him, because the possibility of sexual play had entered his consciousness. A second incident occurred as he left the casino and headed to his car. He passed a woman with a phone in her hand and an expression of exasperation. He asked if she needed a ride. She answered,

"Yes. I came with a friend and I think he left without me."

"A friend?"

"I thought so."

" Hmm... Well, my car is over there." So, they walked to it.

She lived in an apartment that was on his way home, and on the way they talked. She asked

"Do you go to the casino often"

"I do."

They chatted about the casino games they liked. She asked

"What do you do?"

"I'm retired from the university and now have my own business."

"Doing what?"

"Statistical analysis. My company supports government research. What do you do?"

"I do escort services."

"Really. What does that involve?"

"I accompany men to events or go on dates with them."

"Do you have sex with them?"

"It depends on what they want... but if they want to have sex, I am willing."

The conversation lapsed into silence as he pulled into her apartment complex and she directed him to a spot close to her apartment. She asked,

"Would you like to come in for a bit?"

"I can come in for a few minutes, sure." While they talked and as they walked to her apartment, the idea that he could play with her occupied his thoughts. Inside, she offered him a drink, which he declined. She swept her hand around to show the extent of her home and said,

"This is it?" He asked,

"Do you bring men here?"

"Usually not."

"Why me?

"I am not sure, but you seemed safe." To which he responded,

"Yes… I will not beat you up or kill you." She laughed – a bit nervously. He opened his mind, then his mouth to the idea central in it, and asked,

"Would you have sex with me?"

"For escorting, I get $200 per hour."

"And for here and now?"

"Depends on what you want."

"Oral sex."

"I usually do not do that. I am not so good at it."

"But would you, do it?"

"Yes."

"I have $40. Would you do it for forty?"

"Yes." A feeling of power surged through him. He liked the feeling and put aside misgivings about its morality. The feeling persisted as she performed fellatio. He put the experience, his feelings, and misgivings in a mental box that he closed with the thought: this was play, not intercourse, not love, and that it took nothing from his love for Her. Doing so, he got her phone number which he used to arrange future encounters. Over time,

He would see her for a half hour about twice a month. Across meetings, he pursued fantasies that stoked his sense of power. First, he asked her to be naked when he arrived. She did. From the start, he asked her to masturbate and experience orgasm before she performed fellatio. She did so with enthusiasm. He asked her to have multiple orgasms. Something about watching a woman have orgasms pleased him: it brought a feeling of tranquility. She complied. He asked if she liked being spanked. She said she did. Sometimes he spanked her.

He asked if he could slap her lightly as she masturbated. She said yes. Sometimes he slapped her. He asked if she would wear a dog collar and leash and learn to heel, sit, and beg on his command. She said, "If you get me a sparkly collar." He did. She did. He asked her to respond to the question, "Who are you?" with the answer, "I am your whore?" and to the question, "Who owns you?" with the answer, "You do." She did. Always he experienced a sense of power, received sexual release, and had misgivings. Each encounter he locked away in his mind. Across the times he met with her,

Twice she said she wanted to get a regular job ("But, I would still see you,") The first time, he gave her a thousand dollars and did not see her for months. When they met at the casino, she was still hustling. The second time, he gave her two thousand dollars, and did not see her for nearly a year. She had been arrested and spent time in jail. Toward the end of their relation, she lived in motels and wanted to get into an apartment. He gave her $2400 for an apartment in her original complex. She had a male roommate. The last time the maintenance man saw her, she said her roommate had abandoned her, and that she needed money for rent. He gave her nine hundred dollars and told her he could afford no more, and would not see her again. During the time he saw her, he occasionally engaged in the same behavior with other women – in one-time meetings – in pursuit of the rush of a sense of power and the pleasing sensation of watching them have orgasms. Finally, the weight of negative emotions from these encounters convinced him that pursuing a sense of power was empty and false, and did diminish his ability to love. He abandoned the pursuit of that feeling of power and chose a different path. He tried to shift to acts of forgiveness and compassion. When he thought of these women, he felt that they were like birds with broken wings. He felt the same about himself.

In his sexual play with these women, he detected misogyny. He pursued them for the rush of feeling powerful – of being in control – for his own enjoyment, and agnostic to the woman's wishes. Corroborating this judgment, his early extra-marital encounters were with students, or, in one case, a junior faculty at another school. Being in control was addictive. He was selfish. He was not evil. Should he have behaved with more compassion? Probably. Would he have been better off not engaging with them? Well…perhaps. Yet, the incongruency between his general feeling toward women, and his behaviors toward these specific women did not concern him. In the end, he judged himself to have been a misogynist.

FAMOUS PEOPLE

HE MET ALLEN GINSBURG, TIMOTHY LEARY, and B. F. Skinner. He listened to Allen talk with students at breakfast. He learned Allen liked his eggs scrambled. By the time they met, Timothy had left acid and mind trips of "turn on, tune in, and drop out." on earth, and spent his time in space, his mind orbiting earth in a huge satellite. In a chance crossing of paths on campus, their gazes met. They immediately knew each other, but had nothing to say. He and Morris met Burrhus, then in his 80's, at the top of a down escalator in a hotel at a conference on aging. They chatted. Burrhus proffered the single, most functional, advice about old age. He said, "When you think of something, or have something to do, write it down, so you remember it later."

ON THE WINGS OF CHANCE

O N BOY SCOUT CAMPOUTS, AFTER scout leaders fell asleep, like-minded boys played blackjack and poker in their tents, under flashlight illumination, with stakes of pennies and nickels. Learning, losing more than won, the maintenance man loved playing. During high school,

He gambled for nickels and dimes. One boy, Dee, without objection from other players, dealt blackjack. Although a dealer's advantage soon became obvious, the maintenance man enjoyed winning against the odds. In adulthood, card-counting and academic studies of optimal, zero-memory, playing strategies, transformed playing blackjack. To make money or minimize losses while playing, one used the strategies. The elements of risk and chance were reduced by working the strategies, but doing so bored him. It became a slog.

High school poker games required a table, chips, four or more players, and parents' permission to host. He participated in several, and hosted one, during which he enjoyed the comradery more than the outcome. In college, he played poker after hours on Friday and Saturday night, given he had six or more dollars as a stake. When She could, She staked him. He learned the game and his opponents well. His math classes added knowledge of probability; cognitive growth increased his skill of observation; and analytic intuition fostered timely, rapid, correct decisions: most weekends, he won money and funded trips to the union for snacks. But these games were more work than fun.

When he learned the farmer's game, pitch, happiness arrived. In pitch, a lot of information is hidden. Accurate, intuitive estimates of game points available, players holdings, and the likelihood of making a bid were crucial to success. He and Tom, excelled, and when they partnered in games, they were nearly unbeatable. At a quarter a game, a quarter a set, just plain fun! And money for snacks!

He tried bridge and whist. The former, with bidding systems and all cards dealt, was too formal and the latter, with strict rules of play reminiscent of pinochle, too rigid. After a deal, the role of chance was small. Once he mastered play, he lost interest, and only continued to play because Larry and Doug insisted on rubbers of bridge, they not being gamblers.

In graduate school, cutthroat hearts became the game of choice. Games occurred at lunchtime. Faculty and graduate students participated. Losers paid the winner a quarter for the game plus a penny per point of score difference. For one game, winnings averaged several dollars. Existence of a multi-card blind, and the strategic and tactical goals of each player during each trick heightened uncertainty and risk. He played daily throughout graduate school.

He did not gamble when they lived by the shallow Great Lake, nor during the bus trip, nor the first two years he worked at the university by the dry river bed. One year they went to Las Vegas to celebrate his birthday on New Year's day. Her birthday present to him was a $1000 stake. He lost it in a single session at the craps table. He understood the mathematics of all the bets on the table, accepted them and played, however the table betting minimums and the obvious work of the dealers to turn over as many rolls as possible both turned him off. It too was a slog. They never visited Vegas again.

During the years at the university by the dry river bed, he participated in two different, regular poker games. The first was a penny-ante game with five other faculty, of whom he was youngest. That game literally died player by player. The second game was a quarter, half-dollar, dollar game with students and acquaintances. He stopped going when talking between hands increased to long, unacceptable periods. In the early 90's, Native American casino gambling came to the state. He loved video poker –a game of pure chance with choices available to the player. The presence of choice captured his interest. He played regularly once he started. Many friends and acquaintances asked,

" You know the odds are against you, why do you keep playing? Are you an addict?" At first, he answered,

"I like to play."

"But you lose more than you win."

"That's true. It's my money." Such exchanges prompted him to examine more closely what it was that drew him to the game. It was not the chance of winning a big jackpot, although doing so was fun. The explanation that satisfied him, and he felt represented what drew him to video poker, as well as games like pitch and cutthroat hearts, was a feeling he described as "floating on the wings of chance." In video poker this feeling emerges during play.

After selecting a betting stake– constrained by available, disposable income – and playing, his actions became rhythmic: draw cards, examine cards, select those to hold, draw again, and examine the result. Repeat. repeat, repeat…. As hands go on, sometimes a pattern of winning and losing hands takes on a distinct characteristic. He thinks about specific cards that make a good draw; they appear.

When the rhythm of the cards matches the rhythms of his play and thoughts, he experiences a sense that play might continue so forever. When this sense surfaces, the world falls away, the maintenance man is enthralled. He almost believes it will last forever. It never does, because the pattern itself is an epiphenomenon of chance, dependent on the draw of cards in the sequence that created the rhythm. Other draws create other patterns – some not so good, some simply terrible. But oh my, floating on the wings of chance kept him playing.

When he had a lot of disposable income, he chose high stakes. When he had less, he chose small stakes. His gambling never threatened family finances. In late life, living on a fixed income, he limited both stakes and occasions. He allowed his rational self to control his behavior more carefully. But he still thought about floating on the wings of chance, and, as he did, he realized that most of the choices he made in life were like this floating. At each choice, there was risk. The outcomes were not determined. Sure, he set himself, and them both (because She was always with him), on a different path, and each path determined how a period of his life transpired. He accepted what each path brought, and kept on. For him,

He always floated. He is floating still.

THE MAINTENANCE MAN'S
LAST LAMENT

WHEN THEY MET, SHE REACHED 5 foot 4 inches tall, weighed 145 pounds, looked out from soft, piercing, gray-green eyes, and smiled, like Mona Lisa, in a shy way tinged by sadness. Over the years she shed 20-plus pounds of fat she brought to college from home. Once gone, She kept Her weight between 115 and 125 pounds that fit well on her slight frame. She had wonderful small breasts – the right a bit smaller— that she wished were larger and symmetrical. She spoke with a marvelous, crackling, sense of humor. She kept pun-filled conversations going longer than anyone. He never could utter the last pun in these contests. She trounced him at backgammon. To bolster his sense of superiority playing games of chance and choice, he blamed his backgammon failure on tactics: He liked to play a back game.

A prolific crocheter, Her baby afghans warmed more than a thousand newborns during their first months and years on earth. A constant reader, they visited a local used-book store three or four times a year with shopping bags filled with novels She had recently read, to exchange for those She had not. Mystery, horror, intrigue, suspense were favorites. She read so much, She had to keep a list of authors and works read, so as not to pick duplicates when rummaging book exchange stacks. She read and watched TV at the same time. He could not. A 50-year smoker, She quit the last 6 years of Her life and missed the contentment that smoking brought. Caring for Her, by himself,

The eight months She traveled, beset by bullous pemphigoid, from constant itches, to blisters, to body-wide skin sores, to death, taught him, with complete certainty, that, in life, ensuring well-being and happiness in those you love is most important. As for himself,

He felt content with life, and Her in it. He forgave himself for his misdeeds. He felt ready for what came next.

Uncertainty was a companion his entire life. Perhaps it underlay his lack of life goals. Yet, despite the presence of doubt, he made choices, moved from moment to moment, and accepted the consequences. His mother, grandmother, and wife demonstrated love of him in words and deeds. He believed the LSD trip crystalized memories of those words and deeds into a global love of women. Yet, many times he behaved with individual women contrary to that global feeling. With Her, he came closest to loving in a manner consistent with that feeling of global love. Close, but not complete consonance. He knew and accepted there was more he might have done, then forgave himself for his shortcomings.

As autobiographer, he felt satisfied that his report here was honest, direct, and parsimonious. He was left with a single last lament: She was not alive to share Her side. She would have Her own perspective.

Smiling at that thought…

AND HIS DILEMMA?

WHEN YOU FIND THE ONE, treat her/him so. Be content, compassionate, and caring. He tried to do so once. He intended to try again. Otherwise, if not, do what you want, selfish person, you will anyway.

HIS POEMS HE LIKED

Real people

Some people are diplomats
– all the time smiling,
never showing how they really feel.
All the time smiling, never crying,
Like plastic flowers at an alligator's wake.

Together forever

We are nowhere together,
everywhere together,
the same.
Our hearts beat out of phase, in phase, and race ahead.
We are nowhere together (two people butting heads),
everywhere together,
the same.

Zen ken yen

Drippa droppa, tippa toppa, that's the way of ken. In and out, and out and in, that's the way of ken. If you've looked or if you're hooked then perhaps you ken. Or perhaps you cant. And if you have or if you will or even if you cant then, of course, you ken. My mother could. My father can. Then again, perhaps they cant. But then again, they ken. Rich man can. Poor man can. Middle man can. And some of each who cant. And some of each who ken. If you ken you cant. If you cant you ken. Flip flop, a paradox? Then, of course, you cant. Because it's all a silly chant. Out and in, and in and out, that's the way of ken. Drippa droppa, tippa toppa. That's the way of men.

Protection

I remember those hurts.
(The one she did to me,
The one I did to her.)
The one I did so well.
Each taken from a pool of loneliness,
dropped on a plane of thoughtlessness,
showing my soft heart
needs a tungsten shell.

In 1971,

Utopia is a street in Cleveland
just two block long.
With houses on both sides, big old houses,
and a Red Barn restaurant
across from a post office
-- all full of people
-- all very busy.

Revelation

Here I stand, trying to pee and brush my teeth
at the very same time it hits me
that I do need a woman.

I Am

Like Fly Agaric
with a big, colorful,
wide-spreading, head.
Straight and narrow
from there on down.

All around Dallas

Dallas?! Well....
Give me Tampa, Ames, or Cleveland,
Any place I lived.
Give me Portland, Seattle, New York,
Any place I been,
Even a place in hell.
Any place but Dallas
. Geez! Dallas?
Where my brother is?

Wily night.

Wily night slipped his fingers around the light,
and walked off across the land
with it clutched in his hand,
a messenger very bold,
advance man for the coming cold.

Distance

Being far from friends
is hard on the soul,
like loving two people
who will not love each other.
Being far from friends,
hold them close to your heart,
like a newborn child
or the rich warm earth.
I do not want to be,
a friend your heart will never see.

Nickotime

I'd been smoking a very long time.
Smoked so much, it smogged my mind.
Day before yesterday,
I quit to save my mind.
All day yesterday,
It was on my mind.
Most of today been a pretty good time,
Because most of today,
I've had most of my mind.

Sitting here, high

I am death bearer,
death seeker,
death knower.
Life singer.
Highbinder?
I am death bearer.
"See" I said.
"Look what you said!" she said.
"I am death seeker."
"Not me."
"I am death knower."
"I am life singer" "Happy"

FOOTNOTES

[1] Lao Tsu (1974). *Tao Te Ching* (Gia-Fu Feng & J. English, Trans.). Alfred A. Knopf, Publisher. (Original work publication date unknown).
[2] Grateful Dead (1970). Uncle John's Band (Song). On Working Man's Dead (Album). Warner Brothers, Inc.

ACKNOWLEDGEMENTS

THANKS, JEREDITH. HAD YOU NOT said what you did, this work would not exist. Thanks Keith, for showing what good sentences do. Thanks Ray, for knowing important matters differ from ritual. Thanks Harold, thanks Clive, for clear thoughts and the ability to read his mind. Thanks Jerry, for distinguishing appropriate behavior from dysfunctional emotions. Thanks Mom, thanks Dad, for a loving upbringing. Thanks Elmo, a friend in a time of need. Thanks Doug, a friend in deed. Thanks Morris, Ray, Brian, Geoff, and Colonnade and Fry's coworkers, all comrades in work. Thanks to all who gave purpose to large and small moments in his life. Thanks to each woman who helped him behave with greater compassion. Thanks Sharon, for love.

These folks are not responsible for flaws in this work. The maintenance man is.

Gambling man.

I had a pair of patch pants,
all made of leather,
durable and rugged.
Each patch singly,
separately sewn,
as a side bet
against the biggest winner of all.

15 forms of happiness

Bubbling mindless gurgling baby warm glowing gushing home free spirit
no pain shit-eating grin finally know you getting ready to give it up
fishing just for fun stoned mashed potato happiness

About the Author

Raised in a rollicking family – arguing its most engaging entertainment – Bill Stock became brash and outspoken. His wife Sharon smoothed his edges. Loving risk, he embraced gambling and a career in statistics without contradiction. Early on, he read westerns, science fiction, and works about mysticism – creating a mish-mashed view of life. He tried psychedelic drugs, made a Merry Prankster's inspired bus trip, backpacked across Oregon, learned Spanish with friends in España, rode a bicycle from Canada to New Orleans, and visited the dirt-floor cottage where his grandmother was born in Ireland. He worked last as a maintenance man in a supermarket. Since Her death, he seeks to accept life, resolve his dilemmas, and attain serenity. A lover of oceans and forests, for some reason, he lives in an Arizona desert.